Palgrave Philosophy Today

Series Editor: **Vittorio Bufacchi**, Ur

The *Palgrave Philosophy Today* series provides concise introductions to all the major areas of philosophy currently being taught in philosophy departments around the world. Each book gives a state-of-the-art informed assessment of a key area of philosophical study. In addition, each title in the series offers a distinct interpretation from an outstanding scholar who is closely involved with current work in the field. Books in the series provide students and teachers with not only a succinct introduction to the topic, with the essential information necessary to understand it and the literature being discussed, but also a demanding and engaging entry into the subject.

Titles include:

Pascal Engel
PHILOSOPHY OF PSYCHOLOGY

Shaun Gallagher
PHENOMENOLOGY

Simon Kirchin
METAETHICS

Duncan Pritchard
KNOWLEDGE

Mathias Risse
GLOBAL POLITICAL PHILOSOPHY

Joel Walmsley
MIND AND MACHINE

Forthcoming Titles

Helen Beebee
METAPHYSICS

James Robert Brown
PHILOSOPHY OF SCIENCE

Neil Manson
ENVIRONMENTAL PHILOSOPHY

Chad Meister
PHILOSOPHY OF RELIGION

Matthew Nudds
MIND AND THOUGHT

Lilian O'Brien
PHILOSOPHY OF ACTION

Don Ross
PHILOSOPHY OF ECONOMICS

Nancy Tuana
FEMINISM AND PHILOSOPHY

Palgrave Philosophy Today
Series Standing Order ISBN 978–0–230–00232–6 (hardcover)
Series Standing Order ISBN 978–0–230–00233–3 (paperback)
(*outside North America only*)

You can receive future titles in this series as they are published by placing a standing order. Please contact your bookseller or, in case of difficulty, write to us at the address below with your name and address, the title of the series and one of the ISBNs quoted above.

Customer Services Department, Macmillan Distribution Ltd, Houndmills, Basingstoke, Hampshire RG21 6XS, England

Global Political Philosophy

Mathias Risse

Harvard University, USA

© Mathias Risse 2012

Softcover reprint of the hardcover 1st edition 2012 978-0-230-36072-3

All rights reserved. No reproduction, copy or transmission of this publication may be made without written permission.

No portion of this publication may be reproduced, copied or transmitted save with written permission or in accordance with the provisions of the Copyright, Designs and Patents Act 1988, or under the terms of any licence permitting limited copying issued by the Copyright Licensing Agency, Saffron House, 6–10 Kirby Street, London EC1N 8TS.

Any person who does any unauthorized act in relation to this publication may be liable to criminal prosecution and civil claims for damages.

The author has asserted his right to be identified as the author of this work in accordance with the Copyright, Designs and Patents Act 1988.

First published 2012 by
PALGRAVE MACMILLAN

Palgrave Macmillan in the UK is an imprint of Macmillan Publishers Limited, registered in England, company number 785998, of Houndmills, Basingstoke, Hampshire RG21 6XS.

Palgrave Macmillan in the US is a division of St Martin's Press LLC, 175 Fifth Avenue, New York, NY 10010.

Palgrave Macmillan is the global academic imprint of the above companies and has companies and representatives throughout the world.

Palgrave® and Macmillan® are registered trademarks in the United States, the United Kingdom, Europe and other countries

ISBN 978-0-230-36073-0   ISBN 978-1-137-28344-3 (eBook)
DOI 10.1057/9781137283443

A catalogue record for this book is available from the British Library.

A catalog record for this book is available from the Library of Congress.

10 9 8 7 6 5 4 3 2 1
21 20 19 18 17 16 15 14 13 12

Transferred to Digital Printing in 2013

Contents

Series Editor's Preface   vi

Preface   viii

Introduction   1

1 Human Rights   9

2 Universalism vs. Relativism   40

3 Why States?   62

4 Global Distributive Justice   88

5 Environmental Justice   119

6 Immigration   144

7 Fairness in Trade   168

Epilogue: Pluralist Internationalism   193

Notes   197

Bibliography   199

Index   209

Series Editor's Preface

It is not easy being a student of philosophy these days. All the different areas of philosophy are reaching ever increasing levels of complexity and sophistication, a fact which is reflected in the specialized literature and readership each branch of philosophy enjoys. And yet, anyone who studies philosophy is expected to have a solid grasp of the most current issues being debated in most, if not all, of the other areas of philosophy. It is an understatement to say that students of philosophy today are faced with a Herculean task.

The books in this new book series by Palgrave are meant to help all philosophers, established and aspiring, to understand, appreciate and engage with the intricacies which characterize all the many faces of philosophy. They are also ideal teaching tools as textbooks for more advanced students. These books may not be meant primarily for those who have yet to read their first book of philosophy, but all students with a basic knowledge of philosophy will benefit greatly from reading these exciting and original works, which will enable anyone to engage with all the defining issues in contemporary philosophy.

There are three main aspects that make the Palgrave Philosophy Today series distinctive and attractive. First, each book is relatively short. Second, the books are commissioned from some of the best-known, established and upcoming international scholars in each area of philosophy. Third, while the primary purpose is to offer an informed assessment of opinion on a key area of philosophical study, each title presents a distinct interpretation from someone who is closely involved with current work in the field.

In contemporary political philosophy, questions of global justice have increasingly come to dominate the discipline, a fact that is reflected in the decision to devote a whole book to this topic in the present series. As one of the upcoming stars in contemporary political philosophy, and global justice in particular, Mathias Risse was the obvious choice for this title. Over the years Risse has published in all the most prestigious journals of political philosophy, and his forthcoming book *On Global Justice*, to be published by Princeton University Press later this year, is destined to be a fundamental point of reference in the literature on global distributive justice for many years to come.

Risse's book in the Palgrave Philosophy Today series is distinctive for its approach to global issues. In this growing body of literature the standard methodology is to take a theoretical framework originally devised for issues of domestic justice and expand it to cover global concerns. Risse's line of attack is fundamentally different: in *Global Political Philosophy* he starts with the global domain directly. Risse's political philosophy is not merely compatible with global concerns, but devised specifically from the perspective of global justice. As a result, Risse is able to develop an original insight on all the key issues in global political philosophy, including human rights, the international political order, distributive justice, environmentalism, immigration and trade.

Vittorio Bufacchi
General Editor, Palgrave Philosophy Today
Department of Philosophy
University College Cork

Preface

Questions of genuinely global reach have become central to political philosophy in recent decades. What does distributive justice require at the global level? Why would people have human rights? What does fairness in trade require? Why should we live together in states rather than in some other form of political organization (or should we)? What constraints on the flow of immigration are justifiable? What obligations does the current generation of human beings have towards subsequent generations? In spite of the increasing prominence of such questions, introductions to political philosophy normally focus on questions that arise domestically – one state at a time, so to speak, rather than across states. Quite often there is also a chapter that addresses questions that arise at the global level, but that is not where the focus is. This book proceeds differently, by starting off at the global level right away and going back to domestic questions where appropriate.

Global Political Philosophy draws on classes on global justice and human rights that I have taught at the Kennedy School of Government and in the Faculty of Arts and Sciences at Harvard University over the past decade. I am grateful to the students who have taken these classes and to the teaching fellows who have worked with me in the course of the years for their insightful questions and thoughtful contributions to these classes. My assistant Derya Honça has been much involved with all these classes, as well as with the writing of this book, and I am very grateful to her for all the help she has provided over the years. I also thank Eric Cavallero and three referees for their generous comments on the proposal for this book. I am grateful to Vittorio Bufacchi for inviting me to contribute to this series and for his helpful comments on the penultimate version of the text.

Introduction

The work of the 17th century philosopher Thomas Hobbes set the stage for the next three and a half centuries of political philosophy by focusing on the confrontation between individual and state. Do there have to be states? What are the scope and limits of legitimate state power? What is a just state? How do values like liberty, equality or community apply within states? Who should rule? Questions like these – beyond what Hobbes himself explored – have preoccupied philosophers throughout these past centuries, and they remain significant. But questions about the relationship between state and individual, and about the relationship among individuals sharing a state, are no longer quite as central to political philosophy as they once were. In recent decades, questions about the relationship among states and among distant individuals, including questions concerning basic patterns of political organization on this planet, have become increasingly important. It is on such questions that this book focuses.

To be sure, such questions too have been around for centuries, but real-world changes, grouped together under the label "globalization," and have forced philosophers to pay more attention to them than they previously had. "Globalization" denotes processes that erode the political and economic importance of national boundaries and increasingly affect life chances through the system of rules that constitute the global political and economic order. Talk about a "global order" and an "increasingly interconnected world" has become commonplace and appropriate. While this global order has no *government*, it comprises treaty- and convention-based norms that regulate territorial sovereignty, security and trade, some property rights, human rights, and the environment, and that thereby provide for global *governance*. Politically, the UN Charter codifies the most significant rules

1

governing this system. Economically, the Bretton Woods institutions (International Monetary Fund (IMF), World Bank, and later the General Agreement on Trade and Tariffs (GATT)/World Trade Organization (WTO)) form a network intended to prevent war and foster worldwide betterment. Jointly with the more powerful states, these institutions shape the economic order.

The presence of global structures expands the agenda for political philosophers. Human beings have irreversibly encountered each other. We cannot help but negotiate common arrangements on this globe. One outcome of such negotiations – taken literally, given that it has emerged from the efforts of a culturally diverse commission – is the Universal Declaration of Human Rights (UDHR). Adopted by the United Nations in 1948, the Declaration provides a moral vision for the future of humanity. At this time, no other vision has gained as much traction around the world as the human rights movement. One philosophical question that arises with great urgency in an increasingly interconnected world, especially one with a single most visible moral vision, is whether universal moral values are acceptable to begin with. After all, the success of the human rights movement might just be the most recent expression of Western hegemony. Bible-wielding missionaries and civilization-spreading colonial officials might no longer disembark at faraway shores, but human rights activists and World Bank functionaries do. Both universalism of values as such and the idea of human rights require careful philosophical scrutiny. We interrogate these ideas in Chapters 1 and 2.

States now cover all inhabitable regions of the earth and lay claims to many uninhabitable ones. Nonetheless, states have delegated much decision-making to transnational structures. Such structures do not just include formal international organizations like the WTO, but also transnational networks among national regulatory officials, administration by hybrid intergovernmental-private arrangements, and private institutions with regulatory functions. For much of history, large parts of the world were ruled by empires with considerably less immediate control over and access to their subjects than states have today. Institutions that pre-date states also include city states, city leagues and complex feudal structures. So apparently, states are historically contingent forms of political organization: power can, and has been, organized differently. The more one reflects on the historical contingency of states, the more one wonders why, and whether, there ought to be states at all. Perhaps they are not merely historically contingent, but a moral aberration. Perhaps human affairs had better be organized differently: in a world state, in federative structures much stronger than the UN, or ones with a more comprehensive system of collective security, or where border control is collectively administered or abandoned altogether. Chapter 3 takes up this challenge.

A theory of distributive justice explains why certain individuals have particularly stringent claims to certain relative or absolute shares, quantities or amounts of something. Shakespeare's Shylock, in the *Merchant of Venice*, makes his demand to a pound of his delinquent debtor's flesh in terms of justice. Until the clever Portia finds a device for voiding the contract, the presumption is that it must be granted. Demands of justice are the hardest to overrule or suspend. One common view is that these especially stringent claims (and thus any principles of distributive justice) only hold among those who jointly belong to a state. The kind of redistribution required by distributive justice then would only apply within states. Whatever moral obligations one has to those with whom one does not share a state would then have to be of a different nature. Belonging to a state means to be involved in an intensely cooperative endeavor, one that is regulated by rules that are coercively enforced. But the global order too includes coercive and cooperative structures. The WTO regulates most international trade, and increasingly pushes intrusive policy harmonization across countries. If countries fail to comply, trade sanctions may be imposed. The IMF makes loans to economically troubled countries dependent on the acceptance of often demanding conditions. One may wonder therefore whether principles of distributive justice should not apply across the global order, rather than merely within countries. Governments would then have to give much more priority to people beyond their borders than they currently do. Chapter 4 explores these matters.

The real-world changes that have affected the relative importance of certain questions within political philosophy do not merely concern political and economic structures. Our relationship with the environment too has undergone considerable changes. It is said that we live in a new geological era: the Anthropocene. This term characterizes the period where humankind has surpassed the rest of nature in its impact on the structure and function of the earth system. Humans have long been able to undermine the environmental conditions on which their survival depends. For instance, many centers of the highly advanced Maya culture in Central America declined, and ultimately collapsed, during the 8th and 9th centuries. Environmental causes appear to have played a major role. Humankind as such now has a parallel impact at the planetary level. Until the next asteroid hits, it is likely to be people more than other forces that determine the future of all known life, to a large extent through climate change. If average temperatures rise by more than 3 or 4 degrees celsius, the way we live now on this planet could change dramatically. Low-lying regions might be permanently flooded. Previously fertile regions might no longer be usable for agriculture. There could be more severe storms, droughts and floods than before. They could occur in areas where they were previously unknown. Vast regions might become uninhabitable, and there might be considerably fewer humans than there are now.

The world is currently balanced on a precarious edge. Global violence is at a lower level than it has been in decades. Hundreds of millions have been lifted out of poverty. Science and technology are opening up new vistas with amazing speed, democracy is spreading, and global support for human rights is rising. Still, many economies around the world are suffering, and we seem to be unable to bring lasting change to them. Small groups of extremists are increasingly capable of inflicting massive destruction. Conflicts in Asia, the Middle East, Africa and Latin America continue to ferment. The US is no longer the dominant power, and a return to dangerous great power rivalry is possible. Yet unless our planet encounters a disaster of epic proportions, it is climate change that poses the single most significant challenge we face in the 21st century, and plausibly beyond. One need not despair entirely: as long as sunlight reaches us and humankind stays connected with its scientific, cultural and technological legacy, there will presumably be ways for us to continue to exist, in some form or other. Still, the noticeable likelihood of the sort of changes that climate change triggers renders questions of environmental justice, as well as questions about our relationship to the rest of nature, central to political philosophy. Chapter 5 explores this subject.

Global interconnectedness makes it possible for people to move more freely. Tens of millions live outside of their countries of birth. Many move involuntarily, such as refugees or victims of human trafficking. But many more emigrate in search of better economic prospects, or to escape from oppressive or incompetent governments. The most attractive destinations for would-be emigrants accept considerably fewer people than those who wish to enter. If such barriers did not exist, many more people, than are currently able to, would leave their homes. Immigration constraints limit human freedom and prevent the increase of remittances that have become an important engine of growth in poor countries. Such constraints are also problematic from a standpoint that regards the earth as a collective property of humanity and thus views immigration policy not as a privilege that countries may or may not bestow on newcomers, but as standing in need of a global policy approach. Chapter 6 explores moral issues about immigration.

Chapter 7 deals with fairness in trade. At least in a broad range of circumstances, trade theory recommends liberalizing trade since doing so benefits participating countries. Every country should find its comparative advantage on the word market and assess what goods or services it can contribute more efficiently than other countries and import goods and services they can obtain more efficiently elsewhere. But if countries follow this advice without restrictions, the effects on some domestic producers might be pernicious even if the country as a whole benefits. Therefore the dismantling of tariffs and subsidies continues to be the subject of intense negotiations among countries. The WTO provides the forum for extended rounds of trade negotiations that determine the conditions for future trade. These negotiations and their outcomes raise fairness issues. While there is some disagreement about just how important trade and trade liberalization are for development, it is because of the importance of trade for development that concerns about fairness in trade loom large in the minds of those who, in some sense, oppose globalization.

Each chapter explores what I take to be some major issues and positions about the topic at hand and ends with some suggestions on how to pursue our questions further. I present the views developed by others, but also offer views of my own. In fact, it turns out that, in the course of the book, step by step I have developed an overall view of global justice that I call *pluralist internationalism* and that explicitly appears in Chapter 4. The epilogue looks back at the book and assembles what has been said about this view throughout. I develop that view more fully in *On Global Justice* (Princeton University Press, 2012).

When in the 4th century BC Aristotle – one of the towering figures in the history of thought – wrote his treatise on political philosophy, the *Politics,* he discussed the Greek city state and its constitution. We owe the word for "politics" to the Greek term for city state. Hobbes wrote about the importance of the state to guarantee peaceful and secure living arrangements, and explored the rights of the state and the duties of its subjects. Today many problems concern the ways in which humanity can live together on this planet, as well as our relationship with this planet itself. We are still concerned with cities and states, but many urgent questions now arise at the level of the global order or at the planetary level. It is such questions that this book explores to introduce readers to political philosophy. It is quite feasible to teach an introductory course in political philosophy focusing on normative questions that arise in the context of globalization. This book is intended to provide support for such a course. At the same time, writing an introduction with this focus inevitably neglects some of the long-standing questions about the domestic context that normally set the stage for such an introductory course. But it is equally inevitable that introductions that focus on the domestic context neglect the increasingly relevant questions this book is concerned with.

There are two ways of thinking about introductions to academic fields. According to the first, an introduction resembles a staircase: one starts at the bottom and cannot reach the top without passing over every step. According to the second, providing an introduction is like making one's way with a candle into a very large dark room. By and by one sees more and more, but one could readily have chosen a different path, and as one advances, one touches left and right on much that must remain unexplored, and realizes how much there is to explore to begin with. Introductions to mathematics or physics are more of the first kind, but introductions to areas in the humanities are more of the second. For this reason it is unproblematic if readers who choose this book as their first book on political philosophy do not fully understand everything. Moreover, inevitably many arguments proceed too quickly or are left without a complete defense. Note also that the more traditional kind of introduction to political philosophy that focuses on the state can draw on a substantive body of theories, including several major theories of domestic justice. Views of other philosophers can be introduced as contributions to some of these theories, or as logically possible stances in an already well-understood conceptual space. But in the domain of philosophical reflection on questions of global scope it is not the case that there are a few established theories that one could think through for a number of questions. The field is relatively new. In such a case one will often simply have to report that philosopher X asked a certain question and offered a certain response. Moreover, it is unavoidable that the author's understanding of the field will be strongly present in an introduction of the sort I am offering here. The nuances of my own understanding of the field of global political philosophy are developed at length in *On Global Justice*.

The only distinctively introductory book I know that extensively deals with questions of global political philosophy is Cecile Fabre's *Justice in a Changing World* (Polity, 2007). But whereas Fabre takes different stances on domestic justice as her starting point and expands them to the global domain, I begin with the global domain directly. We are fortunate to have several excellent introductions that approach political philosophy through the lenses of the more traditional questions. These include Jean Hampton's *Political Philosophy* (Westview, 1996), Will Kymlicka's

Contemporary Political Philosophy: An Introduction (Oxford, 2001); David Miller's *Political Philosophy: A Very Short Introduction* (Oxford, 2003), John Simmons's *Political Philosophy* (Oxford, 2007), Adam Swift's *Political Philosophy: A Beginner's Guide for Students and Politicians* (Polity, 2006), and Jonathan Wolff's *An Introduction to Political Philosophy* (Oxford, 2006). Any of these could be read by way of supplementing this book.

1 Human Rights

The Universal Declaration and the impact of human rights

The UDHR was passed by the General Assembly of the United Nations on December 10, 1948. It was only a few years before, that the UN had been founded, according to its preamble, with the intention "to maintain international peace and security" and to "achieve international co-operation in solving international problems of an economic, social, cultural, or humanitarian character." The idea that persons have rights *simply by virtue of being human* has a long history. However, the idea that individuals have moral rights for the realization of which there is an institutionally acknowledged global responsibility and that, moreover, can serve to assess the success of political and economic institutions, is a 20th century conviction. Two world wars have taught us that we need organizations designed to help with global problem-solving, and that the protection of individuals cannot be left exclusively to the countries in which they live. Legal scholar Mary Ann Glendon aptly calls the UDHR "a declaration of interdependence ... of people, nations, and rights" (2001, p 174).

It was the Lebanese diplomat Charles Malik who introduced the UDHR to the General Assembly. He directed its members to places where they could find the influence of their culture on this document. For instance, India had played a key role in advancing the principle of non-discrimination that is so prominently placed in Article 2 ("Everyone is entitled to all the rights and freedoms set forth in this Declaration, without distinction of any kind, such as race, color, sex, language, religion, political or other opinion, national or social origin, property, birth or other status."). The UK and the US had shared their long experience with political and civil liberties. Among other countries the Soviet Union had championed social and economic rights. The UDHR had been constructed, as Malik put it, on a "firm international basis where no regional philosophy or way of life was permitted to prevail" (Glendon 2001, pp 164f). Its preamble characterizes the UDHR as "a common standard of achievement for all peoples and all nations," one to which "every individual and every organ of society" was asked to contribute. The preamble also stresses that, in the first instance, these contributions must amount to "teaching and education to promote respect for these rights and freedoms." The drafters – a remarkably diverse group by the standards of the time – were aware that much intellectual engagement was needed to secure the success of the UDHR.

The idea of any universal morality has often been criticized, and such criticism also surfaced while the UDHR was being drafted. In a document published in 1947, the American Anthropological Association insisted that

> standards and values are relative to the culture from which they derive so that any attempt to formulate postulates that grow out of the beliefs or moral codes of one culture must to that extent detract from the applicability of any Declaration of Human Rights to mankind as a whole. (p 542)

Indeed, some have suspected human rights of being 19th century standards of civilization in disguise, designed to determine the conditions under which the benefits of interacting with Europeans and their descendants can be enjoyed. This chapter explores the philosophical foundations of human rights. Chapter 2 addresses general concerns about the existence of universal values, but still with an eye on the fact that the UDHR is the only promising attempt at creating a broadly shared moral vision for the future of humanity.

"Human rights is the idea of our time, the only political-moral idea that has received universal acceptance," writes the legal scholar Louis Henkin, perhaps with some exaggeration, while "the suspension of rights is the touchstone and measure of abnormality" (1990, pp xvii–xviii). But indeed, human rights talk has become the common language of emancipation and moral progress. When organized power is criticized for harming those whom it ought to benefit, appeals to human rights are normally deployed, rather than other languages that have also been used to that end (which the readers may or may not be familiar with), such as the language of Marxism, critical theory, modernization theory, dependency theory, or other moral languages, such as the language of justice or plainly of rights and duties as opposed to "human" rights. Only decades after 1948 did the UN follow suit with legally binding documents. It took even longer for human rights organizations to have a major presence in international politics. But especially since the end of the Cold War, the human rights movement – earlier often confined to candle light vigils – has established such a presence. Organizations such as Amnesty International, Human Rights Watch, and Doctors Without Borders have become highly visible, and human rights standards have entered foreign policy making on a large scale.

In the first instance human rights are not prescriptions of positive law, but moral demands. Moreover, the UDHR itself was just that – a non-binding *declaration*. But in the last half century, multiple international treaties have been passed that are binding on their signatories. The most significant ones (which together with the UDHR form the major human rights documents) are the International Covenant on Civil and Political Rights (adopted in 1966), the International Covenant on Economic, Social and Cultural Rights (1966), the International Convention on the Elimination of All Forms of Racial Discrimination (1965), the Convention on the Elimination of All Forms of Discrimination Against Women (1979), the Convention Against Torture and Other Cruel, Inhuman or Degrading Treatment or Punishment (1984), and the Convention on the Rights of the Child (1989). These documents have also inspired national constitutions and regional intergovernmental organizations, and have encouraged states to use the observance of human rights as a criterion for selecting policies towards other parties.

Social scientists have started to explore whether the use of the human rights language correlates with improvements in people's lives. For instance, they have asked whether a country's signing of human rights conventions is linked to improvements in the conditions of the population (fewer civil rights violations, improved abilities to make a living, etc.). Case-study-based inquiries have identified mechanisms through which human rights documents and organizations could make a difference in domestic politics. For example, to improve their reputation abroad and perhaps obtain better access to foreign aid, oppressive regimes might ratify treaties incorporating human rights standards. Domestic opposition might then challenge the government to abide by rules it has ostensibly accepted. International organizations could contribute to this process of "naming and shaming," or provide logistic support or training. Eventually the government can no longer ignore these pressures, and first has to engage the activists politically and eventually make changes for the better. Success stories of this sort have been reported, for instance, in Eastern Europe and Central America. However, more quantitatively oriented researchers – statistically analyzing cross-country data-sets – have failed to confirm this optimism. This area of research is still emerging, and much more work needs to be done. However, even though we should acknowledge the world-historical relevance of the existence of the major human rights documents and the enormous inspiration they have provided, and even though the global consensus on human rights appears to be growing, we must not confuse the recent ubiquity of human rights language with actual impact.

Human rights: concept and conceptions

We have gotten used to talk about human rights, but it is important to take a step back to realize that we are making rather nontrivial claims if we insist that all human beings have certain moral rights regardless of where they live and what culture they belong to. If people have certain rights, then others (or organizations like states) must make it a considerable priority to do certain things for them or refrain from doing certain things to them, as the case may be. Since we are talking about moral rather than legal rights, they must do these things even where there is no legal enforcement of any kind. Moreover, if people have human rights, then presumably they do indeed have them even if their culture does not acknowledge human rights. Therefore sometimes the question of intervention arises in cases of human rights abuses in cultures that insist that human rights standards are not *their* standards. So we had better have good arguments to explain why there would be such rights. The Cambridge philosopher Raymond Geuss, for instance, has called human rights "a kind of puffery or white magic" (2001, p 144), making it rather clear that he does not believe we could find such arguments. As we are turning to the philosophy of human rights, let me warn the reader that the remainder of this chapter will be denser than most of the other chapters. Much contemporary moral and political philosophy bears on the foundations of human rights. For that reason, we will briefly encounter many theorists and ideas at a much higher frequency than in subsequent chapters. But here indeed we must also lay the foundations for the very idea of a global political philosophy, and that will require some in-depth discussions. However, what we get out of this kind of inquiry richly repays the efforts.

Human rights are rights that are invariant with respect to local conventions, institutions, culture, or religion. Human rights language focuses on abuses committed by those in positions of authority: of two otherwise identical acts, only one might violate human rights, namely, the one that amounts to an abuse of authority. Human rights claims are moral claims on the organization of society. Human rights "can be violated by governments, certainly, and by government agencies and officials, by the general staff of an army at war, and probably also by the leaders of a guerilla movement or of a large corporation – but not by a petty criminal or by a violent husband" (Pogge 2002, pp 57f). There is a difference, say, between thefts committed by petty criminals and thefts that are part of abusive patterns of government behavior or otherwise expressions of socially entrenched or violently enforced oppression. I take the *concept* of human rights to refer to rights (vis-à-vis entities or agents who, in virtue of their power, size, etc., can intelligibly be held responsible for this matter) *with regard to the organization of society* that are invariant with respect to local conventions, institutions, culture, or religion.

A host of philosophical questions arises about human rights. Why would we hold such rights? Is there a set of features of human beings on which they are based? What ought to be their function in the global order, and does this help define what they are? What rights arise in this way? Who must do what to realize them? Political philosopher Joshua Cohen (2006) proposes that human rights have three features: they are universal and owed by every political society to everybody; are requirements of political morality whose force does not depend on their expression in enforceable law; and are especially urgent. Any account of human rights must meet these three constraints, as well as two methodological assumptions: fidelity to major human rights documents, so that a substantial range of these rights is accounted for (granting that major human rights documents play a significant role in fixing the meaning of human rights talk); and open-endedness (we can argue in support of additional rights). However, these criteria (which I agree characterize the *concept* of human rights) do not entail commitments with regard to a range of questions about such rights.

The function of a *conception* of human rights is to provide a fuller set of answers. A conception of human rights consists of four elements: first, a list of rights classified as human rights; second, an account of the basis on which individuals have them (an account of what features make individuals rights-holders); third, an account of why that list has that composition, a principle or a process that generates that list; and fourth, an account of who must do what to realize these rights, an account of corresponding obligations. One should think broadly about the term "features of individuals," to include bases formulated purely in terms of a distinctively human existence and bases that talk about membership in particular associations.

Conceptions will often take, as their starting point, a stance on the first, second, or third component and add the others, which may be trivial (if the basis readily determines these rights, say), or may require argumentative work. I say that conceptions "will often" have such starting points because this classification may not be exhaustive. But it does serve as a useful way of classifying many commonly discussed views on human rights. These first three components are logically tied (choices constrain what one can coherently choose for the other components). With which component one begins depends on what one thinks one can defensibly claim about human rights.

Conceptions that start with a list are *list-driven*, those that first specify a basis are *basis-driven*, and those that use some principle to generate a list are *principle-driven*. For such a conception to be "principle-driven" means that it is guided by some idea of what ought to be on the list of rights other than the specification of a basis; the primary example is a specification of their function in international politics (e.g., determine conditions of appropriate outside interference). Bases specify features of individuals in virtue of which human rights are held. In basis-driven accounts, that basis also gives rise to a principle that generates the list, but there can be principle-driven accounts that do not make use of any basis at all, or that consider the principle, rather than any basis, as authoritative for what human rights are.

Conceptions of human rights

Let us look at some conceptions to illuminate this classification. Political theorist Charles Beitz distinguishes "orthodox" from "practical" conceptions. What renders conceptions *orthodox* is "the idea that human rights have an existence in the moral order that is independent of their expression in international doctrine" (2004, p 196). Philosopher John Simmons, for one, offers what Beitz regards as a paradigmatic version of an orthodox view of human rights, thinking of them as rights that are possessed by all human beings at all times and at all places simply in virtue of their humanity. Human rights so understood "will have the properties of universality, independence (from social or legal recognition), naturalness, inalienability, non-forfeitability, and imprescriptibility" (Simmons 2001a, p 185). Orthodox conceptions form a subset of *basis-driven* conceptions. Orthodox accounts begin with the second component (that basis), which leads to the third (a principle generating the list), which in turn leads to the first (that list). The fourth component (whose duties?) remains to be settled separately.

One will adopt such a conception if one can defend a view of what it is about our humanity, or the distinctively human life, that makes us rights-holders and turn this into an overall plausible conception. The choice of the second restricts the choices for the first and third component. However, the second component may not uniquely fix the list. In disagreements about what shared humanity entails, political practice or views about the function of human rights in global society may help generate a list. But it can only be in a *supplementary* manner that considerations other than those drawing on the basis affect that list. Rather than appealing to "common humanity" one can develop basis-driven accounts in terms of political structures, for instance starting with a view on membership in any defensible domestic order, or on membership in the global order, as I do below.[1] Such accounts are basis-driven but not orthodox. Basis-driven conceptions vary enormously.

In a "practical" conception, it is the purpose of human rights talk in international discourse and practice that defines the idea of human rights. On such a view, we are not saying that human beings at all times have always held human rights. Instead, we are saying that references to human rights play a certain role in international law and politics. We obtain a conception of human rights by starting with the third component (an account of why the list of rights is what it is), in this case, by assessing what ought to be their *function* in the global order. The most plausible example of such a function or purpose would be the creation or preservation of an international order in which peaceful democratic societies can flourish. Thereby we generate a list, thus adding the first component. This is a *principle-driven* conception. There does not seem to be an interesting case of a principle-driven conception that is not practical in Beitz's sense. Such an approach is consistent with a range of ways of providing the basis on which rights are held, and different cultures may have different ways of doing so. A principle-driven conception will be chosen if claims about what generates the list can be made with more certainty than claims about possible bases.

Richard Rorty's (1993) "sentimentalist" view provides a *list-driven* conception. Rorty plainly dismisses reflections on the basis on which rights are ascribed. As far as he is concerned, the question whether human beings really have human rights is not one that is worth raising. Rorty takes a similar stance with regard to the third component, saying only that the emergence of a human rights culture owes everything to hearing sad and sentimental stories. The list of rights has emerged through a process of broadening compassion. Rorty focuses on the fourth point (whose duties?) through an appeal to the need for education to enable people to see similarities between themselves and others. Rorty belongs to an anti-foundationalist, practice-oriented philosophical movement known as *pragmatism*. Pragmatists believe that disagreements about the philosophical foundations of concepts or theories make no practical difference, and that this is a reason not to engage in such disagreements. Rorty applies pragmatism especially to the search for foundations for human rights. As a result, for instance, he thinks no useful work is done by insisting on a purportedly ahistorical human nature, and that therefore there either is no such nature in the first place, or that at least nothing in that nature is relevant to our moral choices. More generally, he considers the second and third component of a conception of human rights dispensable since neither helps *explain* why we endorse human rights.

There is unlikely to be a single most plausible conception of human rights, a single most plausible set of answers to the questions to which a conception offers answers. Coherent answers support each other, with disagreements between conceptions occurring along different dimensions. Human rights discourse is too amorphous to allow for one uniquely best conception. The universality captured by the idea of human rights allows for different elaborations. Nor would such pluralism be problematic. Different conceptions may help "to command reasoned support and to establish a secure intellectual standing" for human rights, as the philosopher and economist Amartya Sen put it (2004, p 317). Securing the intellectual standing of human rights, again, is also what the preamble of the UDHR urges all individuals and organs of society to do.

The distinctively human life

"'You do not interest me.' No man can say these words to another without committing a cruelty and offending against justice." So the French 20th century philosopher and social activist Simone Weil once wrote, "At the bottom of the heart of every human being, from earliest infancy until the tomb, there is something that goes on indomitably expecting, in the teeth of all experience of crimes committed, suffered, and witnessed, that good and not evil will be done to him. It is this above all that is sacred in every human being" (1986, pp 50f). Let me survey, then, different ways of developing conceptions of human rights that are both basis-driven and orthodox, with common humanity being the basis. So these are conceptions that develop the idea that human rights are moral rights individuals have simply in virtue of being human. I sketch different ways of developing an orthodox conception throughout the next sections. However, it turns out that orthodox conceptions are unsatisfactory. Towards the end of this chapter I sketch an alternative way of thinking about human rights.

At the core of any orthodox approach there will be a view of what counts as a *distinctively human life* (which provides contents to the idea of common humanity) and the insistence that such a life is *valuable*. As the moral philosopher James Griffin (2008) helpfully explains:

> Human life is different from the life of other animals. We human beings have a conception of ourselves and of our past and future. We reflect and assess. We form pictures of what a good life would be – often, it is true, only on a small scale, but occasionally also on a large scale. And we try to realize these pictures. This is what we mean by a distinctively *human* existence ... And we value our status as human beings especially highly, even more highly than even our happiness. This status centers on our being agents – deliberating, assessing, choosing, and acting to make what we see as a good life for ourselves. (p 32)

Some theorists think the idea of human rights is ineliminably religious. Legal theorist Michael Perry (2000), for instance, argues that the conviction that each human being is sacred is foundational to human rights, that the idea of the sacred is ineliminably religious, and that therefore the idea of human rights is equally so. Perhaps we can resist this argument also by denying that the idea of the sacred is ineliminably religious. But more importantly, for present purposes, we can resist the proposal that the idea that each human being is sacred is foundational to human rights. Foundational to human rights on the approach we are exploring is the distinctively human life. Attempts to develop a conception of human rights from that starting point must address especially these two matters: first, we must explain *just what* it is about the distinctively human life that generates rights. We must explain the *basis* in this basis-driven conception. Second, we must show that features of the distinctively human existence lead to human rights, that is, to *rights* rather than goals or values, and to *human* rights according to the concept adopted from Cohen (2006). Both questions are quite central to the foundations of morality in general because they are concerned with exploring why human beings can make claims on each other independently of any legal enforcement. It should be unsurprising then that much work has recently been done on both of these tremendously important questions.

One approach to the question of what it is about the distinctively human life that generates rights is a revitalized *natural law tradition*. Roughly speaking, according to the natural law tradition, moral prescriptions are part of the infrastructure of the world around us in much the same way in which laws of physics are, except that it may take different methods to understand what they are. Natural laws are norms whose justification depends on natural attributes of persons and facts about the non-human world. Justifications of natural law do not exclusively involve human conventions or institutions, nor do they exclusively involve any transactions, such as promises or contracts. (Similarly for natural *rights*.) A commitment to natural law involves an objective theory of a good life – and hence of a vision of a good life that every person has reason to realize – that typically includes basic goods such as health, knowledge, or friendship. What makes the distinctively human life valuable in this view is its ability to realize these objective goods. As an example, consider a natural law theory inspired by Christian theology, an inspiration that is implicit (and often explicit), for instance, in the work of the influential 17th century English philosopher John Locke. Locke's *Second Treatise of Government* talks about humans as

> being all the workmanship of one omnipotent, and infinitely wise maker; all the servants of one sovereign master, sent into the world by his order, and about his business; they are his property, whose workmanship they are, made to last during his, not one another's pleasure. (section 6)

Locke also thinks that all human beings are morally equal. The origin of this moral equality is never really explained – and after all, why should all human beings be morally equal given the enormous differences among us? The answer that is implicit in Locke is that we are all equal as *children of God* who were created in the divine image. Natural rights are rights that individuals have, and have equally, as children of God. These natural rights (whose contents Lock limits to the preservation of life, liberty, health, limbs, and goods) constrain any legitimate state power.[2]

Another response to our question of what it is about the distinctively human life that generates rights is that it gives a central role to dignity and its connection to *freedom* and *reason*, a response often referring to Immanuel Kant. An 18th century German philosopher, Kant is one of the pivotal figures in the history of philosophy. I will say a bit more about his work in Chapter 3. According to Kant, what makes the distinctively human life valuable is our possession of reason. Kant understands reason as a capacity for free choice, and it is this capacity that is the only source of value. In this view, things in the world are valuable not because they are so by nature or because God made them so. Instead, nothing in the world has value unless reason has bestowed it. Kant uses the term "dignity" to capture the particular significance of being endowed with reason. Also enlisting dignity, James Griffin (2008) argues the crucial feature of a distinctively human life is "normative agency:" "what we attach value to, what we regard as giving dignity to human life, is our capacity to choose and to pursue our conception of a worthwhile life" (p 44).

Contemporary authors have given pride of place to other features of human beings that would explain what it is about the distinctively human life that gives rise to rights. Philosopher and economist Amartya Sen and philosopher Martha Nussbaum champion *capabilities* as the relevant feature of the distinctively human life, stressing values like freedom, empowerment, or choice (Sen 2004, 1985); Nussbaum (2006, 2000). The moral significance of human capabilities (and thus the significance of *increasing* these capabilities) has also had a considerable impact on thinking about economic development and policies useful for promoting development (for instance through the work of the United Nations Development Programme, whose annual Human Development Reports have been much influenced by Sen's thought). One of Amartya Sen's most influential books is tellingly entitled *Development as Freedom* (Sen 1999). To mention one other answer to the question of what feature of human beings gives rise to right: among others, David Miller (2007), a political theorist at Oxford whose work we will encounter in several chapters of this book, bases a conception of human rights on the significance of *basic needs*, "the conditions that must be met for a person to have a decent life given the environmental conditions he faces" (p 184). Such needs are tied to ideas of the necessary, unimpeachable, or inescapable. They include but are not exhausted by "food and water, clothing and shelter, physical security, health care, education, work and leisure, freedoms of movement, conscience, and expression" (p 184).

Common humanity and human rights

So these are some plausible responses to the question of what features of the distinctively human life generate rights. I return to these approaches below, but for now let me proceed to the second question, just *how* features of the distinctively human existence lead to human rights. Precisely why is it that human beings have human rights and corresponding duties vis-à-vis each other?

One way of generating rights takes us back to Kant. According to what one may call the *Kantian self-consistency approach*, an agent falls into a contradiction with herself when not treating others in a manner that involves respect for rights. Others too are endowed with reason, and thus possess what Kant regards as the sole source of all value. The source of all value can only lie within beings endowed with reason, but not outside of them. According to Kant, that is, the source of value cannot be divine, nor can it somehow lie in the infrastructure of the world (independent of beings who possess reason) as natural law theorists would have it. Courses of action are acceptable, following Kant's Categorical Imperative (the formula meant to capture the essence of moral requirement), only if they are acceptable from the standpoint of all beings endowed with reason ("always act in such a way that the maxim of your own action could be the principle of universal legislation"). There are certain things that must never be done to such beings: they must never be used as mere means to somebody's ends, and thus without any regard for the fact that they too are endowed with reason, for instance through deception and unjustifiable coercion.

Suppose I am treating somebody merely as a means. The person whom I am so treating must rationally understand herself as a source of value. However, the capacity in virtue of which she must do so is the same one in virtue of which I too am rationally compelled to understand myself as a source of value. Disregarding the other person's capacity (by treating her as a mere means to my ends) amounts to disregarding a capacity I find in myself and must value if I am to see value in my own goals (which after all could get their own value only from my capacity to bestow, and thus be a source of, such value). To disregard another person is to draw a distinction between myself and that person that on rational grounds is unacceptable. Kant himself of course did not think in terms of human rights, but his approach can be used to derive a list of such rights. Kant's approach leads to human rights because certain rights are required to give adequate consideration to beings endowed with reason. We would be falling into a contradiction with ourselves if we were to violate these rights of others and thus treat other people's rational nature as less worthy than our own.[3]

However, many philosophers have become doubtful of the enterprise of deriving substantial prescriptions from self-consistency. As far as the argument in the last paragraph is concerned, that I value certain things only permits the inference that I must value *my having the capacity to value.* By the same reasoning, *you* must value *your* having the capacity to value. I must value the capacity to value, or to set ends, *insofar as it is a capacity that I possess.* You must value that capacity insofar as it is a capacity *you* possess. I do not need to value *your* capacity to value, and vice versa. Neither you nor I must value the capacity to value *per se.* No contradiction arises if *I* am using *you* as a means to ends that have value because *I* have conferred it upon them. What the argument demonstrates is how you become *intelligible* to me as an agent, how I come to see your actions as more than mere chance events – by coming to realize that, in a fundamental way, we are alike. But if no contradiction arises in this way, we cannot derive human rights in this way either. So the Kantian approach cannot tell us why we would have human rights.

But perhaps what we should seek to establish is the *unreasonableness* of treating people merely as means or even of treating them as moral unequals, rather than an *inconsistency* that lies in doing so. Consider the following illuminating statement by the American philosopher Joel Feinberg that addresses the idea of moral equality across human beings:

> The real point of the maxim that all men are equal may be simply that all men equally have a point of view of their own, a unique angle from which they view the world. They are all equally centers of experience, foci of subjectivity. This implies that they are all capable of being viewed by others imaginatively from their own point of view. They 'have shoes' into which we can always try to put ourselves; this is not true of mere things. It may follow (causally, not logically) from this way of so regarding them that we come to respect them in the sense tied to the idea of 'human worth.' ... In attributing human worth to everyone we may be ascribing no property or set of qualities, but rather expressing an attitude – the attitude of respect – towards the humanity in each man's person. That attitude follows naturally from regarding everyone from the

'human point of view', but it is not grounded on anything more ultimate than itself, and it is not demonstrably justifiable. (1973, pp 93f)

In the spirit of this statement, we should seek to show that it would be unreasonable to disregard human rights, rather than inconsistent. This move would abandon a major ambition of moral thought, to offer an unassailable demonstration of morality. It would mean to give up on the idea that being immoral involves a particular kind of mistake, the mistake of thinking about oneself vis-à-vis other people in a self-contradictory manner. But we have found some indication that it is asking too much to want a grounding of morality, and specifically of human rights, such that being immoral means to fall into a contradiction with oneself.

Several philosophers have recently attempted to provide accounts of human rights that make their violation *unreasonable* rather than *self-contradictory*. Approaches that proceed in this way (as e.g., the aforementioned James Griffin, David Miller, Amartya Sen and Martha Nussbaum do) begin with an appeal to the normative significance of the feature of common humanity that they stress. The contemporary philosophical literature contains fair number of ways of making such an appeal. It is interesting to look at a few statements to see how different philosophers have spelled out the sense in which human rights violations are unreasonable. For instance, James Griffin states that it is "the mere possession of this common capacity to identify the good that guarantees persons the protection of human rights" (2008, p 46). David Miller (2007) insists basic needs are both morally urgent and of universal reach and thus generate rights (p 197). Gillian Brock, a philosopher from New Zealand, explains that "if the needs are not met, we are unable to do anything much at all and certainly are unable to lead a recognizably human life" (1998, p 15). Moreover, the British philosopher Onora O'Neill (1986) argues that the needy are unusually prone to coercion and that it is a matter of respect for their autonomy not to let people fall into such a situation.

The question then becomes *just how* an appeal to the significance of features of the distinctively human life establishes *rights*, rather than goals or values. One response to this challenge, that one finds philosophers pursue, is to introduce limitations on the range of conditions under which this appeal to moral significance creates rights, and thereby to limit implausible implications. James Griffin talks about "practicalities," empirical insights about limits of human understanding and motivation which ensure that normative agency does not ask too much of individuals. David Miller offers several limitations on what can be demanded on behalf of needs satisfaction, such as limits imposed by what human agency cannot provide at all; what cannot be demanded of others; and what could be provided only if the needs of others were unacceptably violated.

However, Miller's strategy of *limiting unsatisfactory implications* provokes the question of why these features whose significance is made central should have a sufficient grip on others to generate rights *at all*. One might say that pursuing this strategy is like being told, in response to a request for directions, how to avoid going too far while one is still unsure the direction is right. However, crucially, nothing more than what has been said up to this point needs to, or can, be said to show that individuals have rights. To see this, let us look at a very plausible understanding of what is actually involved in arguing for the claim that there is a (moral) right to something. T. M. Scanlon (2003a), (2003b), for one, thinks of an argument for rights as involving an empirical claim about how individuals behave or how institutions work in the absence of particular assignments of rights; a claim that this result would be unacceptable, based on valuations of consequences in a way that takes into account considerations of fairness and equality (as appropriate); and a further empirical claim about how the envisaged assignment of rights will produce a different outcome. Within this approach, one can articulate ideas about needs or normative agency and their importance (and thereby then bring to bear Scanlon's analysis of *rights* on the particular topic of *human rights*), and then indeed also block implausibly strong implications. But after *all this* is said and done, Scanlon submits, and plausibly so, that there is nothing *more* to say to address the question whether such an argument *really* delivers rights. We have reached the limits of what a theory of rights can provide.

The British philosopher David Wiggins (1987) offers a slightly different response to the challenge of why this kind of approach could generate rights. Wiggins argues (within the confines of a theory of needs) that needs must be met for us to be able to maintain any social morality. If, for instance, somebody is denied what is vitally needed, she has reason to withdraw support from society. Rather than emphasizing that respect from others is the appropriate response to certain features of our common humanity, Wiggins stresses what reactions are appropriate for those who are mistreated. The implications of Wiggins' standpoint may be quite striking. If society has nothing to offer to a group of people (think of slums or inner city ghettos or despised minorities, as the case may be), they do not owe society any allegiance.

Orthodox conceptions: obtaining a list of rights

To obtain a *principle* that generates a list of rights, we must explain in more detail what facets of our distinctively human life generate rights. Moreover, we must assess what duties apply to whom given this basis and principle. As far as the first matter is concerned, the answer will vary depending on which of the proposals reviewed above we adopt. If we endorse the distinctively human life as basis, it may, for instance, be considerations of both agency and needs that generate rights to protect such life. However, for *any* of the candidates it will be hard to specify a reasonably determinate list of rights (and to specify the *principle* that generates it).

As far as *agency* is concerned, for instance, we must ask at what level to protect individuals to ensure they can exercise agency. Slaves can exercise some agency, and this is why their owners acquired them. But is the agency dimension of a distinctively human life sufficiently protected if slaves are sheltered from more cruel forms of violence? As far as the needs approach is concerned, note that one can conceive even basic needs at different levels. In their influential work on needs, Len Doyal and Ian Gough (1991) distinguish fundamental needs (physical health, mental competence to choose and deliberate) from intermediate needs (which spell out what is required to satisfy fundamental needs: nutritional food, clean water, protective housing, non-hazardous environment, appropriate health care, security in childhood, significant primary relationships, physical security, economic security, appropriate education, safe birth control and childbearing). One can ask whether what is *needed* for a distinctively human life is protected sufficiently if satisfaction of fundamental needs is guaranteed. The capabilities approach too leads to such a question since we can identify certain basic capabilities as especially urgent.

A general difficulty in identifying a list of rights emerges. I have identified facets of a distinctively human life that supposedly generate rights. For this approach to generate natural rights (which human rights are on this conception), the basis must apply to all humans, and must permit reasonably precise and uncontroversial inferences to duties of others. But if there are competing interpretations of the level at which to protect agency, needs, or capabilities to allow for a distinctively human life, we should accept one that generates the *weaker* set of rights. Otherwise one could reasonably object (and so make the relevant rights controversial and, crucially, render doubtful their status as *natural* rights) based on the availability of a weaker interpretation, which *exhausts* the argumentative force of the starting points, that too many duties are imposed.

This difficulty arises about the *lower* boundary of required protection. We must determine such a lower boundary of protection when we are engaging those who doubt that the idea of the distinctively human life does much work at all to generate human rights. We reach the upper limit of a list that we can derive from such an approach once we reach rights for which we cannot argue by reference to what it takes to protect the distinctively human life, but whose defense essentially requires references to transactions that individuals have made, or to features of membership in associations – and requires such references not just for specific assignments of duties, but for establishing entitlements *in the first place.* For instance, if the derivation of a right crucially depends on references to features of membership in states, the rights so derived are better regarded as citizens' rights, rather than human rights.

Among the rights on the UDHR that clearly cannot be derived within orthodox conceptions of human rights are a right to freedom of residence (in Article 13), a right to protection against attacks on one's honor and reputation (in Article 12), a right to equal pay for equal work (in Article 23), and a right to holidays with pay (Article 24). Moreover, drawing merely on the protection required for the distinctively human life, we cannot obtain any rights associated with liberal democracy, as opposed to other forms of governments; with the secular state, as opposed to other forms of political organization; or with the value of equality, as opposed to other forms of distribution or status. Such rights will plausibly be *rights of citizens*: claims that individuals have against their respective states wherever they live, but that do not come with responsibilities for those with whom citizenship is not shared, and that do not come with the especially high degree of urgency of *human rights*. No matter what proposal we adopt, for what precisely matters about that kind of life, the distinctively human life is available to those who do not live in a liberal democracy or a secular state or do not enjoy a status of equality. Trying to derive the protection of such values from the distinctively human existence hopelessly overextends that idea.

Among the rights that are plausible candidates for human rights according to orthodox conceptions are a right to life and security of the person; a voice in political decision; free expression, assembly, and press; the right to worship; the right to basic education and minimum provisions needed to be functioning as a person (which is more than what is needed for mere physical survival); and the right not to be tortured. But again, there are considerable problems about drawing the lower boundary of required protection. These problems are hard to resolve. We should therefore move beyond an orthodox conception. Further on, I offer a conception in which rights can receive support also based on considerations other than a distinctively human life. But let us explore a different subject first.

Who ought to do what?

The question of who ought to do what to realize human rights has come up for a good deal of discussion in recent years. This question arises according to any conception of human rights. I discuss it at this stage so that I can then end this chapter with my own proposal for how we should think about human rights. What is crucial is that it is not merely states that need to contribute to the realization of human rights. The *general* obligation is for all individuals and institutions to do what they can (within limits) to realize human rights. After all, according to at least paradigmatic orthodox conceptions, human rights are natural rights. Their justification, unlike that of rights of citizens that are not also human rights, does not depend on political or economic structures in any way. Therefore in principle all entities – individuals and institutions – in the global order are duty bearers. Legal theorist Jeremy Waldron plausibly suggests that rights are "best thought of not as correlative to one particular duty...but as generating successive waves of duty, some of them duties of omission, some of them duties of commission, some of them too complicated to fit easily under either heading" (1993, p 25). What this amounts to for entities within the global order depends on their nature. It was true long before there was a global order that the general duty is for all entities to do what they can (within limits) to realize human rights. But it would not have amounted to much because what they *could* do was rather limited. Increasing global political and economic interconnectedness matters greatly when it comes to spelling out the content of obligations.

All entities in the global order – including individuals – have the duty to "refrain" from human rights violations.[4] Since human rights are held against those in positions of authority (rather than against individuals as such), we must be careful in assessing what obligations individuals as such have. Individuals ought to refrain from violating human rights in two senses. First of all, they should not do the kind of thing against which the rights protect – not because they are held against individuals, but because the weight of reason that establishes that these rights are held against those with authority *also* creates a duty for individuals not to do the sort of thing against which the rights protect. Second, individuals should comply with reasonable measures that those in positions of authority take to protect human rights. Given the urgency that characterizes human rights, this much seems plausible as a duty of individuals as such.

States provide the immediate environment for people's lives to unfold. Primary responsibility for realizing human rights thus lies with states. States must "protect" and "provide" human rights to their citizens. They must not only refrain from violating rights, but also protect individuals within their jurisdiction from abuses by third parties. When it is in the nature of the rights in question – think of social and economic rights – states must provide them in the first place. Since human rights are a global responsibility, states must also "assist" *other* states with the realization of such rights in their (the other states') jurisdiction if those states are incapable of doing so themselves. They must "interfere" if other states are unwilling to maintain an acceptable human rights record. Such duties of assistance and interference are held alongside other states, and may well be exercised through international organizations. Since states have these duties of assisting and interfering, they must also "record" the human rights performance of other states, especially those with which they interact regularly (e.g., through trade).

But crucially, obligations also pertain to institutions others than states. International organizations too must "assist" states in discharging duties, and "interfere" if states are unwilling to maintain an acceptable record. They have the additional responsibility of "supervising" the human rights records of states, in any event in the domain of their activities (e.g., the WTO in the domain of trade). Businesses too have duties, especially transnational corporations with great impact on societies. A 2008 UN report plausibly distinguishes between a duty of states to "protect" human rights and that of businesses to "respect" them (Ruggie 2007, 2008). According to the view developed in that report, transnational corporations should be accountable for human rights without being directly under the purview of international law, with its ensuing complications. States must set appropriate incentives. Companies should be legally obligated to adopt due-diligence standards to ensure human rights are respected. Responsibilities for human rights are differential.

If an entity is in a position to realize human rights but chooses not to, intervention may be appropriate. In spite of the ready connotation of "intervention" with military interference, it is important to recognize that intervention could take on a range of forms. In the case of a state, intervention might amount to using incentives to get the government to change policies, to supporting domestic opposition, or to exerting diplomatic pressure and enforcing economic sanctions. Intervention might also involve the provision of educational opportunities for younger people who might later act as agents of change. International entities that make for more accountability (such as the International Criminal Court) also in a sense "intervene" in domestic politics by changing the incentives of government officials.

Human rights as membership rights in the global order

Orthodox conceptions develop the idea that human rights are rights individuals hold simply in virtue of being human. Perhaps this is the most natural way of thinking about *human* rights. But there are other conceptions as well, and orthodox conceptions have difficulties establishing a lower boundary of required protection. Let me therefore end this chapter by sketching an approach to human rights I offer in *On Global Justice*. This approach does not really abandon orthodox conceptions but proceeds at a more general level that leaves room for what is right about orthodox conceptions.

According to orthodox conceptions, human rights are natural rights. For natural rights, all human beings could be duty-bearers, regardless of the conditions under which we live. Therefore the protection of the distinctively human life is a global responsibility, and now the global order is the obvious addressee of these rights. But we may ask: how *else* could rights become a global responsibility (and thus how else could the differentiated way of thinking about responsibility become applicable that we explored above)? Instead of thinking of human rights exclusively as rights individuals hold *in virtue of being human*, one could understand them as those rights for which there is a genuinely global responsibility. Or as one may say, one could think of human rights as *membership rights in the global order*. Human rights thus understood are rights that are indeed accompanied by genuinely global responsibilities, rather than rights people would hold everywhere but that are accompanied only by respectively local responsibilities. (Rights of that second sort would be rights of citizens and thus a matter of social justice, rather than human rights concerns.) Being a member of the global order (the system of states plus network of organizations charged with global problem-solving) means to live on the territory covered by it and to be subject to those bits of the global interlocking system of jurisdictions that apply to one's situation. All humans are now members in this sense. Membership rights in the global order are rights held vis-à-vis that order. Enough structure to render the term "global order" applicable, as well as an accompanying capacity for coordinated action, is a condition for the existence of rights held within that order. Indeed, there is enough structure because of the existence of organizations that are designed for, and concern themselves with, global problem-solving.

We can develop a basis-driven conception of human rights using membership in the global order as basis. Such rights derive from different *sources*, one of which is the distinctively human life. As we saw, the distinctively human life can by itself be the basis of a conception. But if there are other ways of deriving rights that entail a global responsibility, it is plausible to think of the distinctively human life as one in several sources of membership rights in the global order. The additional sources also help with the problem of drawing a lower boundary of required protection: such sources could provide additional support for rights that seem plausible according to orthodox conception, but about which it is doubtful whether they really are required to protect the distinctively human life. Orthodox conceptions do not appeal to contingencies other than laws of nature, general facts about human nature, or the fact that certain beings are human. A conception in terms of membership in the global order, by recognizing other sources, uses contingent facts more freely, by way of enlisting features of an empirically contingent but relatively abiding world order.

One additional source of membership rights is humanity's collective ownership of the earth. Whereas reflection on ownership of the earth has not been prominent in recent political philosophy, it was the pivotal theme of 17th century political philosophy. Philosophers such as Hugo Grotius, Thomas Hobbes and John Locke disagreed about what precisely this ownership status amounted to. At that time intellectual support for this view came from the biblical book of Genesis, where we read that God gave to humanity "dominion over the fish of the sea, and over the fowl of the air, and over the cattle, and over all the earth, and over every creeping thing that creepeth upon the earth" (Genesis 26).

The motivation for thinking the earth is collectively owned by humanity is easy to obtain without any theology. What is at stake is ownership of, as the philosopher John Passmore put it, "our sole habitation... in which we live and move and have our being" (1974, p 3), or in the 19th century political economist Henry George's words, of "the storehouse upon which [man] must draw for all his needs, and the material to which his labor must be applied for the supply of all his desires" (1871, p 27). Suppose the population of the US shrinks to three, but they control access through border-surveillance mechanisms. Nothing changes elsewhere. Surely these three should permit immigration since they are grossly under-using their area. We can best explain this view by the fact that all of humanity has claims to the earth. The resources and spaces of the earth are valuable to and necessary for all human activities to unfold, most importantly to secure survival. Moreover, to the extent that resources and spaces have come into existence without human interference, nobody has claims to them based on any contributions to their creation. If we assume that the satisfaction of basic human needs matters morally, it follows that all humans have some kind of claims to original resources and spaces (resources and spaces that have come into existence without human interference) that cannot be constrained by reference to what others have accomplished.

What humanity's collective ownership amounts to must be worked out in detail. But what is straightforward is that this ownership status grants individuals entitlements against living under political and economic arrangements that deprive those subject to them of opportunities to satisfy basic needs (by using resources and spaces, or else in some other way). However, the arrangement to which individuals are subject is not merely the state in which they live, but the global order as such. Each state, in virtue of its access to their bodies and assets, might deprive individuals of opportunities. But so might other states by refusing them entry if they cannot satisfy basic needs at home. Other states that could provide this ability but refuse would not merely fail to offer aid; they would deny an opportunity to satisfy needs. Co-owners must have guarantees that institutional power will not be used to violate their status. Responsibilities must be allocated at the level of the state system per se, as collective responsibilities, rather than resting exclusively with the individual states. The flip side of these responsibilities is a set of rights individuals hold vis-à-vis the global order. This is how reflection on ownership of the earth leads to membership rights in the global order, and to human rights.

The reasoning in the preceding paragraph generates two fundamental guarantees whose realization is a global responsibility: first, states and other powerful entities must ensure their power does not render individuals incapable of meeting basic needs; second, they must create opportunities for them to meet basic needs. Such guarantees neutralize the dangers that the global order poses for individuals' co-ownership status. The first guarantee leads to rights to life and bodily integrity as well as to individual liberties (e.g., freedom from forced labor, of conscience, of expression and association, of movement, and freedom to emigrate) and political rights (e.g., to accountable representation), and due process rights (e.g., to a fair trial). The second guarantee leads to the need for a guaranteed opportunity to enjoy a minimally adequate standard of living, as far as food, clothing, and housing are concerned. At least in societies with sophisticated economies we must add an elementary right to education and a right to work understood as a right not to be excluded from labor markets.

Collective ownership does not add rights that did not at least seem plausible when we only considered the distinctively human life as a source, and it allows for the derivation of rights only if we already assume that the satisfaction of basic needs matters morally. Nonetheless, it is useful to integrate into an account of human rights reflection on the contingent fact that every satisfaction of a human need depends on some use of the earth's resources and spaces. We can then derive rights in a way that rests on a broader foundation than an exclusive appeal to the moral significance of basic needs. We have *more* to work with than merely the significance of needs or other aspects of the distinctively human life. Appealing to collective ownership helps with the problem of drawing the lower boundary of required protection for the distinctively human life by rendering a number of proposed human rights intellectually more secure.

Another motivation for recognizing this source of membership rights is that there is good reason to integrate theorizing about ownership of the earth into global political philosophy anyway. We increasingly confront problems that concern our use of the earth as such. For instance, the preamble of the 1992 UN Framework Convention on Climate Change begins by acknowledging "that change in the Earth's climate and its adverse effects are a common concern of humankind." And decades before, in a speech at American University in Washington D.C. in June 1963, US President John F. Kennedy stated that "in the final analysis, our most basic common link is that we all inhabit this small planet." The future will only bring more problems that concern our use of the earth as such. Later in this book too we return to collective ownership of the earth.

Human rights as membership rights in the global order: additional sources

Different sources of membership rights in the global order provide different ways in which X may be a right with accompanying global responsibilities. Proposed "rights" may receive support from any or all sources, and the strength of this support may vary. A critical discourse can occur if proposed rights fail to receive support from all sources. Conclusive support from one source is enough to establish a human right. Insufficient support from other sources then illuminates its disputed nature, but does not undo its status as a human right. Conversely, insufficient support from one source only defeasibly establishes that X is not a human right. Inquiries into other sources might still show that X is a human right after all. Its ability to account for contestation and pluralism confers additional plausibility on my conception.

Let me briefly discuss three other such sources. One additional source is enlightened self-interest. For this source, one must show that certain matters give rise to rights domestically (the idea of human rights being a moral one), and a self-interest argument would then show why this matter is globally urgent. The preservation of peace may require that authority is exercised in certain ways (or would be very difficult otherwise), perhaps because unchecked governments will also be abusive vis-à-vis others, or create negative externalities (refugees, etc). ("Necessary/very difficult without:" the closer we come to necessity, the stronger an argument we produce.) Concerns about peace, and the impossibility of limiting certain evils to domestic affairs, were motives behind the founding of the League of Nations after the First World War and what limited recognition human rights had then. Such concerns also triggered more expansive efforts to incorporate human rights in a framework of institutions and treaties after the Second World War. The preamble of the UDHR acknowledges the ties between "justice and peace in the world."

Troubled states are a global liability. They spread refugees and draw others into conflicts. Financial crises are internationally transmitted. Drug-trafficking, illegal immigration, arms trade, human trafficking, money-laundering, and terrorism must be fought globally because the networks behind them often operate globally. Disease control is a global problem as much as environmental sustainability. Conversely, development delivers gains from trade, and from co-operation in science, culture, business, or tourism. Martin Luther King overstates the matter in his *Letter from a Birmingham Jail* insisting that "injustice anywhere is a threat to justice everywhere" (1963, p 79). Nonetheless enlightened self-interest is a powerful way of showing that something is globally urgent.

Another source is *interconnectedness*. Something may be globally urgent if somehow the global order as such is causally responsible for certain problems for people in country A for which an assignment of rights would be the solution, as well as the sense in which this imposes obligations on people in countries B_1, B_2, etc. Enlightened self-interest and interconnectedness often apply jointly. To illustrate, consider the following argument for a human right against any form of slavery, no matter how benign. To begin with, considerations about membership in states show that individuals have a claim against their state for protection also against benign slavery. The increasing intensity of transnational interactions creates opportunities, and triggers demand, for human trafficking and thus modern day slavery. Millions are smuggled across borders and kept in bondage to work in the sex industry, in private households or in sweatshops. Since in any given country (especially in those that are major destinations of human trafficking) individuals have a right to protection against enslavement, it is in every country's enlightened self-interest to combat human trafficking. Otherwise the number of de facto slaves *in their midst* will increase. Regions where certain groups are held in contempt and kept in dependency are among the likely origins of such trafficking. The combination of enlightened self-interest and interconnectedness supports a human right not to be enslaved in any way.

Finally, one way in which concerns can become common within a political structure is for them to be regarded as such by an authoritative process. We can enlist *procedural* sources to argue that human rights express membership "as the global order sees it." For X to become a human right in this way we must determine what counts as authoritative acceptance of a global responsibility across the world. Such acceptance presupposes domestic mechanisms to empower governments (or conceivably other entities) to consent to global duties, as well as international structures within which countries can authoritatively accept duties. While we may well not need to be skeptical about the authenticity or relevance of certain governmental commitments to human rights, such commitments would not readily show that there is a commitment *to global membership rights*, with accompanying duties of *global* reach. It is one thing to show that a government is committed to respecting human rights domestically, another to show that it is also committed to promoting human rights elsewhere.

There are some recent examples of proposed duties of global reach. To begin with, one may think of the "responsibility to protect." This notion captures a state's responsibility to prevent genocide and other massive violations, as well as the international community's responsibility when states fail in this regard. Second, there is the principle of universal jurisdiction, whereby states may claim jurisdiction over certain criminals regardless of their relation to them. Finally, one may think of the International Criminal Court, which prosecutes individuals for genocide, crimes against humanity, war crimes, and the crime of aggression. Yet in light of the difficulties involved in getting duties of global reach credibly accepted, the best we can say is that the duties involved in these efforts are accepted by countries that have explicitly endorsed them *as* such duties and whose authenticity in making international commitments cannot be doubted as merely driven by a desire to be *perceived* as committed.

There is currently no good example of an actual *membership right in the global order* (with accompanying duties of global reach) that has been accepted through authoritative processes both domestically and internationally. This is only something to look forward to in the future. Nonetheless, at least conceptually, procedural sources are an important component of my account of human rights. However, given the constraints on that notion, there are limits to what any kind of process could declare a *human right*. For this reason, presumably, plausible candidates will be limited to cases where substantive sources seem inconclusive. At the same time, rights could be authoritatively accepted as global responsibilities although, conceptually speaking, we would not want to classify them as human rights. It could only be through global authoritative acceptance that something approaching the whole list of rights on the UDHR could offer a truly legitimate moral blueprint for the future of humanity.

Further reading

This has been a dense chapter. Subsequent chapters will be easier to take in, partly thanks to the work that we have now done in this chapter. But since the idea of human rights is the starting point for our journey, and since foundational inquiries about human rights turn on much recent philosophy, a lot needed to be said. For case studies that inspire optimism about the impact of human rights, see (Thomas) Risse et al. (1999). For statistical pessimism, see for instance Hathaway (2002). Making sense of these diverging findings is an area of ongoing research. For a recent contribution, see Simmons (2009).Simmons argues that human rights treaty commitments make a difference in countries that are undergoing democratic reforms anyway. Respect for human rights is driven by large-scale social and political processes (democracy, peace), historical macro-phenomena that are not easily affected by policy makers. Nonetheless, international human rights treaties have helped to nudge human kind in the right direction. Kant's moral philosophy appears most succinctly in his *Groundwork for the Metaphysics of Morals* that exists in many editions. How to make sense of human rights has become an active area of philosophical research. Key contributions include Beitz (2009), Cohen (2004) and (2006), and Griffin (2008). For the history and impact of the UDHR, see Morsink (1999) and Lauren (2003). Forsythe (2006) offers an account of the role of human rights in international relations.

2 Universalism vs. Relativism

Moral relativism explained

In Chapter 1 we encountered an objection to the UDHR raised by the American Anthropological Association. The anthropologists insisted that "standards and values are relative to the culture from which they derive," and took this fact to "detract from the applicability of any Declaration of Human Rights to mankind as a whole." Chapter 1 interrogated the idea of human rights without addressing the subject of universalism vs. relativism of values. This chapter now does so. However, we do not discuss that subject in abstraction from the idea of human rights. At this stage in history, the UDHR is the most promising moral blueprint for the future of humanity. It behooves us, therefore, to focus our exploration of relativism on that idea. At the same time, the growing global consensus for human rights also means the UDHR stands in strong need for philosophical scrutiny. To be clear, strictly speaking we have formulated a response to the charge of relativism: if the account of human rights in Chapter 1 is persuasive, it establishes the existence of universal values. However, since this matter is so important we should explore the issue explicitly.

An initial way of formulating relativism is that "values depend on the culture: there are no universal values." To be more precise, we must distinguish between cultural relativism and moral or normative relativism. *Cultural relativism* is the thesis that different societies abide by different moral codes. *Moral* or *normative relativism* is the thesis that *fundamental* values and ethical beliefs are culture-bound in a sense that does not allow for critical engagement with people who do not belong to that culture, and makes it the case that there is no right and wrong, but merely a "right for" and "wrong for." Cultural relativism does not entail moral relativism. Anthropologists have written about societies where people treat each other with little kindness, where even parents show little concern for their children. They have also written about societies that call on the elderly to retreat to the mountains to die, or leave handicapped children to perish. But to the extent that such treatment differs from how other societies deal with their weaker members, it might well be due to differences in living conditions. If people must worry whether they find enough food to survive another day, they might reveal no disagreement at the level of fundamental values or moral beliefs with those who treat the weak with more consideration: they merely do not find themselves under conditions that allow them to combine their own survival with kindness towards the weak.

Moral relativism is what we are interested in. Universalism is the opposing view: it holds that there are values or norms that apply across cultures, even where the cultures themselves do not accept them. Anybody who endorses human rights as discussed in Chapter 1 believes there are certain rights everybody should accept. Anybody who endorses such rights ipso facto endorses some universal values connected to the distinctively human life. Note carefully that moral relativism differs from *moral skepticism*. Moral skepticism holds that there is no sense in which anybody "ought to" do anything unless legal prohibitions are involved. "You ought not to steal" then only means the law prohibits it. That ought- statement becomes false as soon as applicable law permits stealing. No argument is then available for the conclusion that one ought not to steal that is recognizably moral, that is, an argument that leads to a negative evaluation of stealing simply based on considerations of how we have reason to treat others regardless of whether there is enforcement. Moral relativism recognizes that we are social creatures who live in societies and are subject to norms; but those are norms that only hold within particular communities.

Moral relativism also differs from tolerance. Tolerance is a permissive attitude towards practices of which one disapproves. A tolerant person may or may not be a moral relativist. Somebody might be convinced that Confucianism or Kantian philosophy includes all relevant truths about human affairs, especially moral prescriptions. But she might also believe that intellectual or cultural limitations keep many sincere people from reaching that insight, and thus take a tolerant attitude towards them. Alternatively, a tolerant person might be a committed relativist. Tolerance might be her attitude towards those with whom she shares a network of conventions but who interpret some of its aspects differently, or towards those who reject relativism. A relativist might be intolerant, either because he finds the denial of moral relativism deplorable or because he has a rigid understanding of the conventions that guide his life. Moreover, moral relativism requires of its advocates to accept cultures that are deeply intolerant. Tolerance captures a person's ability and willingness to endure people who act or think differently from how she believes they should. Moral relativism is a view about how morality applies. These notions have little to do with each other.

A moral relativist may offer the following view of what we are doing when passing moral judgment. Suppose I say to you ought not to kill people or assault them, or behave in certain ways in a church or a temple. By making such statements I make clear that I endorse this standpoint, and that I assume you too have reason to do so. Moral judgments occur before a network of conventions we have reason to keep as long as most people around us do. The presumption is that we have a shared motivational structure that makes the relevant kind of moral judgment accessible to all of us. Samurai in Japan in earlier centuries acknowledged codes of conduct vis-à-vis their own group that involved a fair amount of considerateness. But they had little hesitation killing peasants for minor slights. No judgment to the effect that such behavior was morally unacceptable would have made sense to them. Similarly, telling a member of a contemporary crime family that he ought not to execute an assignment to assassinate a member of a rival outfit would be a misuse of moral vocabulary. The hit man lacks any motivational structure to refrain him from carrying out the killing.

In his *Letter from a Birmingham Jail*, Martin Luther King explains that civil disobedience in a racist society seeks to create "a tension in the mind." That tension arises when those who wish to maintain such a society must ask themselves whether they are willing to use force against others merely for demanding rights or opportunities that the racists themselves readily embrace for their own kind. According to moral relativism, if moral judgment does not even have the potential to create a tension in somebody's mind (say, where it conflicts with his selfish purposes), that judgment does not apply to this person.

Indeed, if moral judgments make sense only before the background of a shared network of conventions and a motivational structure in which some people have reasons to do something, others may disobey or ignore moral judgments without being ignorant, without any form of irrationality, stupidity or confusion. Nonetheless, those who participate in the relevant network can engage in sustained moral debate aimed at creating more coherence within that network. In a culture where the Bible is the shared foundation of moral convictions, people might disagree about the moral status of animals. Are human beings overlords of the earth and thus entitled to use other species for food and other self-serving purposes? Or are we in a care-taker role vis-à-vis the rest of nature? Similarly, there might be disagreement about the acceptability of the death penalty. Has God reserved the ultimate judgment for himself and are we therefore under an obligation not willfully to take life he has given? Or are some kinds of behavior so offensive that God's justice requires that the perpetrators not be permitted to live amongst us? One would try to settle these disputes by assessing what makes the overall system of belief most coherent.

Moral relativism: motivation and difficulties

Einstein's special and general theories of relativity revolutionized physics in the early 20th century. They may also have greatly increased the popularity of an unreflective form of moral relativism in public culture ("All things are relative"). However, the reasoning involved in drawing support for moral relativism from Einstein's theories is utterly mistaken. Einstein teaches that both velocity and gravity influence the passage of time. The time lapse between two events varies among different observers. It depends on the relative speeds of their reference frames. Moreover, processes occurring close to a massive body run more slowly than those further away. However, theories about how velocity and gravity influence the passage of time do not bear on the question of whether there are universal values.

But even though Einstein's theories should not be taken to enhance its plausibility, moral relativism is easily motivated. "Different peoples live according to different norms; when in Rome do as the Romans do, and who is to judge anyway:" in the eyes of many, such attitudes capture an enlightened modesty that especially Westerners with their harrowing history of forcing others to copy their ways had better adopt. "The aims that guide the life of every people are self-evident in their significance to that people," so the American Anthropological Association wrote in 1947 (p 542). Moral relativism has much intuitive attraction.

But this intellectual attraction quickly meets equally straightforward problems. Moral relativism, again, is the thesis that *fundamental* values and ethical beliefs are culture-bound in a sense that does not allow for critical engagement with people who do not belong to that culture, and makes it the case that there is no right and wrong, but merely a "right for" and "wrong for." Although this sounds simple, the exposition of moral relativism involves difficulties. It is difficult to determine what counts as the "culture" to which values and beliefs are bound. Cultures tend to be heterogeneous, and it will be hard to assess who has the authority to determine values and moral beliefs on behalf of a culture. Individuals may participate in various cultures simultaneously: they may be integrated into practices shared by ethnic or racial groups, but also belong to a religion that is not limited by ethnicity or race.

Unless we have a reasonably clear sense of how to identify the kind of culture that counts as a context to which values and beliefs are bound, moral relativism is not a well-defined thesis. Those who wish to justify behavior by appeal to the acceptability of such behavior in particular cultures often do so because "culture" is seen as a source of values and norms. However, the more we have trouble identifying what these cultures would be individually, the more it becomes clear that for strikingly many actions there would be *some* kind of culture that supports it. The less one can then resort to appeals to culture to justify actions. Cultures themselves stand in need of justification.

But let us assume this problem is solvable. What is also problematic is that moral relativism makes it impossible to bring up moral criticisms of another culture even if that culture endorses revolting practices. Female genital cutting is a wide-spread practice in parts of Africa and elsewhere. It typically involves the partial or total removal of the clitoris, an operation normally performed on four- to eight-year old girls. The practice is locally deeply entrenched and tied to social status and marriage prospects. Unlike male circumcision it has no known health benefits. It is advantageous only as long as social sanctions hit those who refuse the procedure. Relativism would not permit outsiders to criticize such practices. But this is an odd conclusion. To reach a moral assessment of genital cutting one should understand what is involved in undergoing the procedure, and what the cultural and social significance of the practice is. However, what it is like for girls to undergo this procedure should not be much harder to understand for people who are not part of the culture than it is for the men who are. While grasping such social and cultural significance presupposes an unbiased and sensitive approach, a person with appropriate sensibilities, and some patience, should be able to muster the required understanding. Many outsiders will be unable to do so. But some will.

Moral relativism would also prevent us from critically assessing changes internal to our own culture. Americans could merely observe that the abolition of slavery amounted to a change of customs. They could not praise it as a change *for the better*. After all, one could assess what is right or wrong only by consulting standards of one's own "moral network." Suppose a society undergoes considerable changes that significantly worsen the economic situation of a particular group, as for example revolutions do, or as the abolition of slavery in a country does. In both cases some segments of society would suffer from the changes even though others benefit enormously. It is natural to say that there was moral progress within a society between times t_1 and t_2 if the changes that occurred in between (and that by t_2 have turned into the status quo) create a situation that is more broadly, and freely, accepted in the population than the status quo was at t_1. For centuries the transatlantic slave trade was a mainstay of the economies on both sides of the ocean. When it was abolished, the prospects of potential victims improved, but many whose livelihood depended on it bore heavy losses. But several decades later, perhaps only after those whose prospects suffered had died out, the new situation was overall more broadly acceptable to the people involved (including especially those previously subject to enslavement). The later situation was not simply different, but better. Moral progress took place. But if moral relativism were true we could not talk about moral progress this way.

Is moral relativism inconsistent?

Let us look at one common refutation of moral relativism that proceeds as follows. Instead of abiding by universal principles, moral relativism advises people to act in accordance with the moral principles of their own group. But by doing so moral relativism accepts a universal principle, to wit, this one: "one ought to act in accordance with the moral principles of one's own group." So there is a contradiction that arises from the fact that relativists hold both (a) that there are no universal principles, and (b) that one ought to act in accordance with the moral principles of one's own group. So (b) is the kind of thing that (a) rules out.

But this contradiction is easily avoided. The relativist – speaking as moral theorist – is not committed to (b). Instead, she would endorse something different, namely that (c) *people think* they ought to act in accordance with the principles of their own group. There is no contradiction between (a) and (c). For any given agent what matters in any event is only what network of norms and corresponding motivational structure speak to her. Moral agents have no need to formulate views on morality from a more theoretical standpoint (and thus to consider endorsing (b)). So neither the moral theorist nor the moral agent falls into a contradiction according to the understanding of morality that relativism offers. Whatever else is true, moral relativism is not plainly inconsistent.

So far we have seen that moral relativism is easily motivated, but encounters considerable difficulties. We have also noted that moral relativism is not inconsistent. The best sort of response to relativism is constructive, an answer that makes clear how there can indeed be universal values. I now offer such a response, specifically with an eye on the UDHR.

A first response: the need for universal values

Human beings have irreversibly encountered each other. We live in an interconnected world, and the question of what distant strangers ought to do for each other arises in numerous ways: we *must* confront it. Distant individuals might be tied by complex trade chains. The cotton used for a T-shirt might grow in Texas, but the T-shirt itself is manufactured in China. It is exported later to Brazil and sold in a Carrefour supermarket, as part of a major purchase negotiated in France. Eventually the T-shirt finds its way to a used clothing market in Nigeria (Rivoli 2005). Often the clothes people wear have travelled much farther than they themselves ever will, and the same is true for the food they consume, the cars they drive, and other machinery they use. A family in a small German town might make a middle class living through employment at a weapons manufacturing plant that uses spare parts from Thailand and Korea and exports its products to the Arab world. Via back-channels that pass through Ethiopia these weapons reach fighters in the Somali civil war. The fates of people working in the auto industry around the world are connected because cars are exported globally. How well cars made in Michigan sell depends to some extent on the quality of cars made in Hiroshima. Whether it makes sense for African countries to invest in the agricultural sector to be able to bring high-quality cotton to international markets depends to some degree on what the US decides with regard to subsidies for domestic cotton producers. At a much larger scale, the WTO provides the umbrella for trade negotiations that decide what kinds of products are sensible for countries around the world to try to sell. The IMF might approve a loan for Greece that involves Canadian taxpayer money. The World Bank channels funds from donor countries into development projects around the world.

We are also connected to individuals in distant parts of the world through TV coverage, newspaper reporting and social networks. Even presidents and prime ministers have become Facebook users. Unless governments take measures to disable cell phones and internet connections, videos of police crackdowns reach audiences worldwide within minutes. Victims of atrocities, natural disasters and ordinary state violence are already connected to us in virtue of the fact that we see them on our screens. Natural calamities like earthquakes, tsunamis and typhoons attract instant media coverage, as do major military engagements or terrorist attacks. As opposed to that, lingering problems attract much less attention. But even though the ongoing internal conflict in Congo is not subject to much reporting, anybody who takes an interest can easily find out what is going on. Similarly, one does not need to travel to Haiti to see what havoc the 2010 earthquake wreaked there, and one did not need to visit East Africa in 2011 to know that millions are starving there. We know or could easily know about their plight. Those who observe such suffering could take numerous courses of action, ranging from participating in relief efforts themselves to writing letters to politicians to make sure the plight of distant strangers bears on policy choice. Victims of calamities are making claims on us already because we are so connected to them. Since they are making these claims we need moral standards to assess what and how much we owe them.

Given the numerous ways in which people are connected, these moral standards must be universal. They must be universal at least in the sense that they must apply to all human beings in the present age. If the question arises of whether we can apply the same standards to people in the distant past – whether for instance we should pass moral judgment on Japanese samurai for killing peasants for minor slights – the answer might well be that we had better suspend judgment. Unlike the question of what we owe to distant strangers *now* the question of how we should pass moral judgments on people from the past does not force itself upon us and so can be set aside. As far as our current situation is concerned, the relativist says moral judgments make sense only before the background of a shared motivational structure, and we do not have any such structure at the global level. Therefore, she concludes, universalism is false. But a first response is that *it is the other way round:* we are stuck with the necessity of passing moral judgment at the global level, and must create the motivational structure needed to sustain such judgments.

Recall that the preamble to the UDHR ends by saying that "every individual and every organ of society...shall strive by teaching and education to promote respect for these rights and freedoms and by progressive measures, national and international, to secure their universal and effective recognition and observance." One way of understanding such efforts at education is that they are geared towards creating such a motivational structure. This could happen in many ways. A straightforward but perhaps slightly naïve picture of how human rights norms could receive broad acceptance across the world is as follows. At the first stage, states commit to international treaties. At the second stage, there would be "trickle-down" mechanisms through which the citizens themselves eventually internalize the human rights aspirations codified by these treaties. One way in which this could happen is through education in schools. Such education should make sure that children become aware of how people in other parts of the world live and that they relate sympathetically to these people's plights. Such education should also make sure that people understand that the multifarious ways in which human beings are now interconnected generate obligations for the maintenance of our shared life, and that individuals in this interconnected world are vulnerable in relevantly similar ways. Education of this sort should render the idea of human rights straightforwardly intelligible to children.

Another way in which children could internalize human rights aspirations is via the penetration of domestic legal systems by human rights norms or by explicit appeals to human rights standards in domestic policy discourse. Local concerns that previously had not been understood as human rights concerns could be recast in human rights language. Doing so would make it easier to show that the issues at stake are not local idiosyncracies, but commonly shared concerns. For instance, it is for this reason that in recent times gay rights issues have often been recast as human rights issues. Perceiving issues as commonly shared concerns, in turn, would make it easier to attract outsiders to witness how the concerns are treated, and would also make it easier to appeal to broadly shared standards about how the concerns should be remedied.

As I said, what I described is a straightforward but naïve picture of how human rights norms could get broad acceptance across the world. However, there are many ways in which this could and does happen, ways that are not mutually exclusive and are not excluded by the picture I just gave. Non-governmental organizations could help with the spread of human rights norms in countries that do not yet accept them by providing support to domestic opposition, or by "naming and shaming" the government. Such NGOs could also do grassroots work in poverty stricken areas; they could teach basic skills of self-help and simultaneously empower disadvantaged groups (such as women or ethnic minorities) for instance by talking about human rights standards. Governments and international organizations could make aid dependent on human rights standards, or could exert diplomatic pressure to get such standards accepted. Universities could award stipends to students from countries where human rights are not broadly accepted to increase intellectual engagement with such countries, or they could give scholarships to academics who are persecuted at home because they stand up for human rights standards. International accountability structures such as the International Criminal Court also contribute to the spread of these standards.

Moreover, intellectuals across different religious and cultural traditions could offer fresh elaborations of their traditions to show how human rights may find room within these traditions. They could work out how human rights protect the kinds of tasks individuals are assigned within such traditions. For instance, in religious traditions that want their believers to reach an authentic endorsement of the basic propositions of the faith human rights can be thought of as making sure individuals have the freedom of conscience, and material goods at least at the subsistence level, to engage with their religion. In religions or philosophies that ask their members to do certain services to the community human rights could be thought of as protecting individuals in these roles. Such fresh elaborations of religious traditions could preserve the integrity of the particular cultural contexts in which human rights would then be realized while also making clear that there are many common concerns that arise for us because we are human. Measures such as these could contribute to the creation of motivational structures supportive of universal norms.

A second response: elaborating on the distinctively human life

One might object that this first response is beside the point, that the discussion with the moral relativist is about something else. "Too bad if we need it," objectors might say; "a motivational structure and network of conventions at the global level is not there to be had, political and economic interconnectedness notwithstanding. There are no sufficient value similarities." Or one might complain that the sense of "universal values" the first response has deployed is unsatisfactory. To rebut relativism we do not merely need to show that moral questions that arise in an interconnected world require answers. We must also show that there is a sense in which moral considerations apply to human beings as such. So an additional response to moral relativism will be useful.

That second response takes us back to the idea of a distinctively human life that we encountered in Chapter 1 (drawing on the work of James Griffin) while exploring different conceptions of human rights. To the best of our understanding, there indeed is a distinctively human life that differs from that of other animals. This theme requires more elaboration now to show why it also provides a response to relativism. Before I talk more about this theme, let us note that all human life of the sort we would readily recognize has unfolded over a period of several ten thousand years, a period during which human possibilities were limited by the geological and climatic constraints that were imposed by this planet during that era. Perhaps in the future humanity will be able to leave this planet and migrate to different parts of this universe. Our species might divide into populations that end up living under vastly more diverse environmental conditions than provided by our current ecological niches on earth. It is important to keep this in mind since one way in which relativism could be false is if it just *happens* to be false under the circumstances under which we live on this planet. That is, even if values are culture-bound, it might so happen that human values now are relatively similar since the cultural trajectories our species has so far taken have been bound by the (geologically speaking) recent conditions on earth. Nonetheless, I think that the considerations I am about to present show that relativism is false also in a stronger sense.

So let us turn to what is distinctive about human life. Human beings have conceptions of themselves, and reflect on their past, present and future. They deliberate about, and assess, the different courses of action available to them and then opt to pursue some of them. Humans can see themselves in the world. They can envisage different ways of being in the world, and can think about the world without themselves in it. Humans can comprehend how their being in the world is seen by other beings (human or other). In the course of their lives, human beings acquire knowledge of many things and a myriad of memories, learn skills and find themselves in a complex web of interactions with others. We normally participate in complicated cultures which we preserve or modify, and which we embody in our own ways. Considerable similarities notwithstanding, it is a noticeable feature of humanity, and thus of the distinctively human life, that genetic components and environmental influences interact to produce highly unique individuals with distinguishing features. This idea of a distinctively human existence that I just sketched is not culture-bound.

But there is more to this distinctively human life. To begin with, persons across cultures share vulnerabilities: they suffer from physical pain, require food and water to survive and are susceptible to disease and malnutrition. Human beings are frail complexes of highly perishable tissue. We die after several days without water and after several weeks without food. We are easily crushed by heavy objects. We need oxygen to survive and cannot keep ourselves afloat in water without aid even for a few days. Our biological systems deteriorate quickly in extreme temperatures. Moreover, people across cultures aspire for at least a limited set of common goods: bodily health, bodily integrity and a desire to be treated with some respect in one's affiliations. Not literally everybody seeks to have these goods, but the most common counter examples are people who have chosen a life of self-sacrifice that is designed to deviate from what is (and what those people would themselves regard as) normal, or who have been brainwashed into believing they do not deserve to partake of these goods. Minimal human flourishing is not culture-dependent. Common vulnerabilities and common goods make intercultural exchange intelligible. Needless to say, culture matters greatly for who people are. But different cultures are different cultures *of human beings* (and indeed of humans *as they have so far existed on this planet*, with the kind of evolutionary processes that its recent geological past has made possible). It is in light of our commonalities that we are intelligible to each other, and that we are enormously much better positioned to understand "what it is like" to be part of another culture than "what it is like" to be a member of a different species.

The existence of a distinctively human life that is decidedly not culture-bound creates difficulties for moral relativism. If fundamental values and ethical beliefs were culture-bound, the distinctively human life itself would not come up for any particular moral consideration. The distinctively human life would not be valuable as such then, and would require no special protection. Human life itself would deserve protection only to the extent that it is life that participates in specific cultures. However, cultures are indeed cultures of human beings, built and developed by individuals that in many ways are strikingly alike and that bring distinctively human abilities to bear on the evolution of these cultures. Different cultures are different manifestations of the distinctively human life. It would therefore be tremendously implausible to say human life deserves protection only to the extent that it is life that participates in specific cultures.

It is presumably also for this reason that most if not all sophisticated cultures produce some form of universalist thinking. That intellectual streak might not be dominant in the culture. Cultures are inherently diverse, and different streaks are dominant at different times. To mention a striking example, Germany has been home to both the decidedly universalist Kantian philosophy and the highly racist and thus anti-universalist Nazi ideology. But, indeed, universalist thinking comes naturally to sophisticated cultures: in light of the existence of a distinctively human life the plausibility of particular religious, ethnic or racist categories that are being used to argue for supremacy or other forms of moral distinction, declines. History abounds in failed attempts to defend such categories, fascism, sexism, and racism being egregious examples of recent and to some extent ongoing prevalence. Eventually the thought must emerge that other people are in many significant ways just like those with whom one shares a culture.

Speaking up for the victims

So relativism is ultimately implausible. It is striking that those who speak in support of relativism and against the alleged "value imperialism" associated with universalism are often those in power or their acolytes. "We do things differently around here" is a statement that serves those who in fact get to do things. Those who reject relativism often take the standpoint of those who are being victimized by the practices in question. Victims of torture will always have difficulties conveying to others the pain a tortured person undergoes. However, these difficulties are not culture-bound but turn on whether somebody ever found herself entirely at the mercy of another's arbitrary will. The kind of pain involved would be felt by all humans even if some are better able to withstand it than others. Malnutrition, disease and extreme temperatures do not normally affect human bodies differentially depending on which culture they belong to, even though, again, some will be better able to bear it than others.

To the extent that representatives of certain cultures reject human rights by saying something like "around here *we* do things differently," their argument often rests on an attribution of unanimity in their own culture that does not exist, and is especially implausible when egregious human rights violations are involved (Scanlon 2003b). After all, if P speaks on behalf of a collective "we," this presupposes two things. First of all, there must be a "we" that is somehow constituted and can be consulted. Countries that lack any kind of democratic or otherwise consultative traditions and where over generations people have become used to being treated by their rulers with contempt and distrust will rarely be organized as a group in a way that allows anybody to consult "them." It is therefore impossible to assess what "they" think about anything. Second, speaking in this manner also presupposes that P finds himself in the position of credibly speaking *for* the relevant collective "we" (where it does exist). We would need to assess why of all people it would be P who would be privileged to do so. Both of these points may generate doubts if P claims to speak on behalf of a collective. A population that is systematically abused or undernourished is unlikely to be sufficiently well-constituted as a group to generate views on anything. If in addition the abuse or malnourishment is caused or tolerated by the government it would be preposterous to believe a government spokesperson who claims "we do things differently around here."

However, statements of the sort "we do things differently" do not always come from those in power. They might be made by those whom outsiders would characterize as victims. In the 20th century political machineries have largely perfected the use of propaganda to reinforce their messages. Children might be exposed to governmental propaganda from a young age on, and might never encounter anything to which they could compare these messages. A strong personality cult around a leader could deprive people of any mental capacities even to formulate criticism of the leader's decisions. Instruction at schools and universities might be streamlined, opposition oppressed, the media state-controlled, and the influx of information and materials from the outside world tightly regulated. A society might be organized in such a way that full allegiance to the regime is amply rewarded, and the political credo of the regime itself might even be embedded into an erudite intellectual system that has considerable breadth and depth (involving sophisticated distortions of recognizable moral ideals), and thus offer tools to withstand intellectual scrutiny.

All of this was true of the fascist and communist dictatorships the world has seen in the 20th century, and to some extent continues to see. Such systems can hold their populations captive also because they could capture the minds of many intelligent and experienced people. But if a whole generation can see the world only through the lenses of an oppressive regime, that generation might be deeply persuaded that they have found the one and only right way to live and that it is the ignorance or maliciousness of the outside world that seeks to interfere with their progress towards utopia. Under such circumstances, a governmental spokesperson might be right claiming that "around here, we do things differently", as a result of intensive governmental penetration of all areas of life, people's attitudes towards their oppressors are actually positive. But should outsiders respectfully accept the reality of these attitudes? Or should one nonetheless think of those *as victims* who actively endorse such attitudes and even ponder suitable ways of interfering? It is under such circumstances that, as Scanlon (2003b) put it, we must wonder:

> which is the more objectionable form of cultural superiority, to refuse to aid a victim on the grounds that 'they live like that – they don't recognize rights as we know them,' or to attempt to protect the defenseless even when they themselves feel that suffering is their lot and they have no basis to complain of it? (p 119)

It is the second alternative that more naturally attracts the objection that somebody who thinks like that is guilty of inappropriate feelings of cultural superiority. After all, in such a case one regards certain people as victims and thinks that intervening is appropriate even though those who are classified as victims, and thus on whose behalf the intervention would take place, are okay with what is being done to them and oppose intervention. But if indeed their acquiescence has arisen as a result of brainwashing by the government, then it would be highly problematic to abandon the victims. What seems like an enlightened attitude – "do allow them to become happy as they see fit" – might in fact capture a complacent and self-congratulatory attitude. One might even take offense at the thought that such people are even called "victims" because it would be demeaning and disempowering to do so. One might be utterly convinced of the righteousness of one's alleged tolerance, and obtain so much satisfaction from the idea of being a genuinely enlightened person that one loses sight of the fact that people are being victimized in this way. It is then this kind of complacency vis-à-vis victims of oppression that captures the truly problematic attitude of cultural superiority.

Note two things. First of all, making the judgment that such manipulation occurs and thus that the alleged victims have a clouded sense of judgment will be difficult in most cases where the question arises. What is involved is a judgment of *false consciousness*, that is, a judgment that people have been persuaded to support a regime that, contrary to their own perceptions, works to somebody else's benefit and has no other rationale. Such an assessment involves judgments that the victims were brainwashed and manipulated. One could try to make such judgments applicable by arguing that the population itself, once it is through the transition, would presumably approve of the changes (and thus appeal to the idea of moral progress we encountered earlier). One should indeed keep in mind that fascist and communist dictatorships offer good case studies for this kind of judgment. Nonetheless, the burdens of judgment are very high in this kind of case. After all, one would have to conclude that people are indeed victims of abuse although they themselves do not merely disagree, and disagree about a rather fundamental matter about themselves, but might have rather sophisticated reasoning to offer to explain why they do.

Second, these reflections have taken us naturally to the subject of intervention. It is a small step from thinking of certain people as victims to thinking about suitable ways of interfering. So I hasten to remind the reader of a point already made in Chapter 1, that intervention can indeed take many forms. One might intervene by using incentives and offering assistance if certain conditions are met. One might apply diplomatic pressures or engage intellectually. One could offer educational opportunities. But one might also support domestic resistance and engagement, and in extreme cases consider different kinds of economic sanctions. Of course military intervention is one way of intervening, but an extreme way indeed. All of these could be suitable forms of intervention given the circumstances. Sometimes any kind of intervention might be impracticable even when morally permitted or required.

Who are *we* to criticize?

Even those who do not endorse relativism might be reluctant to intervene in other cultures: "after all, who are *we* to criticize, considering how many flaws we have ourselves?" We have noted that there is a considerable range of possibilities for what intervention might amount to, and the appropriateness of intervention must always be carefully considered. But, indeed, some might express a strong reluctance to intervene in any way under at least most circumstances. This attitude contrasts with a rather too aggressive attitude towards intervention, one that stands in a natural succession to an earlier affirmative view of colonialism. That earlier attitude understood the spread of European culture as the "white man's burden" (which is originally the title of a poem by the British poet Rudyard Kipling), and was informed by prejudiced outsider interpretations of other parts of the world. Edward Said (1978) has coined the term "orientalism" for this kind of interpretation. Other cultures were not interpreted on their own terms, but in terms of what they appeared to be to Westerners, and in ways that allowed Westerners to make sense of them. That aggressive attitude towards intervention informed by orientalist or similar views is misguided, and I take it no further discussion of that point is needed. But let us discuss the view that holds that, partly in response to the earlier prevalence of this other view, at least Westerners should be *extraordinarily reserved* when it comes to any kind of intervention.

In 1996, the *Boston Review* published an intriguing and still timely exchange on female genital cutting (FGC, also known as clitoridectomy). According to philosopher Yael Tamir, critics of FGC often belong to societies with their own mechanisms of keeping women at a lower status, to cultures that foster a view of women in which those continue to be seen primarily as sexual objects and producers of children. "One cannot help thinking," she writes,

> that the gut reaction of many men against clitoridectomy reflects the fact that in our society the sexual enjoyment of women is seen as a measure of the sexual power and achievements of men. Men in our society are more intimidated by women who do not enjoy orgasms than by those who do. In societies in which clitoridectomies are performed, men are more intimidated by women who do enjoy their body and their sexuality. In both cases, a masculine yardstick measures the value of female sexuality.

Her point is that, oblivious to our own failings, we ask: "How can *they* (the perpetrators in the other society) do that to *them* (the victims in that society)?" Nonetheless, there is considerable cultural continuity between the societies that are involved here. So we should not primarily aim to understand *them* and correct *their* ways, but to understand and improve our own culture.

Tamir's point is easy to illustrate. One of the most popular TV series of recent times is *Baywatch*. Much of the success of that series is due to the prominence given to attractive females in bathing suites moving gracefully along California beaches. Moreover, if one does a google image search for "woman," chances are the first image one encounters is one of a woman who might as well appear on *Baywatch* (with only slight modifications in her wardrobe). The critics whom Tamir has in mind presumably belong to societies where this kind of display is being made of the female bodies, and which is thereby indicative of a view of women in which they continue to be seen primarily as sexual objects and producers of children.

Tamir is right that successful intervention depends on the credibility of interveners. If for instance we wish to intervene (in whichever way, and if only through the educational work of NGOs) in societies that practice FGC, much soul-searching is required on the side of intervening agents and those who support their actions. We must indeed wonder what our motivations are, and whether we are not ourselves guilty of offenses similar to those we wish to eradicate in other societies.

But consider now philosopher Martha Nussbaum's response to Tamir. We must not "indulge in moral narcissism when we flagellate ourselves for our own errors," she writes, "while neglecting to attend to the needs of those who ask our help from a distance." We might well find ourselves guilty of certain faults. But we must also realize that in different scenarios different reactions are appropriate. It is important to keep in mind the contrast between a society that practices FGC and one that glorifies a certain male ideal of the female body and thereby contributes to a view of women as limited to being objects of sexual desire. After all, FGC is carried out by force on children too young to consent, is irreversible and often performed under dangerous conditions, is linked to health-problems and often performed in countries with low female literacy and tied to other customs of male domination. If we do not keep these differences in mind, we make these matters too much about us: we refuse to aid the victims of practices that are much worse than what goes on in our own societies by drowning in what would indeed be narcissistic reflection on our own shortcomings.

A concluding thought on the UDHR

The discussion in this chapter does not show that all the rights in the UDHR are universal. As we noted in Chapter 1, we can come near the full list of rights in the UDHR only if they are authoritatively accepted around the world. But what we have seen is that relativism as such is not a threat to the moral blueprint that has been envisaged by the UDHR. We need not worry that the idea of universal values as such is flawed.

Further reading

There are some additional ways of critically approaching the idea of human rights that we do not discuss in this book. One of them is *realism* in international relations, a position that holds that states are self-interested, power-seeking rational actors whose aim is to maximize their security and their survival chances. Realists leave little room for cooperation among states other than what states perceive as necessary to such ends. Thus they leave little room for any universal values that might genuinely guide international politics. An insightful discussion of realism (and a response to it from the standpoint of a moral philosopher) can be found in chapter 1 of Michael Walzer's (1977) classic book on just war theory. *Utilitarianism* provides a competing moral outlook to a rights-based approach. Utilitarians advise moral agents to choose a course of action that brings a maximal amount of happiness into the world. Utilitarians think of the overall amount of happiness as having been summed up from individual amounts of happiness. While there is much intuitive plausibility to utilitarianism, this way of thinking might also require heavy sacrifices of certain individuals if such sacrifices are necessary to bring about the highest overall amount of happiness. Utilitarians can make some room for rights (including human rights), but primarily as devices of social coordination that can be readily set aside if necessary. For a contemporary introduction to utilitarianism, see Shaw (1999).

Turnbull (1972) is a classic anthropological treatise of people whose behavior seems to deviate radically from what one would hope is normal (e.g., by not attending much to their children). For philosophical discussions of relativism, see also Timmons (2002) and Williams (1993). My account of relativism draws on Harman (2000), but he offers a more sophisticated account and defense than I do. For a discussion of relativism in the context of human rights, see Williams (2005). Merry (2006) discusses the fascinating subject of the vernacularization of human rights norms, and (Thomas) Risse et al. (1999) discuss different feedback mechanisms between domestic and international organizations. For the idea of "fresh elaborations" of religious traditions in the context of human rights norms, see Cohen (2004).

3 Why States?

Justifying the State

It is the most basic but also the most striking fact about the political organization of humanity now that we live in states. Individuals are generally unable to choose their state, but which states they are born into shapes their life prospects. So it is unsurprising that the main task for Western political philosophy in the last several centuries has been to theorize the relationship between the state and its citizens. What are the scope and limits of legitimate state power? What is a just state? And why should there be states in the first place? Chances are that extraterrestrial visitors would be quite astonished to find us living under an organizational pattern that seems designed to maximize mutual indifference at the global level. What *justifies* the existence of states? That is our question now.

Most people remain citizens of the same state all their lives. There are emigrants, asylum seekers, dual citizens, refugees and stateless persons. But their numbers are small compared to those who are none of these. Many states cannot effectively control their territory, have disputed boundaries or are not widely recognized. Nonetheless, the world's political reality continues to be shaped by states, and their number has only recently reached its maximum to date. Historians disagree about why states arose. For instance, Hendrik Spruyt (1994) argues that territorial states, alongside city-leagues and city-states, emerged in response to economic changes in the late Middle Ages. "States won because their institutional logic gave them an advantage in mobilizing their societies' resources" (p 185). Charles Tilly (1990), for one, disagrees, claiming that states succeeded because France and Spain adopted forms of warfare that temporarily crushed their neighbors and introduced a political model that others were compelled to adopt.

States, then, have emerged in response to historical conditions in Europe and spread from there to other parts of the world through decolonization and later wars of independence. Quite possibly states will disappear in response to other historical conditions. Perhaps an exacerbating ecological crisis will bring about a world state that rules over a dwindling human species. The more one reflects on the historical contingency of states, the more one wonders whether there ought to be states at all. In any event, we must explore how states might be justified.

To offer a *justification* for X (e.g., acts, policies, institutions) is to argue that X is rationally or morally acceptable (Simmons 2001b). We offer justifications if there is opposition, and thus in response to objections. We seek to justify states because we cannot take for granted that human beings live in states simply because it suits their nature. Justifications may include comparative and non-comparative considerations: entities can be praiseworthy for prudential or moral advantages in a manner that does not involve comparisons, or vis-à-vis alternatives. However, "justifying the state" cannot mean showing the prudential or moral superiority of *any* state over all *possible* alternatives. It means to show the superiority of *particular* forms of the state over all *relevant* alternatives.

Much political philosophy following Thomas Hobbes argued that, under a broad range of circumstances, founding a state – rather than organizing their lives some other way – is what individuals should do in non-state situations. Justifications offered for states were designed to defeat particular kinds of doubt, captured by what we may call *skepticism from below*, the view that denies that there morally ought to be any form of organized power, including states. Philosophical anarchists consider organized power illegitimate and favor living arrangements that lack certain features of states, especially their coerciveness. These are called "philosophical" anarchists because, unlike some (but certainly not all) of the political groups known as anarchists, they do not necessarily advocate for violent opposition to states. The philosophical anarchist has been to modern political philosophy what the moral skeptic has been to ethics: a constant source of doubt about the validity of the major claims made by those who develop theories about those areas.

Debates with anarchists have normally assumed that what was at stake was merely the founding of *one* state. However, more is needed to "justify states" in an interconnected world than a rebuttal of anarchistic objections to the founding of any given state. One may be able to say to each individual in isolation that rationally and morally speaking she ought to join a state. But the overall *system* of states triggers objections of its own drawing especially on competition among states. "Justifying the state" now means to justify a system of multiple states. Thus in addition to skepticism from below, a justification of the state must rebut *skepticism from above*, the view that finds organized power unproblematic but denies that power ought to be organized in multiple states. Alternatives to a system of states include a world state, a world with federative structures much stronger than the UN, with a more comprehensive system of collective security, one where jurisdictions are disaggregated, or where border control is collectively administered or abandoned entirely.

Addressing skepticism from above and below: Hobbes

Let us explore how three distinguished philosophers have responded to skepticism from below and above: Thomas Hobbes, Immanuel Kant and John Rawls. They are among the major contributors to political philosophy in modern times. By looking at how they have responded to skepticism from below and above we also encounter some of the core ideas of their theories. The 17th Century English philosopher Hobbes is famous for his early development of "social contract theory," the method of justifying political principles or arrangements by appeal to agreements that would be made among suitably situated rational, free and equal persons. Notoriously, he used that method to argue that we ought to submit to the authority of an absolute sovereign. Few have agreed with this conclusion, but his method has provided major inspiration, and his results have been a reference point for all subsequent inquiry.

Often taken as the starting point for justifications of the state, Hobbes's *Leviathan* (published in 1651) introduces a view of human nature and envisages humans in a situation without any power that reliably protects them ("state of nature"). Individuals are presumed to be sufficiently similar in mental and physical abilities so that everybody is vulnerable. People are afraid of death, show limited benevolence, have an inclination to partiality, and worry about their reputation. A state of nature populated by individuals of this psychology abounds in violence and insecurity. Persons who might otherwise be peaceful engage in second-guessing and embrace preemptive aggression as rational. After all, "there is no way for any man to secure himself, so reasonable, as anticipation; that is by force, or wiles, to master the persons of all men he can, so long, till he see no other power great enough to endanger him" (chapter 13, pp 87f).

Only the founding of states through social contracts solves the security problem in the state of nature, says Hobbes, and this is his positive case for states. He insists that governments have absolute authority over their subjects, except that those retain a right to resist when their lives are endangered. He believes virtually any government would be better than civil war, and only absolute governments are not prone to dissolution into civil war. Hobbes rebuts solutions to the security problem in the state of nature that dispense with coercive structures, and thereby addresses skepticism from below. In addition to forming states, he considers other solutions to the security problem in the state of nature: lying low to avoid conflict, and forming smaller defense alliances that are less tightly organized than states. Lying low fails because of the rationality of anticipation. Forming smaller groups fails because they are internally unreliable and are in the same situation vis-à-vis each other as individuals are without them.

So according to Hobbes (and those who see themselves as Hobbesians), we agree to the state (including limiting our individual freedoms) because it is in our self-interest to do so. Thus, the state solves a number of problems that are in our self-interest to have resolved. *Leviathan* never pushes the argument further in support of a world state. States are in the same situation vis-à-vis each other as individuals are in a state of nature. This understanding of the relationship among states (which Hobbes thinks is not subject to moral norms) characterizes the "Hobbesian" view of international relations that many still endorse. Yet unlike the life of individuals in the state of nature, the existence of states is not bound to be "solitary, poor, nasty, brutish, and short" (chapter 13, p 89). Instead, wars between states "uphold thereby the Industry of their subjects" (chapter 13, p 90), for which "Industry" there was "no place" in a state of nature among individuals (chapter 13, p 89). A state of nature makes it all but impossible for people to make a living. Wars among states are not equally detrimental. Skepticism from above fails to worry Hobbes since he does not think the security problem at that level is equally urgent. Only states can solve the security problem in the state of nature. But once states exist, that problem is indeed solved.

Addressing skepticism from above and below: Kant

The 18th-century philosopher Immanuel Kant is the central figure in modern philosophy and continues to exercise a significant influence in many central areas of philosophy and beyond. The fundamental idea of Kant's "critical philosophy" is that human understanding is the source of the general laws of nature that structure all our experience; and that human reason gives itself the moral law. Scientific knowledge and morality are secure (and consistent with each other) because they both rest on human autonomy (rather than any aspects of the external world) as their foundation. Kant's political philosophy champions the idea of freedom. According to Kant, every rational being has an innate right to freedom – independence from being constrained by another's choice – and a duty to enter into a civil condition governed by a social contract in order to realize and preserve that freedom. The state is the means for freedom as long as state action is aimed at hindering actions that would undermine the freedom of individuals. The state thereby sustains a maximal amount of freedom consistent with identical freedom for everybody.

Like Hobbes, Kant helps himself to a state of nature (and social contract) argument. He diagnoses similar problems in that state. Without coercive authority, individuals "can never be secure against acts of violence from one another, since each will have his own right to do what seems right and good to him" (*Metaphysics of Morals*, section 44, p 456). Property acquisition can only be provisional in a state of nature. Rights are insecure and indeterminately circumscribed without "external, public, and lawful coercion" (p 137). Yet individuals are not merely prudentially advised to join states, but *owe* it to, and can force, each other to found arrangements where rational wills may live together harmoniously. As Kant says in *Perpetual Peace*, a "man (or an individual people) in a mere state of nature robs me of any such security and injures me in virtue of this very state in which he coexists with me" (p 98n). Not submitting to states is to prefer the "freedom of folly to the freedom of reason," which is "barbarism, coarseness, and brutish debasement of humanity" (*Perpetual Peace*, p 103).[1]

Kant's positive case for the state is like Hobbes' except that he is less focused on plain physical security. He pays more attention to what the removal of insecurity enables persons to do with each other. Unlike Hobbes, Kant does not rest his case once states are established. Kant takes skepticism from above more seriously. Right cannot prevail among persons in their own state if outsiders threaten their freedom. "Perpetual peace," for Kant, is the "ultimate goal of the whole right of nations" (*Metaphysics of Morals*, section 61, p 487). As the seventh proposition in his *Idea for a Universal History with a Cosmopolitan Purpose* states: "The problem of establishing a perfect civil constitution is subordinate to the problem of a law-governed external relationship with other states, and cannot be solved unless the latter is also solved" (p 47). But what political arrangements should exist globally given that states by themselves fail to solve the security problem?

Kant's 1795 *Perpetual Peace* proposes a federation of states opposed to war. While Kant thinks of this as the completion of a project begun with states, *Perpetual Peace* insists that states cannot be forced to submit to an international regime. States have a lawful internal constitution and thus do everything individuals are morally *required* to do. *Perpetual Peace* assumes that states would reject a world state (p 105), and that this suffices not to recommend one. Religious and linguistic diversity plays a role too in Kant's attitude towards the world state. He also finds that "governing [a universal association of states] and so protecting each of its members would finally have to become impossible" (*Metaphysics of Morals*, section 61, p 487). The purpose of the federation is "[not] to meddle in one another's internal dissensions but to protect against attacks from without" (*Metaphysics of Morals*, section 54, p 483). Indeed, without protection from external interference no state can do for its citizens what it is supposed to do.

Since in several chapters in this book we discuss humanity's collective ownership of the earth, let me draw attention to the fact that Kant too adopts a version of that thought. *Perpetual Peace* advocates for what he calls a "cosmopolitan right of universal hospitality." All human beings have the right to engage in commerce with others. No state is allowed to deny foreigners the right to travel through in order to trade with others. Moreover, each country must give people shelter if turning them away leads to "destruction." Presumably this means they must be granted asylum if at home they are threatened with persecution or starvation.

Kant's most complete argument for this cosmopolitan right appears two years later in his *Metaphysics of Morals* (Doctrine of Rights, section 62). The starting point is that each person has a right to freedom (not to be subject to another's will). Therefore, each person is entitled to occupying some space on earth. In virtue of the spherical and thus limited nature of the earth, humans potentially or actually encounter each other. Therefore, there must be moral norms about what people owe to each other when this happens, and about how people may acquire parts of the earth to the exclusion of others. Kant thinks of humanity as forming a community with the (sole) obligation of regulating property acquisition. To that community he ascribes a collective will that is charged with this regulation, and that must do so in a way acceptable to all persons. Such a will, Kant submits, would adopt the cosmopolitan right to make sure each person's right to freedom is preserved given our limited space on this planet.

Addressing skepticism from above and below: Rawls

John Rawls was the most significant political philosopher of the 20th century. His 1971 *Theory of Justice* too uses a social contract argument to approach the question of what principles of justice should govern a state. Since few such contracts have been made, and since it will be no longer binding on the living even where one was made in the past, one may think about a hypothetical contract instead. But Rawls does not employ an argument of either the traditional or the hypothetical form. His "aim is to present a conception of justice which generalizes and carries to a higher level of abstraction the familiar theory of the social contract found, say, in Locke, Rousseau, and Kant" (1999a, p 10).

This generalization involves an expository device Rawls calls the "original position." In the original position people are behind a "veil of ignorance" so that

> no one knows his place in society, his class position or social status, nor does any one know his fortune in the distribution of natural assets and abilities, his intelligence, strength, and the like. I shall even assume that the parties do not know their conception of the good or their special psychological propensities. The principles of justice are chosen behind a veil of ignorance. This ensures that no one is advantaged or disadvantaged in the choice of principles by the outcome of natural chance or the contingency of social circumstances. Since all are similarly situated and no one is able to design principles to favor his particular condition, the principles of justice are the result of a fair agreement or bargain. (1999a, p 11)

The original position models the idea of equality among participants. This device captures reasonable limitations on arguments they can make in support of principles of justice. Referring to his own approach, Rawls talks of "justice as fairness"; he thinks principles of justice are those principles that are chosen under initial condition of fairness. Individuals can enter the original position any time by accepting the constraints that define it. Two things matter greatly here. First of all, all individuals are expected to comply with, and contribute to, the economic, legal and political system under which they live (and their compliance and contributions are coercively enforced if not provided voluntarily). And second, individuals advance in society based on their initial position in it and based on their natural assets. But none of these is deserved in any way; they are morally arbitrary.

It is in light of these points that it becomes plausible to argue, as Rawls does, that behind the veil of ignorance individuals would adopt a "maximin" approach; they want to make sure the group that is worst-off as participants in the political and economic system is as well-off as possible. Individuals behind the veil of ignorance seek to *maximize* the share in social primary goods that accrues to the worst-off – and thus *minimal* – position in society (social primary goods being the goods generated by social cooperation, see below). That is, individuals compare different ways of regulating the distribution of goods, inquire about each proposal which group would fare worst, and choose the one that leaves the respectively worst-off group better off than any alternative. In other words, in the original position, an institutional set-up would be chosen in which the status group that makes the largest concession (fares worst under it) is as well-off as possible. Rawls argues that, given the reasonable limitations in the original position, participants would choose the following two principles of domestic justice (e.g., 2001, p 42):

1. Each person has the same indefeasible claim to a fully adequate scheme of equal basic liberties, which scheme is compatible with the same scheme of liberties for all.
2. Social and economic inequalities are to be arranged so that they are both (a) attached to offices and positions open to all under conditions of fair equality of opportunity, and (b) to the greatest benefit of the least advantaged.

The second part of the second principle is the *difference principle.* Priority is given to the first principle, and within the second to the first clause. Conflicts between the principles are decided in favor of the first. Conflicts between the two parts of the second principle are resolved in favor of the first part.

The rights captured by the first principle are political and civil rights: freedom of thought and liberty of conscience; political liberties (e.g., rights to vote and participate in politics) and freedom of association, as well as rights and liberties specified by the integrity (physical and psychological) of persons; and finally, rights and liberties covered by the rule of law (2001, p 44). The second principle adds demanding conditions regarding socio-economic inequalities. Fair equality of opportunity requires arrangements that enable people to be healthy and well-educated enough to be competitive, regardless of what segment of society they belong to. The difference principle regulates the remaining inequalities in socio-economic status. It asks us to compare feasible institutional arrangements that distribute these goods and identify the respectively least advantaged. We should choose an arrangement that makes *its* least advantaged better off than the respectively least advantaged are under any *other* arrangement. Rawls thinks this condition works out in such a way that remaining differences in primary goods benefit everybody. But even though it is only the difference principle that explicitly states the idea that a social system should be arranged to the advantage especially of the least advantaged, it is really both principles together that capture that idea. Inequalities in the most basic liberties are unacceptable, but other inequalities *are* permissible as long as they are to everybody's advantage as spelled out by the second principle, and thus especially to the benefit of the least advantaged status group.

The driving intuition behind Rawls' approach is the moral arbitrariness of natural assets and social status. As he explains specifically with regard to the difference principle, we are led to that principle

> if we wish to set up the social system so that no one gains or loses from his arbitrary place in the distribution of natural assets or his initial position in society without giving or receiving compensating advantages in return. (1999c, p 87)

Undeserved natural assets and social status should be harnessed to improve the lives of all those who make up the society in which alone these assets can be developed and in which alone this status matters. It should be clear that implementing Rawls's two principles would entail dramatic changes in just about all societies. To illustrate, the fair-equality-of-opportunity principle in 2(a) requires a reform of primary and secondary education to make sure the extent to which individuals are competitive in society depends much less on their social origins than currently it normally does. The implications of the difference principle are much harder to assess since such an assessment involves complex counterfactuals: how well-off would those people be who would be the least well-off under an alternative institutional set-up? But the difference principle, in any event, would only regulate inequalities that remain after the fair-equality-of-opportunity principle has been implemented. And while it is not trivial to think about what precisely fair equality in education would amount to, it is obvious that a school system that offers vastly different educational opportunities to students depending on where they grow up (as the education system in the United States does) would have to be reformed thoroughly in light of this principle.

Strikingly, Rawls does not discuss either kind of skepticism. Rawls apparently thinks modern philosophy has rebutted skepticism from below, leaving to him the design of states. He assumes that states do much more than solve security problems. The principles of justice do not regulate all aspects of life. They regulate the *basic structure* of society, and apply only to people who share such a structure. The basic structure is the way in which the major social institutions fit together, and how they assign fundamental rights and duties and shape the division of advantages from cooperation. Institutions that constitute this structure include the political constitution, the different forms of property, the legal system of trials and other procedures, the organization of the economy (norms enabling production, exchange, and consumption of goods), and also the nature of the family. The goods generated by the basic structure (the goods whose distribution the principles of justice regulate) are the "social primary goods:" basic rights and liberties; freedom of movement and free choice of occupation against a background of diverse opportunities; powers and prerogatives of offices and positions of authority and responsibility; income and wealth; and the social bases of self-respect. That, in addition to solving the security problem, the state provides these goods goes a long way towards justifying its existence.

As for skepticism from above, in his 1999 *Law of Peoples*, which addresses questions of international justice by way of assessing what is required of the foreign policy of just states, Rawls endorses Kant's views in *Perpetual Peace* (1999b, p 10). Taking his cues from Kant throughout, he asserts that a world government would either be a global despotism or else would be beleaguered by battles against various groups trying to gain their political independence. As opposed to that, "two main ideas motivate the Law of Peoples," as Rawls tells us:

> One is that the great evils of human history—unjust war and oppression, religious persecution and the denial of liberty of conscience, starvation and poverty, not to mention genocide and mass murder—follow from political injustice, with its own cruelties and callousness... The other main idea, obviously connected with the first, is that, once the gravest forms of political injustice are eliminated by following just (or at least decent) social policies and establishing just (or at least decent) basic institutions, these great evils will eventually disappear. (1999b, pp 6f)

The most important feature of the "realistic utopia" – a political idea that stretches our ordinary political notions without envisaging ideals beyond our comprehension – that Rawls has in view for the global arena is that the great evils of human history are absent. The most important condition for this realistic utopia to obtain is that all societies have internally just, or at least decent, domestic political institutions. Rawls puts forward eight principles for ordering international relations:

1. Peoples are free and independent, and their freedom and independence are to be respected by other peoples.
2. Peoples are to observe treaties and undertakings.
3. Peoples are equal and are parties to the agreements that bind them.

4. Peoples are to observe the duty of nonintervention (except to address grave violations of human rights).
5. Peoples have a right of self defense, but no right to instigate war for reasons other than self defense.
6. Peoples are to honor human rights (according to Rawls's own rather minimal conception of human rights that generates a list of rights much shorter than what is on the Universal Declaration of Human Rights).
7. Peoples are to observe certain specified restrictions in the conduct of war.
8. Peoples have a duty to assist other peoples living under unfavorable conditions that prevent their having a just or decent political and social regime.

Skepticism from below: the nagging doubt

Our brief look at Hobbes, Kant and Rawls has gone some ways towards a justification of states. After all, justifying the state is to argue that the state is rationally or morally acceptable, and each author has offered arguments to that effect. However, what we have seen so far is consistent with arguing that the problems arising from the sheer fact that there is organized power in the first place outweigh the moral and prudential advantages of a state system. What we have said is also consistent with arguing that the problems arising from the particular way of organizing power in multiple states outweigh these advantages. All things considered, the state system may still lose the argument when compared to no states at all or, say, a world state as competing political arrangements. Indeed, as I will argue now, skeptics from below succeed at creating a nagging doubt about whether there is a moral or rational reconstruction of the existence of states. Skepticism from below (philosophical anarchism) cannot be conclusively refuted. Once we see that point, we must reconsider what a justification of states might still amount to.

Libertarianism is one philosophical view to which we can turn to articulate skepticism from below. Libertarians hold that agents (at least initially) *fully own* themselves and have moral powers to acquire property rights in external things. Libertarianism falls into right-libertarianism and left-libertarianism. While both endorse self-ownership, they differ with respect to the powers agents have to appropriate unowned natural resources. Left-libertarians hold that natural resources are owned in some egalitarian manner. Right-libertarians deny any but at most a minimal moral account of ownership of external resources; such resources may be appropriated (to the exclusion of all others, without compensation) by the first person who discovers them, or mixes his labor with them. The egalitarian ownership status of natural resources leads left-libertarians to take a more positive attitude towards states than right-libertarians do. After all, that ownership status readily generates redistributive claims, and the state is the natural entity to administer such redistribution.

Right-libertarians, however, tend to take a strongly negative view of state power. They resist the idea that there are no alternative ways of securing the benefits guaranteed by states and argue that states have done more harm than good. Murray Rothbard, for one, regards the state as

> the supreme, the eternal, the best organized aggressor against the persons and property of the mass of the public. *All* States everywhere, whether democratic, dictatorial, or monarchical, whether red, white, blue, or brown....And historically, by far the overwhelming portion of all enslavement and murder in the history of the world have come from the hands of government. (1996 pp 46f)

Right-libertarians offer formal models of public choice (mathematical models of how collective decision making could function) that dispense with states. In addition they seek to identify historical societies that realized libertarian ideals. In ancient Ireland and pre-colonial Africa people apparently enjoyed adequate security and had sophisticated property arrangements without the kind of coercive enforcement practiced by states.

But it is not merely right-libertarians who worry about state power. The perception that states create problems has increasingly influenced the debate about whether the state can be justified. "Religion and philosophy have claimed their martyrs, as have family, friendship, and office," writes the political theorist Michael Walzer (1970), but "there has never been a more successful claimant of human lives than the state" (p 77). Introducing the term "democide" (murder committed by governments), the political scientist Rudolph Rummel (1994) insists that a "preeminent fact about government is that some of them murder millions in cold blood" (p 27). The genocide expert Israel Charny adds that

> in total, during the first eighty-eight years of the [twentieth] century, 170 million men, women, and children were shot, beaten, tortured, knifed, burned, starved, frozen, crushed or worked to death; buried alive, drowned, hanged, bombed, or killed in any other of the myriad other ways governments have inflicted deaths on unarmed helpless citizens and foreigners (1999), p 28).

Depending on the estimates the dead could conceivably be more than 360 million people. "It is as though our species has been devastated by a modern Black Plague" (p 28).

Even those rejecting Hobbes' strong claim that just about any state is preferable to non-state arrangements may think abusive states were unavoidable in developing political formations that solved the security problem. However, the suggestion that the security problem is solvable without states raises the possibility that history might not be so reconstructable. If so, the Hobbesian case for the rationality of founding states collapses. We face the disturbing prospect that the advantages that life in states provides could have become available without states and their coercive apparatus and tendency to make war against each other. All things considered, in spite of what we have said towards a justification of a state system, states might be little more than tamed versions of entities that arose when, as the 19th century German philosopher Friedrich Nietzsche strikingly put it, "some pack of blond predatory animals, a race of conquerors and masters" decided to set "its terrifying paws on a subordinate population which may perhaps be vast in numbers but is still without any form, is still wandering about" (*Genealogy of Morality*, Second Essay, section 17).

Doubts about Kant draw on these doubts about Hobbes. Kant never explains, as Simmons (2001b), p 140, argues, why we have a duty to live in states rather than a general duty to respect rights. Nor does Kant explain why anybody inflicts an injury by refusing membership in society if others have accepted it and thus solve each other's security problem. Perhaps Kant would reply that there is no other way of securing these benefits. But then the doubts about Hobbes re-enter. Kant might have concluded too quickly that there were no alternative solutions for the security problem, without duly considering that states generate problems of their own.

The state: justified "by the balance of probabilities?"

So it seems we cannot conclude that it would be irrational or immoral to adopt arrangements other than states. Skepticism from below remains unrefuted. However, maybe we set the standards too high for what counts as a successful refutation. To argue for anarchy, and thus to support skepticism from below, says British philosopher Jonathan Wolff (1996),

> it is not enough to point out the peculiarity of the state and the difficulties with many of the arguments in favor of it. Rather, in contractualist terms, it has to be shown that reasonable people seeking agreement on the nature of the social world would prefer anarchy to the state. ... The defense of the state, we may say, needs only to meet the burden of proof assumed in the civil, not the criminal, courts: not beyond reasonable doubt, but by the balance of probabilities. (p 115)

Wolff appeals to epistemic standards. As far as Hobbes is concerned, Wolff's point is that agents in a state of nature rationally should found a state. "By the balance of probabilities" states solve the security problem best. As far as Kant is concerned, there should be *enough* confidence in the success of the moral argument for states, as well as *enough* abhorrence for the costs associated with omitting the founding of states, to make that case acceptable. Both times skeptics from below demand too much if they ask for more.

Yet once we recognize troubles arising from the interactions *among* states, and thus broaden the conversation with the anarchist, Wolff's conclusion might not follow. Would it *really* be rational to found states "by the balance of probabilities," rather than try to arrange affairs without creating multiple centers of coercive power? Would it *really* be immoral not to do so, given the limited confidence we should have in arguments for states and given the moral costs of founding states erroneously? It seems we are in no position to answer affirmatively. Generally, the strength of skepticism from below is often underappreciated, especially when we update it in light of the existence of multiple states. We first had to concede that such skeptics create a nagging doubt about the success of a major project of modern political philosophy. Now we also have to grant that even after switching to reflection about epistemic standards, we still cannot conclude that skepticism from below fails. It continues to create a nagging doubt about the justifiability of states.

We are entitled to say there *ought to be (multiple) states* only if both skepticism from below and skepticism from above can be refuted. We have seen that skepticism from below cannot be refuted. To say that "there ought to be (multiple) states," in turn, is synonymous with "there is a duty to found states if they do not exist yet and to maintain a system of states if it exists." Since we are not entitled to say that there ought to be states, we are not entitled to say that there is such a duty. However, a state system may still be *justified* all things considered even though we are not entitled to say there ought to be a state system. In other words it may be justified as permissible, even if not as obligatory. Given what I have said about what is involved in a justification of states, we would find ourselves in precisely that situation if the following conditions hold: (1) The state system has certain moral or prudential advantages. (2) To the best of our understanding, no alternative political system has moral or prudential advantages that outweigh those of a state system. (3) Nonetheless, there remain nagging doubts about the acceptability of the state system, and so we cannot conclude that there actually ought to be a system of states.

It is in the moderate sense captured by these conditions that the state system is justified. To that end, what remains to be argued at this stage of our discussion is point (2). If indeed this is all there is to the justification of states, a grand project of modern political philosophy has failed: to establish that there ought to be states without leaving a nagging doubt, a suspicion that there might be no moral or rational reconstruction of the development of states. Nonetheless, if states can be justified in the sense of conditions (1), (2) and (3), we have a response to two kinds of intellectual opposition to the existence of states. We can respond, first of all, to those relatively few who wish to dismantle the state system. But this justification of states also responds to the more common view of those who reply to the question of whether, morally speaking, there ought to be multiple states by saying either that "there ought not, but for pragmatic reasons (and indeed only for pragmatic reasons) this is no conclusive reason to dismantle them now." Talking in this way presupposes that there is an alternative way of thinking of world order, one that does not include a multiplicity of states, and that we can *comprehend* well enough to pursue were it not for practical obstacles (such as that doing so would require wars). I will argue now that there is no such ideal. To argue that there is not is tantamount to arguing for point (2) above.

Limits of utopian thinking

Large-scale utopias, surely those that envisage redesigning the global political system to such an extent that the state system is abandoned, can only be incompletely theorized. Mathematical models can fix basic parameters and "predict" what happens by making derivations. However, comprehensive visions of the future inevitably are incomplete in ways that are hard to gauge from experiences with limited scenarios. Once such visions come to guide many people's actions, certain features that could not have been expected to be significant may become significant. Those who dislike certain effects of states might stipulate a world with certain features (free movement, universal equality of opportunity, etc.). But at the time of conception there is no good understanding of what it would be like to have this vision realized.

We do not understand what a world would be *like* where all state power (except, perhaps, a world state), ranging from border control to maintenance of social insurance, is replaced with other arrangements. We do not understand a world whose distinctive features do not include multiple states. My point is not to enlist any of the conservative attitudes identified by the political economist Albert Hirschman (1991): the perversity, futility, or jeopardy thesis. The first says that purposive action to improve some feature of the political, social, or economic order only exacerbates the condition one wishes to remedy. The second holds that attempts at social transformation fail to "make a dent." The third argues that the costs of change are too high since they endanger previous accomplishments. My point is, instead, that utopian thinking readily involves us in the construction of visions we do not understand well enough to comprehend what their realization would look like.

What is crucial is that utopian thinking can sensibly be action-guiding *only if* we have a reasonable reassurance that changes will not create larger problems than they solve. There can be no such reassurance without a reasonably clear understanding of what the world would be like once those changes occur. Replacing the current order with one where all states are subject to coercive interference by regional or global institutions, or one doing away with states and other coercive structures entirely, is a case in point if ever there was one. The political theorist Isaiah Berlin once wrote that "[u]topias have their value – nothing so wonderfully expands the imaginative horizons of human potentialities – but as guides to conduct they can prove literally fatal" (1992, p 15). One way in which they can prove fatal is if we do not understand well enough what a world would be like once the utopia is implemented.

Political philosopher Raymond Geuss has discussed the kind of limitation of utopian thinking that I am exploring here. He argues that "when a theory is widely believed and has come to inform the way large groups of people act, deeply hidden structural features of it can suddenly come to have a tremendous political impact"

(2005, p 35). His illustration for this phenomenon is Marxism. Theories like Marxism, says Geuss,

> present themselves with a certain prima facie plausibility as theories committed to promoting human freedom... Nevertheless... a deeper account of their political views would reveal hidden authoritarian elements, such as a commitment to a 'positive' rather than negative freedom. It was eventually this hidden structural kernel of the theory, not the private motives of its supporters, that had the last word in the real world of politics. ... The Soviet Union, as it actually was, was the real content of Marx's 'positive' liberty. (p 36)

Let us consider one way of thinking about the phenomenon to which Geuss draws attention. Recall the following passage from the *German Ideology* (jointly written by Karl Marx and Friedrich Engels in 1846):

> For as soon as the distribution of labor comes into being, each man has a particular, exclusive sphere of activity, which is forced upon him and from which he cannot escape. He is a hunter, a fisherman, a shepherd, or a critical critic, and must remain so if he does not want to lose his means of livelihood; while in communist society, where nobody has one exclusive sphere of activity but each can become accomplished in any branch he wishes, *society regulates the general production* and thus makes it possible for me to do one thing today and another tomorrow, to hunt in the morning, fish in the afternoon, rear cattle in the evening, criticize after dinner, just as I have a mind, without ever becoming hunter, fisherman, cowherd, or critic. (McLellan 1977, p 185, my italics)

There are relatively few passages where Marx illuminates communism, and thus the kind of society he believed would eventually replace capitalism. This passage from the *German Ideology* is one of the few that do so. But Marx and Engels mention one crucial matter only in passing, that "society regulates the general production." This point captures a hidden structural feature that arguably did have a tremendous impact. Marx and Engels could not have anticipated the Soviet Union's rigid five-year-plans, Chairman Mao's Great Leap Forward in China, or the excessively cruel measures communist societies would take to squelch opposition as they went about regulating the production. Instead, the paragraph where Marx and Engels assume that such regulation is up to society also envisages individuals happily pursuing multifarious activities, which the authors thought possible only if society takes care of background parameters. In his *Main Currents of Marxism* (Kolakowski 2005), Polish philosopher Leszek Kolakowski has argued with great force that Stalinist Russia was no aberration, but Marxism's logical culmination. Even to the extent that Marxist ideas were misapplied, such misapplications evolved from the very efforts to apply the ideas.

The thesis of the inevitability, or faithfulness to doctrine, especially of Stalin's Soviet Union within Marxist theory is engulfed by bitter argument. "Blaming Marx for the horrors of Stalinism is like blaming Jesus Christ for the Inquisition," one might say. In response to Kolakowski some have claimed that the regulation mentioned in the *German Ideology* is compatible with radical kinds of democracy. But recall Geuss's point that "when a theory is widely believed and has come to inform the way large groups of people act, deeply hidden structural features of it can suddenly come to have a tremendous political impact." Applied to this case, the concern is that Stalinism is one way of developing a recognizable form of Marxism. In the Soviet Union one development of Marxism had come to inform the way large groups act. One view of what it is for society to regulate the production did have a considerable impact under those circumstances.

What is crucial is that, also independently of my presumably controversial illustration in terms of Marxism, the point I am borrowing from Geuss presents a criticism of large-scale utopias.[2] We cannot respond to the question of whether there ought to be a system of states by saying that "there ought not, but for pragmatic reasons, and indeed only for pragmatic reasons, this is no conclusive reason to dismantle them now." (What is meant by pragmatic reasons is that too much harm would be done in the period of transition to a new form of political organization, or that no anti-state platform could possibly hope to win over the hearts of most people.) After all, this statement presupposes an action-guiding ideal of a stateless world (except, possibly, a world state).

Both skepticism from above and skepticism from below create doubts about the justifiability of states. However, we would need an intelligible ideal of a world order without a multiplicity of states for this kind of skepticism to generate intellectual support for the view that states should be dismantled were it not for pragmatic considerations.

More on limits of utopian thinking

To be sure, what I have argued is compatible with a demand for wide-ranging reforms of the state system and the international organizations that states have founded. It is also consistent with the fact that gradual changes will eventually put us in a position to envisage an ideal of a political order without states. What can be a realistic utopia may change over time. But at this stage we have no such ideal of a world without states. So as of now, we should not even argue that such a world should be realized gradually.

My epistemic argument might seem weakest for the global state alternative: at first glance, a world state seems easier to imagine than a world of no states, or than any arrangement of coercive power other than a state system. A global state, one might say, would just be more of what we are used to (a state), only bigger. And a world state, after all, might strike many as an attractive alternative to the system of multiple states. But the thought that the epistemic argument would apply to a world state with less force than to other alternatives to the state system is illusionary. A global state would replace all power centers that have emerged on this planet, one global power that could interfere with the lives of human beings across the world in much the same way in which now multiple states can interfere with the lives of people under their jurisdiction. The point I have borrowed from Geuss paradigmatically speaks to the kind of political, economic, legal and social transition humanity would have to go through in order to build a world state (or any other global or quasi-global structure that would replace the multiplicity of power centers characteristic of our system of states).

Let us consider an objection. When the French Revolution occurred, conservatives like the Irish philosopher and statesman Edmund Burke condemned it because it uprooted an existing order for abstract ideals. Most people would presumably say that, all things considered, it was good that the revolution occurred (showing that social orders can change, in such a way that a new order eventually commands broader acceptance), and that its condemnation expresses a bad kind of conservatism. People used to be unable to imagine a world without slaves, or one in which women vote; what Europe would be like without Germany and France being arch-enemies; what an erstwhile autocracy would be like with its subjects democratically empowered, etc. Presumably the world is the better for these changes.

"Thought achieves more in the world than practice; for once the realm of imagination has been revolutionized, reality cannot resist," the 19th century German philosopher Georg Wilhelm Friedrich Hegel once wrote.[3] But thought is not easily revolutionized. The 20th century economist and philosopher Friedrich von Hayek offers what might count as a reply to Hegel: "The sources of many of the most harmful actions are often not evil men but high-minded idealists" (1973, p 70). It would be impossible to offer an account of what ought to be tried and what not. Much depends on how many people follow suit. Discouragement might be self-fulfilling; it might be only because many people *believe* that something cannot be done that it cannot be done. Nevertheless, we should not explore what the world would be like without countries. We do not know enough to do so. This claim is true even if Burke was wrong about the French Revolution, and even if we do not fully understand how to distinguish between the two cases.

Certain large-scale developments are not the sort of thing on which one can sensibly advise, especially since there is little to learn from smaller scenarios. When Rawls discussed the notion of a "realistic utopia" in his *Law of Peoples*, he finds himself unable sharply to delineate realistic from non-realistic utopias (1999b, p 20). Nonetheless, the change demanded by anarchism and views of world order that dismantle the state system in favor of other structures (including a world state) is too radical. Nor can we credibly assert that we should gradually approximate this goal because we do not understand the goal itself well enough to aspire at approximation. Contrary to what is asserted by John Lennon in one of the most famous songs of recent times, we cannot "imagine" a world without (multiple) countries in ways required for such ideals to be adopted.

Patriotism?

States can be justified, but only in the following sense: (1) The system of states has certain moral or prudential advantages. This point we could take from the classic attempts to justify states in Hobbes, Kant and Rawls. (2) To the best of our understanding, no alternative political system has moral or prudential advantages outweighing those of a system of states. That is the point we established by pondering the limits of utopian thinking. (3) Nonetheless, there remain nagging doubts about the acceptability of the state system, and we cannot conclude that there ought to be a system of states. This point we took from an exploration of skepticism from below, which articulates doubts about the state whose force is often underappreciated.

It is worth emphasizing that what we have argued so far does not undermine all kinds of positive attitude one might have towards one's country. Even if there is no moral requirement to found states in a state of nature, and even if doing so is not the uniquely rational thing to do, one might still feel patriotic attachment to one's own country. But let us conclude by exploring this attitude of patriotism some more. Robert Goodin (1988), for one, explores the question of "what is so special about our fellow countrymen." He responds that there is nothing much special about them at all. States have certain duties vis-à-vis their citizens. However, these are merely duties everybody has towards everybody else, but are most effectively discharged if assigned to individual states. So one might be a *pragmatic* patriot: it so happens that one is "teammates for life" (Wellman 2003, p 270) with a particular group of people with whom one shares language and culture, but one might as well have been part of some other team. Or one might be a *critical* patriot: somebody who is committed to making her country a better place, and feels special pride of those characteristics of her country of which she approves, but who feels shame and embarrassment over its perceived failures.

Australian philosopher Simon Keller (2005) explores a different sort of patriotism, one that is much stronger than these two versions, but nonetheless also much more common. What we might call *intense* patriotism involves loyalty to one's country entangled with a conception of that beloved country as having certain valuable characteristics that make it genuinely worthy of loyalty. Intense patriotism is a kind of love that makes reference to aspects of one's country that are taken to merit pride, approval, affection or even reverence. Intense patriotism does not involve choice and deliberation, is essentially grounded in a country's being one's own, and essentially involves references to valuable defining qualities of one's country that merit loyalty.

Keller finds such patriotism worrisome. Intense patriotism generates a disposition to find certain beliefs about one's country to be true. For these beliefs to be beliefs one can defend, one must take them to be implied by what one knows about the country, and be convinced one's assessment of the evidence is unbiased. At the same time, intense patriotism involves a pre-commitment to certain beliefs. The result is a mental attitude of what (following the 20th century French philosopher Jean-Paul Sartre) has come to be called *bad faith*. That is, intense patriotism requires of the mind to embrace two attitudes that it cannot think together once they are brought into the open – to want certain beliefs to be true but also to want to be able to defend one's beliefs with relevant evidence – and thereby condemns the intense patriot to a kind of inauthentic life. After all, for beliefs to be beliefs one *wants* to have, one must interpret the evidence with a bias. Confronted with negative evidence, the intense patriot will be dismissive of this evidence or downplay its significance. Accordingly, she will reason differently about her own country and other countries.

Patriotism is widely regarded as a virtue. It is especially for this reason that the kind of inauthentic life Keller associates with intense patriotism is so worrisome. After all, the patriot who thinks of himself as virtuous will hardly acknowledge the defensive mechanisms through which he responds to negative evidence about his country. If Keller is correct, intense patriotism is problematic even though, again, what is problematic about it by no means follows from the main argument of this chapter. But I submit that Keller indeed identifies a very worrisome, and rather common, way of feeling about one's country.

Further reading

The question of how states are justified is one of the traditional questions of political philosophy. All introductory books to political philosophy that focus on the state and that I mentioned in the introduction discuss this topic. This chapter has acquainted readers with some core ideas of three of the classics of modern political philosophy: Hobbes, Kant and Rawls. For Hobbes and Rawls it was easy to focus on their main works in political philosophy: the 1651 *Leviathan* for Hobbes, and the 1971 *Theory of Justice* for Rawls (which in 1999 appeared in a second edition that includes some changes and is now authoritative). But Kant wrote down his thoughts on political philosophy in several smaller pieces, and has changed his views on some issues in the process. Still, Kant's piece on *Perpetual Peace* is his most sustained treatment of political philosophy. John Locke's *Second Treatise of Government* (published in 1690) and Jean-Jacques Rousseau's *Social Contract* (published in 1762) too count among the classics of the social contract tradition. Nozick (1974) is the best-known representative of libertarianism, but he is rather hard to classify as either right- or left-libertarian (given that he acknowledges certain moral constraints on the appropriation of external resources). The justification of states developed here is taken from Risse (2012). Rawls (1999b) develops the notion of a realistic utopia.

4 Global Distributive Justice

From domestic justice to global justice

A theory of *distributive justice* explains why certain individuals have particularly stringent claims to certain relative or absolute shares, quantities or amounts of something whose distribution over certain people must be justifiable to them. Alongside distributive justice there is also *rectificatory justice*, and perhaps other kinds. Yet because our concern mostly is with distributive justice, *justice* refers to distributive justice unless otherwise noted. Among moral prescriptions, it is the demands of justice that are the hardest ones to overrule or suspend. Justice plays its central role in human affairs because it enables persons to present claims of such stringency. "We can't leave it to insurance companies to deliver justice," South African writer J. M. Coetzee has the protagonist of his novel *Disgrace* say (2000, p 137). This is amusing precisely because of the stringency of justice (which renders it rather obvious that, indeed, we cannot leave justice to insurance companies). We speak about justice in the family, at the workplace or in competitions. There is justice as a personal virtue, a constitution of character or disposition to help ensure others have, or are, what they should have or be. Domestic distributive justice is also called "social justice."

Justice has been theorized in numerous ways, depending on what the context is where people have claims to shares of something and what it is to which they have such claims. The modern conception of domestic justice incorporates several assumptions (Fleischacker 2004). First, each individual has a good that deserves respect (i.e., each has his or her own idea of happiness and of the good life), and individuals are due certain rights and protections to that end. Justice is not merely a matter of realizing, say, a divine order or a set of prescriptions that are part of nature much as physical laws of nature are. Second, some share of material goods is among the rights and protections everyone deserves. Justice is not exclusively concerned, say, with the distribution of honors. Third, the fact that each person deserves rights and protections is rationally and secularly justifiable. Fourth, the distribution of these material goods is practical: it is neither a fool's project nor self-undermining, like attempts to enforce friendship. And fifth, it is for the state (and conceivably other political entities) to achieve justice. Justice cannot be left to civil society organizations such as churches.

The combination of these commitments about how the fates of individuals are tied together is strikingly unusual by historical standards. But it is also such an understanding of domestic justice that generates a debate about *global justice*. If each individual has a good that deserves respect, we must ask whether justice only applies among those who share a state and whether the corresponding duties expire at borders. If rights and protections require rational justification, we must explore whether such justification is available for the privileged treatment each country gives its citizens. If the distribution of material goods is practical, we must note that numerous organizations now seek to make this true globally. Contemporary logistical capacities are astonishing, and there is much scientific understanding that helps with practical challenges beyond borders. And if it is for the state to achieve justice, we must ask whether international entities also have obligations of justice, or whether the state system as a whole does.

So indeed, we reach questions of global justice simply by reflecting on the commitments that shape our contemporary understanding of domestic justice. The mainstays of the contemporary conception of justice make it unavoidable in particular for us to inquire about whether principles of justice could *only* apply among those who share a state. That question is central to this chapter.

Peter Singer, "famine, affluence, and morality"

A different way of reaching the question of whether justice applies only among those who share a state is to engage with a famous argument from a 1972 article by the Australian philosopher Peter Singer. His argument proceeds in the following steps:

(1) Suffering and death from lack of food, shelter, medical care is very bad.
(2) If it is in one's power to prevent something very bad from happening, without thereby sacrificing anything of comparable moral significance, one ought to do it.
(3) So, if it is in one's power to prevent such suffering and death without sacrificing anything of comparable moral significance, one ought, morally, to do it.
(4) It is in one's power to donate one's discretionary income to charities.
(5) Donating discretionary income to charities will prevent suffering and death from occurring due to lack of food, shelter, and medical care.
(6) By donating (most of) one's discretionary income, one would not be sacrificing anything of comparable moral significance.
(7) So one ought to donate (most of) one's discretionary income.

This striking conclusion is directed at everyone with income to spare. The point is not just that the very wealthy should do without exotic vacations, inhabit smaller (and fewer) houses or drive less luxurious (and fewer) cars. Instead, any income that is not needed for a decent standard of living should be used to help the most destitute, regardless of where they are located.

The argument is *valid*: its conclusion follows from its premises. Statement (3) is derived from (1) and (2), and (7) is the main conclusion. Premises (1) and (4) are trivially true. That leaves premises (2), (5) and (6) for possible objections. If the argument fails, in other words, it must be because one of those premises is false. Let us consider objections to (5). If *everyone* donated most of their discretionary income to charities our economy would collapse, which would render us ineffective in the ongoing battle against avoidable suffering. But Singer does not address whether somebody ought to donate most of her money if her peers are *already* doing so. For any given individual it will be true that her donating her discretionary income *now* can prevent serious harm and will not cause the economy to collapse. Another objection is that keeping people alive today only postpones suffering from starvation and disease. But this concern is met if one donates to charities that promote population control. So it seems premise (5) can be defended against objections.

By way of objecting to (6) one might say that donating one's income brings about a morally significant harm: it enables governments to abdicate responsibility for preventing harms. However, this objection assumes that the more people donate privately, the less likely it is that governments provide aid. But the opposite seems true: the less people donate, the less governments will feel motivated to donate. After all, governments would then not be judged by their efforts to help distant strangers. Or one might object that discretionary income is often spent on pleasures involving entertainment, time with friends and enjoying the "good things in life." Such indulgence contributes to the development of one's character. However, it is hardly credible that one's character is developed, say, by buying designer jeans, owning a large music collection or watching movies in theatres. Entertainment is important, as is time with friends, but there are ways of engaging in such activities that incur relatively modest costs. So this objection is implausible and highly self-serving. Premise (6) too can be defended.

So if we can rebut Singer's argument, it must be by way of objecting to (2): "If it is in one's power to prevent something very bad from happening, without thereby sacrificing anything of comparable moral significance, one ought to do it." Let us call this the Principle of Sacrifice (following Miller 2010). This principle is Singer's central normative premise. It is the idea of *universal respect*, one might say, that generates this principle; respecting each person properly requires that we treat her in accordance with the Principle of Sacrifice. What is most striking is that this principle requires a certain kind of sacrifice on behalf of all and any human being, regardless of whether one would sacrifice on behalf of family members, compatriots or distant strangers in far-flung parts of the world. What matters now is that the principle thereby denies that particularly demanding principles of justice apply (only) among compatriots that would generate obligations that must be prioritized over obligations towards distant strangers. Instead, we must sacrifice on behalf of distant strangers *even if* it detracts from efforts to improve life closer to home.

To assess the Principle of Sacrifice we must therefore investigate the question of how principles of distributive justice apply globally ("with whom do we stand in the justice relationship?") This involves a foundational inquiry about how principles of justice apply that takes up much of this chapter. Discussing Singer's argument has returned us to the point we reached by reflecting on the commitments involved in the contemporary understanding of domestic justice.

Grounds of justice

Let us begin with some basic distinctions. These are abstract distinctions that are nonetheless tremendously useful because they allow us to formulate some major views on global distributive justice. What is essential in our upcoming discussion is the distinction between *relationism* and *nonrelationism*. Paradigmatic relationists think the applicability of justice is based on shared political structures. Paradigmatic nonrelationists think it is based on common humanity. More precisely, relationists think principles of justice hold only among persons who stand in some essentially practice-mediated relation to each other. Nonrelationists think such principles may apply among those who stand in no such relation. A reference to practices keeps nonrelationism from collapsing into relationism. The relation of "being within 100,000 km of each other" is not essentially practice-mediated, nor is, more relevantly, that of "being a fellow-human." I say "essentially" practice-mediated relations because there may be practices associated especially with this latter relation which are dispensable to understanding its content.

Relationists and nonrelationists disagree about the *grounds* of justice, the norm-generating conditions or considerations based on which individuals are in the scope of principles of justice. I use the term "grounds" to stay neutral between relationism and nonrelationism and so arrive at a formulation in terms of "conditions or considerations." I use the term "relationship" broadly enough for relationists and nonrelationists to register as offering different accounts of what one may call the "justice relationship." We may think of grounds in two (roughly equivalent) ways. First, these are the features of the population (exclusively held) that make it the case that the principles of justice hold. ("Our distinctively human life," nonrelationists may say; "shared membership in certain political structures (e.g., states)," relationists may say.) Second, these are a set of premises that entail the principle of justice. These premises can be partly normative (e.g., references to the significance of the distinctively human life, or of membership in political structures). Each member of the relevant population has a stringent claim to what their share of the relevant good would be if the distribution was just.

Relationists may hold a range of views about the nature of the relevant relation. They may disagree about the scope of justice, the range of people in the justice relationship. *Globalists* think the relevant relation holds among all human beings in virtue of the existence of practices that relate all humans to each other within a single global order. Globalists owe an account of what it is about involvement with, or subjection to, the global order that generates demands of justice. *Statists* think the relevant relation holds (only) among individuals who share membership in a state. They owe an account of what it is (exclusively) about shared membership in states that generates demands of justice. Those who accept duties of justice that hold (only) among people who share a state endorse "the normative peculiarity of the state;" those who do not, reject it. Statists endorse the normative peculiarity of the state; globalists and nonrelationists do not. So whereas globalists and statists are united by being relationists, globalists and nonrelationists are united by rejecting the normative peculiarity of the state.

Relevant versions of nonrelationism take the scope of justice to be global, including all of (and only) humanity. Yet nonrelationists may determine the scope differently. One could limit justice to a subset of humanity by insisting on the normative importance of, say, sex or race. Or one may insist that justice must have all sentient beings in its scope, at least higher animals and conceivably rational Martians. Yet the former possibility is implausible, and the latter I set aside. Nonrelationists owe an account of how common humanity generates demands of justice.[1] Relationists think of principles of justice as regulating practices that some persons share with each other. This implies two things. First, for relationists, principles of justice apply only to those who respectively share the practices. Relationists are motivated by the moral relevance of practices in which certain individuals stand. Such practices may include not only those that individuals chose to adopt but also those of which they have never chosen to partake. Second, relationists think of principles of justice as regulating only those practices rather than every aspect of the lives of those who share them.

Rawlsian relationism

To illustrate what is at stake, note that John Rawls is a relationist. Rawls, whose work we already encountered in Chapter 3, famously calls justice "the first virtue of institutions, as truth is of systems of thought" and talks about "justice in social cooperation" (1999a, p 3). Justice is then a characteristic of institutions, which are practices. Recall that Rawls's principles regulate the practices constitutive of the *basic structure* of society. "Distributive justice," says Rawls's sympathetic expositor Samuel Freeman by way of expounding this approach and by way of illustrating Rawls's relationism, "poses the general problem of fairly designing the system of basic legal institutions and social norms that make production, exchange, distribution, and consumption possible among free and equal persons" (2007, p 305). Many aspects of advantage and its distribution are natural facts, but "what is just and unjust," says Rawls in a relationist spirit, are not these facts, but "the way that institutions deal with these facts" (1999a, p 87).

To be sure, relationists can recognize duties to those with whom they do not stand in the justice relationship. Alas, those duties would either differ relevantly from duties of justice or else in some other way differ from those duties of justice that hold among individuals who share the relevant relation. The American philosopher Thomas Nagel (2005) adopts the former approach, insisting that justice only holds within states. Rawls adopts the latter and implicitly acknowledges a distinction between duties of *distributive* justice that hold within states and *other* duties of justice that may hold otherwise. The duty of assistance to "burdened societies" in Rawls' *Law of Peoples* is not one of distributive justice (1999b, pp 106, 113–20; see also Freeman 2007, ch. 9). Duties of distributive justice are duties with regard to shares in a system of economic production and exchange, which Rawls thinks presuppose a basic structure.

Rawls is a statist. His main goal is to offer principles of domestic justice. His *Law of Peoples* adds an approach to global justice by way of sketching the foreign policy of a society within which his domestic principles apply. It is telling that Rawls approaches questions of global justice by way of assessing the foreign policy of such societies. Methodologically in the background is his *political constructivism*. Rawls begins with domestic justice and works "outward" from there to the *Law of Peoples* (2001, p 11). He believes one cannot theorize global justice without first theorizing domestic justice. As Freeman says:

> The principles that appropriately regulate social and political relations depend upon the kinds of institutions or practices to be regulated, and these principles are to be "constructed" on the basis of ideas that are central to the functioning of those institutions or practices and people's awareness of them. (2007, p 270)

Freeman sees this political constructivism as integral to Rawls's rejection of global principles of distributive justice. The convictions and intuitions that can be used to obtain a theory of justice concern the practices and institutions in which we lead our lives. These convictions are less developed outside of domestic settings. A theory of global justice remains unsecured unless we base it on a theory of domestic justice since it is only the latter that we can establish firmly.

Crucially, Rawls believes that "humans should be coerced only according to a self-image that is acceptable to them," which implies that "[s]ince 'global citizens' cannot be presumed to view themselves as free and equal individuals who should relate fairly to each other across national boundaries, we cannot legitimately build coercive social institutions that assume that they do" (Wenar 2006, p 103). Leif Wenar, another sympathetic expositor of Rawls, rightly uses this observation to explain why Rawls did not advocate global egalitarian ideals of a sort that, say, Beitz (1999) and Pogge (1989) had found natural as an extension of his domestic principles. Rawls had good reasons to limit the applicability of his principles to states and to deny that they should hold at the global level.

Grounds of justice: further clarifications

Parallel to what I said about relationists, nonrelationism implies two things: nonrelationists seek to avoid the alleged arbitrariness of restricting justice to the regulation of certain practices, and since they do not limit justice in this way, they will plausibly apply principles of justice to the whole range of advantageous and disadvantageous events in a life. Nonrelationists consider justice a property of the *distribution of advantage*, broadly understood. Whereas for relationists individuals stand in the justice relationship if they have special claims within particular practices, for nonrelationists that relationship is distinguished by the absence of special claims.

"Grounds" differ from the "circumstances" of justice that have long been discussed by political philosophers. "The circumstances of justice obtain," explains Rawls, following the 18th century philosopher David Hume, who first theorized this topic, "whenever persons put forward conflicting claims to the division of social advantages under conditions of moderate scarcity" (1999a, p 110). Circumstances of justice specify the living conditions of human beings under which *any* principles of justice apply *in the first place.* Justice does not apply if for instance all desirable goods exist in unlimited quantities (as they do in paradise), or if there is far too little to satisfy even everybody's basic needs (as e.g., in the post-apocalyptic world in Cormac McCarthy's harrowing novel *The Road*). Under the circumstances of justice the grounds specify *which* principles of justice apply to *which* people.

Let me also explain how the positions I have introduced relate to "cosmopolitanism," a term that is much used in recent debates in political philosophy as well as in popular culture. This term combines the Greek words for universe (kosmos) and for city (polis). The ancient Greeks who bequeathed us this term lived in a world of often hostile city states. Therefore the thought contained in this term is the initially rather radical one that in some sense the whole world is a city and thus all of humanity forms one community. In recent debates the following definition by the contemporary philosopher Thomas Pogge is often used:

> Three elements are shared by all cosmopolitan positions: First, *individualism*: the ultimate unit of concern are *human beings*, or *persons.* ... Second, *universality*: the status of ultimate unit of concern attaches to *every* living human being *equally*—not merely to some sub-set, such as men, aristocrats, Aryans, whites, or Muslims. Third, *generality*: this special status has global force. (1994, p 89)

None of the positions I have discussed (statism, globalism, non-relationism) denies the moral equality of persons. Each has the capacity to make sense of individualism, universality and generality. Therefore this understanding of cosmopolitanism does not discern among the views we have discussed. A crucial issue for each position is how rich a notion of moral equality its advocates wish to endorse, and how the relevant notion of moral equality relates to ideas of political and distributive equality. Moral equality captures the thought that in some fundamental ways all human beings matter equally. Political equality captures the thought that in some fundamental ways all participants in a political system (such as a state) matter equally (e.g., should all have the right to vote). And distributive equality expresses the idea that each person in a certain group should have an equal share of something (e.g., income or wealth).

Statists deny a close link between moral and political equality: all human beings are morally equal, but only in the presence of certain practices (shared citizenship) does political equality apply. Statists may or may not find inequality among individuals in one country (in terms of outcomes, resources, or opportunities) morally problematic, but do not find inequality among countries problematic *as such*. And in any event, one needs strong arguments to derive distributive equality of anything from ideas of moral or political equality. Globalists and nonrelationists may hold a range of views on distributive equality, for instance one according to which it is most important that all have "enough" of a range of goods (in a sense that would have to be spelled out in more detail), and less important that all have the same share of these goods.

In the domain of distributive justice, the term *cosmopolitan* has become the victim of its own success. While it is still suitable to describe a love of humanity or the evanescence or fluidity of culture (and thus in this sense to capture the idea that the world is a city), I submit that the term has outlived its usefulness for matters of distributive justice. We have learned the basic cosmopolitan lesson: moral equality is an essential part of any credible theory of global justice. We live on a cosmopolitan plateau. But we should conduct the philosophical debate about global justice in the more nuanced terms discussed in this chapter.

Nonrelationism

Nonrelationists insist that relations in which particular individuals stand are not important enough to define the moral obligations that pertain to such individuals (and only to them). The British political theorist Simon Caney (2005) suggests a version of this approach. He offers the following thought regarding the relevance of economic interaction, and a similar thought would apply to all practices:

> Consider a world with two separate systems of interaction that have no contact but are aware of each other and suppose that one of them is prosperous whereas the other is extremely impoverished. Compare, now, two individuals—one from the prosperous system and the other from the impoverished system—who are identical in their abilities and needs. The member of the prosperous system receives more. But it is difficult to see why—concentrating on any possible and reasonable criteria for entitlement—this is fair. *Ex hypothesi,* she is not more hard-working or more gifted or more needy. In all respects they are identical (bar one, namely that one is lucky to live in the prosperous society and one is not) and yet an institutionalist approach confers on one more benefits. (p 110)

To make his case, Caney identifies a moral argument of sorts and then argues that that argument appeals to properties that everyone has. Limiting such arguments to particular groups means to commit the "fallacy of restricted universalism: A distributive theory, that ascribes rights and claims on the basis of certain universal attributes of persons, cannot at the same time restrict the grounds for those claims to a person's membership or status within a given society." Attempts to derive principles of justice from universal attributes that nevertheless are supposedly limited to certain groups (e.g., compatriots) commit this fallacy. Consider how Caney applies this strategy to civil and political liberties. He argues for the "scope$_1$ claim: the standard justifications of rights to civil and political liberties entail that there are *human* rights to these same civil and political liberties" (p 66). The scope$_1$ claim holds

> because the standard arguments for civil and political rights invoke a universalist "moral personality." That is, the relevant aspect of persons is the right to be subject to principles to which they can reasonably consent (for contractarians), or their use of moral language (for Habermas), or their humanity and status as persons (for deontologists), or their ability to lead a fulfilling life

(for perfectionists). As such, it would be incoherent to adopt any of these lines of reasoning for a particular right and then ascribe that right only to other members of one's community. (p 77)

Arguments of this sort challenge relationists to explain just what it is about their preferred relation that, in the case that interests us, generates demands of justice that would apply only among those who share that relation. Let us turn to that challenge.

Defending relationism

Statists and globalists disagree about what relation is relevant for the applicability of justice. Nonetheless, they are both relationists, resting claims of justice on nationally or globally shared practices, respectively, and thus to some extent use similar arguments to defend their views against nonrelationists. Let us see what strategies relationists may enlist in their defense.

The first strategy draws on the fact that it is (conceptually) difficult for us successfully to press *any* demands upon each other at all, especially the stringent demands of justice. Relationists can readily deal with this difficulty. They can help themselves to considerations that arise from within the practices they consider central to the applicability of justice. They need not deny that there can be *natural* rights and duties of justice. But arguments in support of such rights and duties critically depend on features of shared humanity. Crucially, however, derivations of *transactional* and *associational* duties (the kind of arguments relationists offer) can enlist a larger set of considerations. Such derivations can use claims about persons having undergone certain transactions under specific conditions (e.g., promises, contracts), or about them living in certain human-made arrangements (associations) that put demands on those involved in them. Associations can normally be organized in different ways, and for a particular arrangement to be justifiable to all, everybody must be granted certain entitlements.

Claims of justice cannot succeed merely based on references to the significance of something for a claimant. (Otherwise everybody would have a claim of justice to the person he falls in love with, regardless of whether she reciprocates.) We need reasons why others ought to *provide* what is significant. Nonrelationists can most readily meet that challenge if they restrict themselves to establishing rights and duties pertaining to elementary human concerns, such as basic-needs satisfaction (see again Chapter 1). Relationists are better equipped to make such a case. In particular, duties pertaining to *relative*, rather than *absolute*, economic status are (at least) easier to establish, and more demanding, if we can resort to shared practices to make that case.

To illustrate, consider T. M. Scanlon's (2003d) influential discussion of objections to inequality and hence to differences in relative economic status. Scanlon identifies five reasons to pursue greater *equality*: (a) to relieve suffering or severe deprivation, (b) to prevent stigmatizing differences in status, (c) to avoid unacceptable forms of power or domination, (d) to preserve the equality of starting places that is required by procedural fairness, and (e) because procedural fairness sometimes supports a case for equality of outcomes. Statements (b) and (e) are the clearest expressions of commitments to equality; (d) is consistent with considerable inequalities and so is only weakly committed to equality, whereas (a) and (c) are not committed to equality at all. Scanlon argues that Rawls uses (b) through (e), and perhaps (a) as well, to argue in support of his principles of justice. So those principles are supported by reasons that are distinctly committed to an ideal of equality but also by reasons that are distinctly not.

Crucially, however, even the force of (c) and (d) depends on the *practices* (if any) that the relevant individuals share. For instance, to explain what counts as unacceptable forms of power, it helps to explore how individuals respectively contribute to the maintenance of an economic system and hence also what the economic ties among them are to begin with. Undoubtedly, some exercises of power are unacceptable regardless of what relations individuals stand in. But the more *ties* there are, the more possibilities there will be for the relevant individuals to contribute to the maintenance of relations, which in turn generate rationales for them to complain about certain exercises of power. Similarly, to assess how much reason there is to preserve the equality of starting places on behalf of procedural fairness, it is essential to assess to what kinds, and range, of procedures the individuals are jointly subject to. Thus if we seek to argue for obligations pertaining to relative standing without making use of relations, there is little we can say. We can derive more demanding obligations if we can resort to relations.

The second strategy in defense of relationism appears in Samuel Scheffler's (2001) account of the link between special relations and responsibilities. Relations create responsibilities because having reason to value relations noninstrumentally just *is* to have reasons to see oneself under, and actually have, special obligations. As Scheffler puts it, to attach noninstrumental value to a relationship with someone means "to be disposed, in contexts which vary depending on the nature of the relationship, to see that person's needs, interests, and desires as, in themselves, providing me with presumptively decisive reasons for action, reasons that I would not have had in the absence of the relationship" (2001, p 100); to call reasons "presumptively decisive" means to grant that, in principle, they could be outweighed, although they present themselves as reasons on which agents must act. Skepticism about such special obligations succeeds only if we have no reasons at all to value our relations noninstrumentally. However, this kind of case is clearest for family ties and friendships but less clear for political relations. Presumably statists can more readily make the case than globalists.

Statism vs. globalism

Statists must develop their version of relationism in a way that supports the normative peculiarity of the state. They could first use the two strategies in support of relationism to rebut nonrelationism and then offer an account of the normative peculiarity of the state to rebut globalists. Two proposed accounts of the normative peculiarity of the state are *coercion-based statism* (i.e., what distinguishes membership in a state is its coerciveness) and *reciprocity-based statism* (i.e., it is its intense form of cooperation). According to the first view, what limits the justice-relationship respectively to those who share a state is that they (and only they) are subject to the enforcement mechanisms of the state, and it is because their lives are constrained in this way that they have particularly stringent claims to a share of the goods they produce under such circumstances (think of Rawls's social primary goods). According to the second view, what limits the justice relationship is that those who share a state jointly create goods through a tight system of relationships (ranging from actual exchanges of goods to social insurance mechanisms that provide background support).

However, forms of coercion and cooperation also hold within the global order as such. Therefore it is problematic to argue that justice governs *only* the relation among those who share a state. To illustrate this point, let us explore the debate between Thomas Nagel (2005) and Joshua Cohen and Charles Sabel (2006). Nagel defends a version of coercion-based statism. What is a characteristic of those who are jointly subject to principles of justice, for Nagel, is that (a) they are, at least putatively, the joint authors of the legal system (b) to whose norms they are also subject. Thus they are expected to accept (and are otherwise coerced to comply with) the authority of these norms even where collective decisions diverge from their preferences. It is the combination of (a) and (b) that creates a special presumption against arbitrary inequalities (inherited social status and genetic advantages) in our treatment by the legal system.

So Nagel argues as follows:

1. Arbitrary inequalities are morally problematic if and only if the affected agents are both (a) putative joint authors of the coercively imposed system, and (b) subject to its norms.
2. Only states, in their ideal forms, satisfy conditions (a) and (b) in (1).
3. Therefore, arbitrary inequalities are problematic only among those who share a state.

"Arbitrary" inequalities are those due to unearned characteristics (inherited social status, genetic advantages), and so the kind of inequalities constrained through principles of justice such as

Rawls's two principles that we encountered in Chapter 3. If this conclusion holds, these principles will only apply among those who share a state. As we noted, Rawls did think that his principles were respectively limited to those who share a state. But he wrote his *Theory of Justice* decades before the debate about the grounds of justice began. For that reason, Rawls himself did not go to much trouble explaining what it was (exclusively) about the state that rendered such demanding principles applicable.

Economic integration is increasing, much rule-making occurs in global settings (security, labor standards, environment, food safety standards, etc.), and transnational rule-making affects behavior of individuals and institutions. Nonetheless, Premise 2 of the argument above insists that international organizations (like WTO or World Bank) do not act in the name of individuals, or do not impose norms that require compliance. They are only indirectly related to individuals. But suppose the IMF lends funds to a country threatened by economic chaos only if it reforms. Or suppose a country changes its trade policies to comply with WTO agreements. "Why not say," inquire Cohen and Sabel,

> that citizens in member states are expected to take account of WTO decisions, which have binding legal force: that they ought not to oppose a new trade regulation that is made pursuant to a WTO finding? (p 168)

By way of objecting to Premise 2, why not say the ideal form of these interactions too satisfies (a) and (b)? Consider another example. The European Parliament is elected by direct vote. While its impact on the EU is much smaller than the impact of national parliaments on domestic politics, the joint presence of this parliament and the European Commission entails that the EU exerts coercion that has EU citizens as authors and subjects. Nagel argues that a difference between citizenship in a state and membership in international organizations is that one does not generally assume the former voluntarily but does so assume the latter. Nonetheless, both involve sanctions in cases of non-compliance. Moreover, once either citizenship or membership has been assumed, resigning may not be a reasonable option.

Statists can respond that the state's normative peculiarity is based on its *particular kind* of coerciveness or cooperativeness. Risse (2012) accounts for the state's coerciveness in terms of legal and political immediacy. (As we will see, I do so on behalf of *pluralist internationalism* rather than *statism*, but statists too can enlist this move.) The legal aspect consists in the directness and pervasiveness of law enforcement. State enforcement agencies have direct, unmediated access to bodies and assets. Since many facets of the dealings of citizens among each other (including all property dealings, ranging from the purchase of a coffee to ownership of firms and conditions on inheritance and bequest) are regulated, enforcement is pervasive for most individuals subject to it. The political aspect consists in the significance of the environment that the state provides for the realization of basic moral rights, a significance that captures the profundity of this relationship.

The state is also cooperative in a particularly intense way. "When well-functioning," writes Andrea Sangiovanni (2007), the basic extractive, regulative, and distributive capacities central to any modern state plus a system of courts, administration, and military, "free us from the need to protect ourselves continuously from physical attack, guarantee access to a legally regulated market, and establish and stabilize a system of property rights and entitlements" (p 20). This system is supported "through taxation, through participation, in various forms of political activity, and through simple compliance, which includes the full range of our everyday, legally regulated activity." We can use the term "reciprocity" to characterize the particular way in which the state is a cooperative endeavor.

However, assuming Risse (2012) succeeds in explaining what is morally special about shared membership in states, one must still wonder whether this account matters *for justice*; whether it can explain why justice applies *only* among those who share a state. Globalists push that point. Charles Beitz, a major advocate of globalism, argues that global interdependence

> involves a pattern of transactions that produce substantial benefits and costs; their increased volume and significance have led to

> the development of a global regulative structure... Taken together, these institutions and practices can be considered as the constitutional structure of the world economy: their activities have important distributional implications. (1999, p 148)

It does not matter precisely what the nature of international economic interdependence is. Beitz argues that in an interdependent world, limiting justice to domestic societies means taxing poor nations so that others may live in "just" regimes (pp 149ff). His target is Rawls. Contrary to what Rawls himself thought about this matter, Beitz argues that if Rawls's case for his principles succeeds, their content should not change as a result of enlarging the scope of the original position to include the global order. Beitz considers two objections. The first insists that interdependence is necessary but insufficient for the applicability of justice. The global order lacks any effective decision-making mechanisms, as well as any real sense of community, and these, the objector says, are also necessary for an order's being subject to standards of justice. Beitz responds that these differences fail to show that principles of justice do not apply globally; instead, they show that it is harder to implement them. According to the second objection, features of cooperation within states override requirements of global principles *even if* justice applies globally. Rich countries may deserve their advantages because of differences in organization or technology. Beitz responds that this entails basing entitlements on morally arbitrary factors such as those that, as Rawls insisted, ought not to affect one's share of social primary goods. Thus he rejects this move much as Rawls rejects principles of justice drawing on undeserved social or genetic characteristics.

Pluralist internationalism

The most sensible way of making progress in the debate between statists and globalists is to deny that there is a single justice relationship in which any two individuals either do or do not stand. One may use *principles of justice* as a collective term for different principles with their *respective* ground and scope. Let us call *nongraded* or *monist internationalism* the view that principles of justice either do or do not apply, that they do apply within states, and thus that they apply among people who share membership in a state and only then. Nongraded internationalism is the same as statism. Introducing this additional terminology allows us to connect statism to other views that endorse the normative peculiarity of the state. Coercion-based and reciprocity-based statism capture versions of monist or nongraded internationalism.

Graded internationalism holds that different principles of justice apply depending on the associational (i.e., social, legal, political, or economical) arrangements. Graded internationalism allows for associations such as the WTO, EU or the global order as such to be governed by principles of justice but endorses the *normative peculiarity* of the state. Among the principles that apply within other associations we find weakened versions of principles that apply within states. We discuss trade in more detail in Chapter 7, but suffice it to say now that all those who live under the WTO are tied to each other much more loosely than individuals who share a state. It is therefore plausible to think the principles of justice that hold within the WTO are weakened versions of those that hold within a state. So globalism would be correct to the extent that there are principles of justice that apply outside of the state. But these would be different principles from those that apply within states.

However, now that we are entertaining a nonmonist view, we must take seriously the idea that some grounds could be relational, whereas others would not be. We must consider the possibility that there is no deep conflict between relationism and nonrelationism. Perhaps advocates of relationism and nonrelationism have overemphasized various facets of one overall plausible theory that recognizes both relationist and nonrelationist grounds. Integrating relationist grounds into a theory of justice pays homage to the idea that individuals find themselves in, or join, associations and that membership in some of them generates duties. Integrating nonrelationist grounds means taking seriously the idea that some duties of justice do not depend on the existence of associations. One nonrelational ground is common humanity. To the extent that we must recognize common humanity as a ground, nonrelationism is correct.[2]

The view that develops these ideas is *pluralist internationalism*. The use of the term *internationalism* for this position acknowledges the applicability of principles of justice outside of and among ("inter") states. The use of the terms "graded" and "nongraded" internationalism captures the logical relationship of these views to pluralist internationalism. Let me sketch how Risse (2012) develops this view. Pluralist internationalism endorses the state's normative peculiarity. Legal and political immediacy plus reciprocity characterize shared membership in a state as a ground of justice and thus render particular principles of justice applicable. Risse assumes that the principles of justice that apply domestically are Rawls's two principles:

1. Each person has the same indefeasible claim to a fully adequate scheme of equal basic liberties, which scheme is compatible with the same scheme of liberties for all.
2. Social and economic inequalities are to be arranged so that they are both (a) attached to offices and positions open to all under conditions of fair equality of opportunity, and (b) to the greatest benefit of the least advantaged.

As we noted in Chapter 3, what is behind Rawls's reasoning is an awareness of the moral arbitrariness of natural assets and social status. Rawls seeks "to set up the social system so that no one gains or loses from his arbitrary place in the distribution of natural assets or his initial position in society without giving or receiving compensating advantages in return (1999a, p 87). Crucially, this intuition is decisive only while we are talking about shared membership in a political system characterized by legal and political immediacy as well as reciprocity. It is only before this background that arbitrary inequalities are problematic to such an extent that principles as strong as Rawls's apply.

Behind the veil of ignorance, Rawls argues, individuals would adopt a *maximin* approach: they seek to maximize their share in social primary goods in the worst-off position. According to Rawls, that reasoning leads to his principles. The resulting distribution should be acceptable to everybody since they would be acceptable *especially* to the worst-off. The first principle guarantees that each person's integrity is protected; the first part of the second principle ensures that society makes substantive efforts to create equal opportunities for all; and the second part makes sure the kinds of advancement in society that natural and social advantages still permit (once equal liberties and fair equality of opportunity have been realized) benefit everybody, including the least well-off. Rawls's principles are controversial. Nonetheless, I assume here that these indeed are the correct principles of domestic distributive justice.

But although pluralist internationalism acknowledges the normative peculiarity of the state, it recognizes multiple grounds, some relational (e.g., membership in a state, subjection to the global trading regime) and others not (e.g., common humanity). Respectively different principles are associated with these grounds, all of which are binding, say, for states and international organizations. Internationalism transcends the distinction between relationism and nonrelationism. In subsequent chapters we encounter other grounds that this view acknowledges, and the epilogue revisits this view. We have already encountered one component of pluralist internationalism: pluralist internationalism incorporates the view of human rights as membership rights in the global order we developed in Chapter 1. Membership in the global order is a relational ground of justice. An associated principle of justice is that human rights understood as membership rights in the global order be realized.

Revisiting Caney and Singer

Caney's nonrelationist argument envisages two people who are identical in all morally relevant ways. Yet according to pluralist internationalism, membership matters morally even if it has arisen in a manner for which individuals deserve no credit. Common humanity is one ground of justice, and to that extent Caney's nonrelationism is correct. However, we can derive only so much from that starting point, and Chapter 1 has already explored "how much" when we talked about orthodox conceptions of human rights.

Recall now Singer's Principle of Sacrifice that we encountered at the beginning of this chapter: "If it is in one's power to prevent something very bad from happening, without thereby sacrificing anything of comparable moral significance, one ought to do it." Singer implicitly assumes that there are no principles of justice that apply only among those who share a state and that thus generate particular obligations among such people. Pluralist internationalism rejects the Principle of Sacrifice. All human beings are owed equal respect. However, particularly demanding principles of justice do apply among those who share membership in a state. Responses to human neediness as such (to needy people wherever they live) should be guided by a less demanding principle than Singer's principle, such as Richard Miller's (2010) Principle of Sympathy:

> One's underlying disposition to respond to neediness as such ought to be sufficiently demanding that giving which would express greater underlying concern would impose a significant risk of worsening one's life, if one fulfilled all further responsibilities; and it need not be any more demanding than this.

That is, one should respond to neediness (only) to such an extent that further efforts would create a great risk that one's own life would go worse, assuming that one also takes seriously one's moral obligations that do not turn on neediness.

We can argue for the Principle of Sympathy as follows. Moral equality demands that we treat everybody with respect. To treat people with respect means especially to make sure they can maintain their self-respect in relationships we share with them. Those who share a country jointly participate in a relationship characterized by legal and political immediacy as well as reciprocity. Under these circumstances, the maintenance of self-respect requires that these laws seek to put all people subject to them in a position to go after meaningful pursuits. Therefore, respect obligates us to take redistributive measures to make sure they are in that position. Thus to the extent that our resources are limited, we are permitted not to respond to the neediness of those with whom we do not share coercive relations.

This argument makes clear why there are considerable domestic redistributive duties *and* at the same time why relative neglect of duties to distant individuals is acceptable. A bias towards those with whom one shares a state is not only consistent with universal respect, but is required. To be sure, this argument does decidedly not preclude foreign aid, but instead passes judgment on its relative importance vis-à-vis domestic duties. I take for granted now that there indeed are demanding responsibilities for the global poor. But it is also true that these responsibilities are globally shared in ways in which domestic responsibilities are not.

Nationalism

Our discussion has accounted for the normative peculiarity of the state in terms of dense relationships of coerciveness and cooperativeness. Appeals to nationality, or shared nationhood, have played no role. In light of the historical importance of nationalism, I should explain why I do not account for that peculiarity by appeal to shared nationhood, and I should explain what relevance shared nationhood may nevertheless have. The political theorist and historian of ideas Isaiah Berlin has suggested that nationalism

> entails the notion that one of the most compelling reasons, perhaps the most compelling, for holding a particular belief, pursuing a particular policy, serving a particular end, living a particular life, is that these ends, beliefs, policies, lives are *ours*. This is tantamount to saying that these rules or doctrines or principles should be followed not because they lead to virtue or happiness of justice or liberty ... or are good and right in themselves ... rather they are to be followed because these values are those of *my* group – for the nationalists, of *my* nation. ... (1981, p 342f)

We must distinguish *civic* from *ethnic* nationalism, depending on how one develops the attitude Berlin expresses. Both allow us to formulate the thesis of the state's normative peculi-arity. According to the civic conception, a nation is a voluntary association of individuals, a kind of daily plebiscite. There are special obligations among fellow citizens because they have actu-ally accepted them. This may not involve an oath or something similarly explicit, but civic nationalism emphasizes the manner in which individual *wills* maintain a closely-knit community. The ethnic conception ties the stance that one ought to follow rules or principles "because these values are those of *my* group" to objec-tive features of social life, such as language and tradition. These supposedly shared features are taken to generate duties.

Appeals to the importance of nationhood of either sort lead to nationalism as the principle "which holds that the national and the political unit should be congruent" (Gellner 1983, p 1). David Miller (1995) argues that shared nationality is a powerful source of identity, although he denies that it generates any clear speci-fication of duties towards compatriots (which must emerge from public discourse). Without bonds of nationalism, Miller suggests, bonds of citizenship are very thin, psychologically *and* norma-tively. I submit that the view developed in this chapter rebuts Miller's stance as far as the normative dimension is concerned. Immediacy and reciprocity make bonds of citizenship norma-tively rather strong.

In addition, there are well-known problems with both versions of nationalism. Shared citizenship (or co-membership in a given society) does not generally possess the voluntary nature on which civic nationalism focuses. Since it is therefore based on a mis-guided understanding of the nature of shared nationality, it can-not give us an account of how shared nationality would generate obligations. Ethnic nationalism is problematic because its central considerations do not generally apply to all relevant people. In any event, it does not provide us with an intelligible way of generating obligations in the first place. Therefore it is a considerable advan-tage of my internationalism that it does not enlist nationhood to explain what is special about membership in a state.

Nonetheless, nations frequently are cohesive groups in which individuals care about each other more than about others (being "teammates in life," Wellman 2003, p 270). The nation's welfare often improves through political autonomy. As David Miller stresses, bonds of citizenship are easier to maintain with support from bonds of nationalism. I accept these points as reasons why people do or do not wish to live together. As the 19th century English philosopher John Stuart Mill put it in his *Considerations on Representative Government*, "[w]here the sentiment of nationality exists in any force, there is a prima facie case for uniting all the members of the nationality under the same government, and a government to themselves apart" (1991, p 310). Appeals to nationality are relevant for drawing boundaries. I submit that they are irrelevant when we ask what duties hold among those who share a state, or where principles of justice apply, and why they do.

Does the global order wrongfully harm the poor?

So far we have only explored distributive justice. However, when discussing global justice one must also wonder whether the global order *wrongfully harms* some people, presumably the global destitute. Perhaps we should think of global justice primarily in terms of obligations to rectify harms that have already occurred, and to make sure that no further harm is inflicted. There are different ways of articulating the concern with rectifying harm that has already occurred.

Perhaps the global order harms the poor because there is an actually feasible alternative under which the situation of the global poor is improved, as presented by Thomas Pogge (2002). It would just take 1.2 per cent of the income of rich economies, $312 billion annually, to bridge the aggregate shortfall of those living on less than $1 per day to the $2 line (2002, p 7). Pogge's proposal for raising some of those funds is the Global Resource Dividend, which taxes extraction of resources.

However, while Pogge's calculations show that abject poverty could be surmounted *if* closing such a gap is a matter of transferring money, it is doubtful whether financial transfers are enough to seriously mitigate poverty. Suppose we have the funds to cover the financial shortfall. We still need reliable ways of distributing funds to individuals who do not simply have bank accounts that they can securely access. We would also need an environment where individuals can actually spend the money on available goods and services. Both of these scenarios involve *institutional* improvements, especially if one wants the changes to be lasting. Similar points apply if one wishes to support medical and educational advancements. One cannot simply start to "work on AIDS" but instead must build and maintain a medical infrastructure. One cannot improve education by building a few schoolhouses but must also invest in teacher training and provide books, supplies, family support and much else.

It has become a guiding insight for many at the intersection between the social sciences of development and its practice that *sustainable* measures for *enduring* change require good institutions. Having funds to close the aggregate *financial* shortfall between the current situation S_1 and a desirable situation S_2 is at best necessary but not sufficient for S_2 to be feasible. Pogge may respond that while it is true that money does not automatically educate or cure anyone, the funds would be used precisely to take care of these issues in appropriate ways. Money is not enough by itself, but the other necessary conditions normally require money. This is fair enough, but the relevant points now are these: There is a scenario in which the poor are wrongfully harmed, namely, if not enough effort goes into exploring possibilities for implementing appropriate institutional change. But while this is presumably a valid charge, it makes it much harder than it appears in Pogge's proposal to ascertain how to go about creating a feasible alternative and who is guilty of what failings in this regard.

Pogge defends what we may call the Strong Thesis (Cohen 2010): "Most global poverty could be eliminated through *minor* modifications in the global order that would entail at most slight reductions in the incomes of the affluent." To appreciate the strength of Pogge's position, note that the Strong Thesis goes much beyond what we may call the Conventional Thesis: "Some global poverty could be eliminated by changes in the global rules that would not themselves result in serious moral injuries." It is indisputable that there is much that wealthy countries and global rule-makers could, and ought to, do in order to improve the plight of the global destitute. It is also indisputable that citizens of wealthy countries share a responsibility for the alleviation of extreme poverty. But to the extent that the Strong Thesis goes beyond the Conventional Thesis, it is speculative and unwarranted by available evidence. There is no reason to accept the claim that changes in the global rules would suffice to lift most of the terrible destitution that persists on this planet.

Rectifying past injustice

A different way of thinking about rectificatory justice is in terms of past violations that cast a long shadow. Lea Ypi, Robert Goodin and Christian Barry (2009) argue that when for instance the British colonized India or the French Haiti, they integrated those areas into their coercive and cooperative systems. Therefore the colonized were owed transfers due to principles of redistributive justice that apply within such a system and that should have compensated for their disadvantaged status. Instead of exploiting India, the British should have thought of the poorest people there as (presumably) among the poorest in their realm and sought to ease their plight. Later, at decolonization, the colonies were again owed transfers, much like in a divorce the more successful partner owes transfer payments to the less successful one. But such transfers did not occur. In different ways and to different degrees colonies were set up for the benefit of the colonizers and often just left to their own devices at decolonization. What the colonized were owed then they are still owed. The current claimants are the heirs of those to whom such transfers were once owed, in whose estates original claims continue to accrue interest.

Haiti has an especially sad history of colonial exploitation. Its native population perished soon after the arrival of the Spanish. At first the Spanish and then later the French colonizers imported African slaves. Eventually Haiti became the shining jewel of the French colonial empire, much more profitable than New England ever was for the British. These profits were made through the backbreaking labor of plantation slaves. In a gruesome rebellion and devastating war of independence the slaves expelled their masters at the end of the 18th century. Several decades later the French threatened to reconquer Haiti. Instead they settled for extorting a huge indemnity and favorable trade terms. In 2003 then-president of Haiti Jean-Bertrand Aristide demanded $21,685,135,571.48 in reparations from France. He calculated this sum from the amount of the indemnity and the interest that amount would have carried over the years. Ypi, Goodin and Barry's argument supports this demand (and would support others of its kind).

One might object that Ypi, Goodin and Barry treat the debts that were once owed to the colonized too much like money that was put in a bank account at some point and has since not only accrued interest, but has been bequeathed to subsequent generations who never touched it (Sher 1980). Let us envisage a rectified world RW in which the past violations did not occur (e.g., past transfers did occur, contrary to fact). In RW, what do we know about how well-off the descendents of those would be who in that world did *not* become victims? Between an earlier time t_1 and the present time t_2, many things would have happened. The longer the interval between t_1 and t_2, the more things would have happened. Where the initial wrong was done long ago, most of the difference between the living conditions of the victims' offspring in the actual world and the living conditions of the offspring of those who did not become victims in RW would stem from actions of intervening agents between t_1 and t_2. Little or none will be the *automatic effect* of the initial wrong. However, compensation is warranted only for disparities in entitlements which are the automatic effect of that initial wrong. Therefore, past debts are precisely *not* like untouched bank accounts. Since perpetrators are accountable only for automatic consequences of wrongs, there will be little or nothing left to compensate. This line of reasoning undermines contemporary claims to compensation. It does so with the more force the longer ago the offending actions occurred. Sher's reasoning would readily apply to Haiti and thus speak against Aristide's demands against the French.

By way of contrast, consider the Democratic Republic of Congo (DRC). There is a link between the lack of good institutions, as well as many other troubles the country has had, and the in this case Belgian colonial occupation. The Congo Free State, first property of King Leopold II and later transferred to the Belgian state, was exploited with ghastly recklessness. No political or economic structures were created to prepare for independence. At independence in 1960, DRC did not even have a basic network of roads. Tensions on Independence Day and a mutiny prompted by the conduct of the remaining Belgian officers led to the murder of Prime Minister Patrice Lumumba, which inaugurated the terrible Mobutu dictatorship, which led to a civil war of deplorable dimensions. These appalling events are rather automatic effects of the dreadful colonial experience, one that ended within living memory. In this case, both Sher and Ypi, Goodin and Barry would presumably support demands against Belgium for appropriate restitution.

However, Sher ignores the extent to which momentous decisions locked in later generations and thus he underestimates the impact of past violations. According to theories of *path-dependency*, events at turning points constrain the range of subsequently available institutional arrangements. Had other events occurred (assuming they were realistically possible), the later range of opportunities would have been different. Crucial events cast long shadows, by creating conditions under which later generations rise and acquire attitudes or inclinations. Therefore perpetrators are accountable not only for automatic effects, but also for the manner in which their deeds shape future opportunities. Specifically, in former colonies institutions have arisen from a history where the range of available options was normally shaped enduringly by concerns other than the flourishing of the colonized. To revisit that analogy, often colonists decidedly were like people who opened an account *and* also created the parameters that shaped the lives and attitudes of future users, as well as the conditions under which they would make withdrawals.

Presumably *some* share of the advantages in which the world's rich indulge would be unavailable to them were it not for past injustice. To that extent these advantages are ill-gotten. Similarly, to *some* extent the misery of the poor has been caused by pernicious interactions with people from other parts of the world, which resulted in institutions that were not geared towards the well-being of those expected to comply with them and that continue to cast a shadow. As William Faulkner famously wrote in

Requiem for a Nun: "The past is never dead. It's not even past." But past violence not only produces ill-gotten gains. It also creates difficulties in making good on what obligations the wealthy have to the poor (a subject we discuss in various chapters). There will often be doubts about whether certain measures are required to satisfy such obligations. In light of what we have now argued, there is a *compensatory* aspect to these duties. That is, in many cases where we have doubts about whether something ought to be done by way of satisfying obligations towards the world's destitute, this compensatory aspect should make us answer the question affirmatively. Past injustice creates considerable obligations for the present.

Further reading

Questions of domestic justice are discussed in all introductions to political philosophy that focus on one state (see again the list in the introduction to this book). Beitz (1999) is the second edition of a work that appeared in 1979 and thus long before philosophizing about global justice became wide-spread. His work is the classic account of globalism. Pogge (2002) defends the provocative thesis that the global order harms the poor; the work appeared in an extended second edition in 2008. See Cohen (2010) and Risse (2005) for critical assessments. Important recent accounts of global justice include Caney (2005), David Miller (2007), Richard Miller (2010), Moellendorff (2002), Tan (2004) and Brock (2009). Rawls (1999b) plays an important role in the debate about global justice, but is not stage-setting in that area as Rawls (1999a) has been for domestic justice. Risse (2012) develops pluralist internationalism. Blake (2001a) is a seminal text on the grounds-of-justice debate. Miller (1995) is an excellent discussion of nationalism.

5 Environmental Justice

The anthropocene

Our species of *homo sapiens* has been around for about 200,000 years. For 50,000 years, our major traits have been fully developed, and our brains have barely changed. The earth, however, is almost 100,000 *times* as old. It has been through a turbulent history that included several mass extinctions. Let me mention a few highlights. According to the "giant impact hypothesis", about four billion years ago the earth was hit by a Mars-sized body. The moon was created from debris that was left over from this collision. About 650 million years ago, our planet was covered by ice, an era known as "snowball earth." About 250 million years ago, in a period called the "great dying," most life perished in a brief moment of geological time. Massive volcanic eruptions may have been at fault. It appears that 65 million years ago, an asteroid the size of Mount Everest hit in the Gulf of Mexico, triggering the extinction of the dinosaurs that had been the dominant species for many millions of years. The biospheric conditions that made the ascent of our own species possible, and even the physical shape and composition of the earth, have resulted from a series of cataclysmic events and periods. In one way or another, the occurrence of natural disasters is a part of our lives. But the short presence of human beings on this planet (geologically speaking) has so far been blessed by conditions that, by and large, are strikingly hospitable to the flourishing of human life. As its history reveals, however, the earth is not inevitably friendly to humanity's ongoing existence.

The relationship between humans and their environment has entered a new geological era, the Anthropocene, a period where humankind has surpassed the rest of nature in its impact on the structure and function of the earth system. Short of events like a head-on collision with an asteroid, massive changes in the earth's interior or vehement sun storms, it is humans that have the biggest impact on the future of all life on this planet. One kind of impact is that humanity has caused a change in global climate. Naturally occurring greenhouse gases, such as water vapor, carbon dioxide and methane, form a thermal blanket that traps sun energy inside the atmosphere and thereby makes the earth inhabitable in the first place. However, in recent centuries human activities have greatly increased greenhouse gas concentrations. Considerable quantities of carbon dioxide have resulted from burning fossil fuels and from deforestation. Increasing evaporation of water amplifies the warming effects of these gases by causing larger greenhouse effects than combustion and deforestation alone. The result is climate change. The Intergovernmental Panel on Climate Change concluded that most of the increase in average temperatures is very likely due to increases in man-made greenhouse gas concentrations. In the Introduction we noted how dramatically an increase of average temperature by more than 3 or 4 degrees Celsius may change the way we live on this planet.

Our brains emerged through an evolutionary process in which survival depended on an organism's ability to navigate its immediate environment. The kind of brain that succeeded in evolution and that we still possess does not naturally prompt us to provide for future generations. As far as our attitude towards nature is concerned, several decades ago, long before climate change became an acknowledged issue, historian Lynn White's article "The Historical Roots of Our Ecological Crisis" triggered some soul-searching. White argued that Christianity created a frame of mind that sees human beings as separate from the rest of nature. The dominant reading of the Christian story of creation granted human beings mastery over nature. Subsequently, the development of science and technology was a sustained effort to exploit nature for human purposes, and it originally proceeded in this Christian frame of mind. This attitude towards nature has since become entrenched at a global level. So evolution has generated a kind of brain that not only did not prepare our species for the need to take care of future generations, but that has also made us susceptible to an attitude that appreciates nature only in terms of its value for us.

In his fascinating and tremendously important 2005 book *Collapse*, the American geographer Jared Diamond looks at several societies that have existed at different times, and disappeared. Several of them were located in remote areas, such as the medieval Viking colonies in Greenland, or the civilization on the Easter Islands that left behind numerous monumental statues. But some were far less isolated, such as several Central American cultures that met the same fate. Environmental disasters always precipitated the collapse. What is remarkable is that the environmental problems that led to such devastation normally will have been as visible to decision makers at the time as they are today. The reason why they took no resolute measures to avert the incipient disaster was because the decision makers had vested interests in the status quo. The earth as a whole, and thus humanity as such, in an era of human-caused climate change is in much the same situation as was the case with these perished human living arrangements. Again the problem is that vested interests prevent decisive action.

Climate change as the perfect moral storm

Moral philosopher Stephen Gardiner's 2011 *Perfect Moral Storm: The Ethical Tragedy of Climate Change* aptly characterizes the challenges we confront when dealing with climate change. A perfect storm involves the unusual intersection of several serious, mutually reinforcing storms. In the case of climate change, three major problems interfere with our ability to behave ethically: the global, intergenerational and theoretical storms. The global storm concerns our difficulties in reaching any kind of international agreement on measures to combat climate change. It is collectively rational for humanity to reach an agreement on how to control emissions. It is nonetheless also rational for each country to exempt itself from such regulation hoping that others take the lead. The intergenerational storm consists in the fact that the current generation has asymmetric power over future generations. Earlier generations can affect the prospects of future generations, but not vice versa. Any generation has incentives to generate front-loaded goods, goods that largely benefit the present but for which later generations pay. All goods whose production generates greenhouse gas emissions are such goods given how long some of these gases stay in the atmosphere. The third storm is the theoretical storm: there are no robust general theories to guide us. Existing theories are underdeveloped in many of the relevant areas, including intergenerational ethics, international justice, scientific uncertainty and questions about the human relationship to animals and the rest of nature.

Let me illustrate the point that our theories are underdeveloped to deal with climate change by discussing Cost-Benefit Analysis (CBA). CBA goes back to the 19th-century development of welfare economics, and thus to a time when social-scientific methods started to bear on politics. CBA systematically captures the different available options, and makes sure all relevant costs and benefits inform the decision process. For instance, CBA registers that money invested into improving life for future generations cannot also be invested into improving the present, with whatever positive spill-over effects on the future that may have. CBA keeps alternative social objectives in view. At the same time, the systematic virtues of CBA might deceive us when it comes to problems of the complexity of climate change, where the needed information is not reliably available and the time horizon too extended.

The common way of integrating future costs and benefits into CBA is by *discounting* them. Discount rates mirror expectations about the economy, and formally are inverse interest rates. Discounting the future means assigning a lower value to future costs and benefits than to those occurring in the present. We can most straightforwardly motivate discounting for individual behavior. An individual should prefer receiving $500 today to receiving $500 at future time t since in between she could invest the $500. Receiving $500 at t is equivalent to receiving x<$500 now, where x delivers $500 at t under the expected interest rate.

The present value of future benefits and future costs thus is a discounted adjustment of future values. Therefore substantial future costs may be acceptable for relatively minor gains in the present.

Similar considerations apply to certain public expenditures of a collective. Among the costs that might arise are those of human lives themselves. A monetary equivalent would be assigned to human life. Because of the effects of compounding, the choice of a discount rate matters enormously, the more so the longer the decision horizon. For a 1% annual rate, one unit of benefit in the present is equivalent to 1.3, 1.6, 2.7, and 144.7 units in the future if the benefits occur after 30, 50, 100, and 500 years, respectively. The corresponding numbers for 3% are 2.4, 4.3, 19.2, 2,621,877; for 5%, 4.3, 11.4, 131.5, and 39,323,261,827; and for 10%, 17.4, 117.3, 13, 781, and 4.96×10^{20}. In policy choices that affect future generations, the lives of people living 100–200 years from now are severely discounted. Moreover, even minor differences in the discount rates make an enormous difference for the extent to which they are discounted.

There are two reasons why one would want to discount future values. First, one might value the future less because it *is* the future ("pure time preference"). Second, one might do so because the passage of time correlates with other phenomena, such as increasing wealth, availability of technology, or more pronounced uncertainty. In support of pure time preferences one finds appeals to revealed preferences (people commonly caring more about the nearest and dearest, as well as their own immediate future), and a corresponding reference to the alleged anti-democratic arrogance of social planners dismissive of such preferences. Another point is that we would be overburdened giving equal consideration to all people across the ages. There are likely to be many more people whose birth is yet to happen than are currently alive. If all of them counted for the same, the interests of the living might carry almost no weight at all.

As far as the second sort of reason is concerned, however, not all future people will be wealthier than all contemporaries. Perhaps if "we" collectively will be richer, "we" can worry about redistribution later. Yet we cannot assume that future people can solve distribution problems more easily than we can. Nor can we know that particular discount rates track increases in wealth. The rationale for discounting in individual behavior does not apply to climate change. We are then talking about people who live across different generations. Unlike in cases of public expenditures for the immediate future, one set of people participate in the decision process, but others bear the costs. Or consider the value of lives (or anything else that is not straightforwardly priced, e.g., wildlife or ecosystems). We often adopt policies that implicitly put a price on human life (e.g., by deciding how much money to invest in safety). We make such decisions in a context where probabilities of death or other harms are of a certain magnitude, as are the benefits of the relevant policies. We do not know if future people will find scenarios acceptable where probabilities of death or disease, as well as gains from certain policies, are much higher, generating the same expected value for which we find the mix of probabilities and benefits acceptable. But we may well bequeath such policies to the future. In a nutshell, we should have considerable reservations about applying CBA to climate change.

The joint presence of these storms also generates a problem of *moral corruption*: we are only all too inclined to accept arguments whose conclusions benefit us. The harms and injustices that might occur are potentially catastrophic, but the future victims cannot make themselves heard. Our own vigilance must protect them. An example Gardiner uses to illustrate the phenomenon of moral corruption is geo-engineering, an area of research that investigates possibilities of intentional interventions in the earth's climate system on a global scale to remove greenhouse gases from the atmosphere. The thought of the possible future availability of geo-engineering offers reassurance that we may go on as we have, assuming there will be a solution in the future. Perhaps there will be, but the joint presence of the three storms makes us unduly willing to believe that it will be so.

Climate change as a problem of justice

As far as climate change is concerned, there are three options: to let the changes happen and suffer the consequences; to mitigate climate change (reduce its pace and magnitude); or to adapt (reduce its impact). The first option – to conduct "business-as-usual" – is motivated by the view that the future is likely to be richer than the present. We will be better equipped to deal with problems then. But the damage might not only be irreversible, but also trigger increasingly problematic consequences. Alternatively, one may favor the "business as usual" option if one thinks there is nothing we can do about climate change anyway, or if one believes climate change simply is not "our" problem and that therefore there is nothing we ought to do about it. However, it is decidedly not true that there is nothing we can do about climate change. And indeed, climate change is "our" problem at least in the sense that we are contributing to it and are thereby causing hardship for others (both now and in the future). For these reasons, I do not further consider the "business-as-usual" option. Possibilities for mitigation include a reduction of greenhouse gases (through changing energy use, reforming agricultural practices, or limiting deforestation), as well as geo-engineering to remove gases from the atmosphere or create cooling effects to offset heating. Possibilities for adaptation include developing crops resistant to climate change; public-health defenses; flood control and drought management; building barriers against sea-level rises; or avoiding development in at-risk areas.

One contribution philosophy can make to an attempt to keep humanity from suffering the same fate as the earlier civilizations in Diamond's *Collapse* is to present arguments for the claim that many matters of global concern are indeed matters of *justice*, and must receive the kind of urgency appropriate for matters of justice. Both mitigation and adaptation (being deviations from the economic business-as-usual trajectory countries would otherwise choose) create burdens. Enlightened self-interest goes a long way towards explaining why these burdens should be shared among all human beings. After all, we are dealing with a problem with unpredictable and potentially cataclysmic effects. But why would this be a problem of distributive justice, and thus why would there be a moral obligation to *share* these burdens *fairly*? Why not say the distribution of burdens should result from rational bargaining in which every country maximizes its national interests?

There are several answers to this question. First of all, there are humanitarian duties in virtue of the moral significance of the distinctively human life. After all, climate change has the potential of threatening the living conditions of many people especially in the regions around the equator, which are already rather problem-ridden. Second, climate change is occurring as a result of human activities and in that regard differs from a disaster caused by an asteroid. Emitters are presumably responsible for the harm they inflict. A third reason appeals to the utilitarian side of moral thinking. Utilitarians seek to bring a maximal amount of well-being into the world compared to other available courses of action. Given the potentially disastrous consequences of climate change, measures to adapt to and mitigate climate change in the long run contribute much to this endeavor. Finally, the distribution of burdens from climate change is a moral problem also because humanity collectively owns the earth, which gives everybody some kind of entitlements to the atmosphere. We have already encountered that idea in Chapters 1 and 3. Let me say a bit more about it now. We will use this idea later in this chapter, and again in Chapter 6.

Collective ownership of the earth

In Europe the 17th century was a troubled period marred by religious wars. But the Old Testament provided as secure guidance as these difficult times permitted. This was also the time when European expansionism started to peak. Questions of global scope arose when the colonizers thought about the conditions under which they could occupy territories, or whether they could also occupy seaways to the exclusion of others. The idea that humanity collectively owned the earth helped with those questions. Outside of a religious context, one might think, this approach makes little sense. After all, we inhabit a planet that was already in existence for longer than four billion years when our species emerged, and the physical and biospheric conditions that enabled its ascent have resulted from a series of cataclysmic developments. Would it not be preposterous to think humans *own* this planet?

The idea that humanity owns the earth has contributed its share to the history of human chauvinism. The American poet Walt Whitman once praised animals by emphasizing that, as opposed to humans, "not one is demented with the mania of owning things" (section 32 of "Song of Myself"). But my secularized understanding of collective ownership does not presuppose the arrogance associated with a reading of the Bible that subjects the creation to the human will, an attitude that emerges, for instance, in the protestant theologian Jean Calvin's view that God took six days to create the world in order to demonstrate to human beings that everything was prepared for them. In that way my approach differs from its 17th century predecessors who advocated for collective ownership based on the Bible and who generally accepted this understanding of human superiority.

Collective ownership insists that all human beings, across generations, have the same kind of claim to the earth, and thus defines a status that human beings have *vis-à-vis each other*. Recall the three claims on which I base the view that humanity collectively owns the earth: the resources and spaces of the earth are valuable to and necessary for all human activities to unfold (the earth being humanity's natural habitat, a closed system of resources everybody needs for survival); the satisfaction of basic human needs matters morally (and, we need to add, matters more than any environmental value, such as protecting the biosphere); and that, to the extent that resources and spaces have come into existence without human interference, nobody has claims to them based on any contributions to their creation. In a nutshell, all human beings, no matter when and where they live, have some kind of claims to original resources and spaces that cannot be constrained by reference to what others have accomplished.

However, what I have said so far about collective ownership can be spelled out in different ways. One of them is an equal division: each of altogether n human beings has a claim to a $1/n$ share of original resources (Steiner 1994). Equal division gains plausibility from the idea that there is a (figurative) heap of resources to which each person has an equal claim. However, the idea of "dividing up" such a heap presupposes an ability to assign values to sets of resources to render them comparable. To that end one must find some way of assessing an *aggregated* value for the over-all heap of resources. This would be complicated because we do not merely have to assess property values of two-dimensional spaces, but instead the overall usefulness of three-dimensional regions for human purposes. But let us ignore this complexity. What is crucial is that we would need a uniquely most plausible way of assessing the value in question, one that everybody could reasonably accept. However, many materials only acquire value through activities that require social contexts. How valuable, say, oil, uranium, or silicon are depends on what people can and want to do with them. So it depends on what technology is available that requires these materials; on how people choose to integrate it into their lives; and on how property rules determine what they can do with resources and technology. These matters are not the sort of thing for which there would be a single most plausible arrangement that everybody could be expected to respect.

Instead of using an equal division approach to collective ownership, we should think of collective ownership in terms of what we may call "common ownership." Common ownership is a right to use something without a right to exclude other co-owners. This was a wide-spread form of ownership when towns collectively owned areas reserved for the feeding of animals. All citizens could take their animals there, perhaps subject to constraints designed to avoid overuse. The core idea of common ownership as a conception of humanity's collective ownership is that the distribution of the original resources and spaces of the earth among the global population is just only if everyone has the opportunity to use them to satisfy basic needs, or otherwise lives under a property arrangement that provides opportunities to satisfy basic needs. My proposal is that humanity as a whole collectively owns the earth in much the same sense in which citizens of such towns owned their town greens.

Let me address a *reductio ad absurdum* through which some seek to ridicule collective ownership. This discussion will be useful when we discuss Singer's argument below. Can anybody sensibly claim, asks right-libertarian Murray Rothbard, that a newborn Pakistani baby has claims to a plot in Iowa that Smith just transformed into a field (1996, p 35)? As soon as we consider such implications of collective ownership, says he, we realize its implausibility. Smith has claims on the strength of his efforts. The baby has none. However, collective ownership does not require that each nugget of gold found on the ocean floor be divided among all humans, or every drop of oil extracted on the Arab peninsula. That the baby has claims on a par with Smith's is consistent with Smith's not having to vacate *that* land (the baby does not have a claim to each object), and with Smith's not having to *vacate* that land (the claim may be satisfied through compensation). Any plausible understanding of collective ownership must block the inference from "humanity collectively owns the earth" to "humanity collectively owns this or that *particular part* of the earth." The common ownership interpretation meets that criterion (as does e.g. equal division). That humanity commonly owns the earth in much as the same way as in which, say, Bostonians used to own the Boston Common does not mean they have shared claims to each object that forms part of it. It just means they should have an equal opportunity to use the commonly owned resources. Once I make use of X to satisfy basic needs, it is impermissible for others to use X for their purposes.

Disappearing island nations

Chapter 1 integrated humanity's ownership of the earth into an account of human rights as membership rights in the global order. Collective ownership is one of the sources from which such rights derive. Let me briefly return to this theory of human rights to apply it to one of the most pressing problems that arise in the context of climate change: how to think about disappearing island nations such as Kiribati (Risse 2009). This gives us an illustration of how to work with the idea of collective ownership.

Straddling the equator, the nation of Kiribati consists of thirty-three coral atolls spread over 3.5 million square kilometers in the Pacific. Rising sea levels and salination caused by climate change might make the islands uninhabitable. As a consequence, Kiribati's president proposed to scatter his people of about 100,000 throughout the world. In 1990, a number of small-island and low-lying coastal countries formed the Alliance of Small Island States (AOSIS), one of whose purposes is to articulate concerns about climate change. AOSIS used to insist on the urgency of climate change *mitigation*, rather than the sort of *adaptation* advocated by Kiribati's president. However, his proposal was cautiously endorsed in the Niue Declaration on Climate Change in 2008.

That inhabitants of Kiribati ought not to be left to drown is morally over-determined. Still, it is illuminating to see precisely what reasoning bears on this matter, and how it engages my conception of human rights. As we saw in Chapter 1, states and other powerful organizations must offer guarantees to neutralize the dangers imposed on co-owners by the global order. One danger is that the existence of states limits opportunities to relocate if individuals cannot make a living where they live. If areas are lost to sea rise, there is no longer a way of respecting the troubled party's co-ownership rights by helping them make a living in their current location. The only way of respecting these rights is to permit immigration.

There is therefore a human right to relocation. It even includes a demand upon host countries to enable new immigrants to make a living. Whether my approach supports the president's wish for his people to move together we cannot know without further investigations that reveal which countries over- or underuse three-dimensional spaces (to use terms from Chapter 6). Kiribati's people have such a claim against countries that underuse resources and spaces to such an extent that they can all be admitted. Now of course we are here talking about an example where there are only 100,000 people. But this argument would also hold if there were 10 million or many more people thus affected. The same reasoning would apply, for instance, if it were decided one day that Japan high earthquake risk and exposure to tsunamis requires the evacuation of much of its population.

Collective ownership and enlightened anthropocentrism about the environment

Collective ownership is a view about the relationship among human beings that can readily integrate plausible accounts of environmental values. Needless to say, not all manners of capturing the value of nature are consistent with collective ownership. In his famous *Sand County Almanac*, the environmentalist Aldo Leopold formulated the following ethical principle: "A thing is right when it tends to preserve the integrity, stability, and beauty of the biotic community. It is wrong when it tends otherwise" (1949, p 224f). By not recognizing any kind of priority for human beings (and thus their basic needs) over other natural entities, Leopold's principle is inconsistent with any version of collective ownership.

This "land ethic" moves outside of *enlightened anthropocentrism,* the view that I think formulates a very plausible view of the value of nature. This view recognizes that, on the one hand, all values must be values to human beings and on a human scale. Enlightened anthropocentrism recognizes that answers to environmental questions "must be based on human values, in the sense of values that human beings can make part of their lives and understand themselves as pursuing and respecting," as the 20th century moral philosopher Bernard Williams put it (1995, p 234). We cannot value in any *other* way. On the other hand, enlightened anthropocentrism denies that instrumental values or values of human flourishing exhaust the range of values on a human scale. Enlightened anthropocentrism can readily acknowledge a number of appropriate attitudes towards valuing nature, for instance, that nature should be valued intrinsically, as sublime or awesome, as providing a context where human life obtains meaning, and even as sacred.

Enlightened anthropocentrism as a view about the value of nature has important implications also for the debate about *sustainability.* "The idea of sustainability is a distinctly modern notion," as the environmental philosopher Dale Jamieson explains, "closely tied to the schizophrenia of modern life that simultaneously persecutes nature while trying to protect it" (2002, p 327). A starting point for the sustainability debate is the 1987 Brundtland Report, *Our Common Future,* which stressed the urgency of fostering growth while paying attention to global equity and environmental concerns. "Sustainable development" was explained there as "development that meets the needs of the present without compromising the ability of future generations to meet their own needs."

Let us distinguish "weak" from "strong" sustainability (Neumayer 2003). *Capital* is whatever forms the capacity to provide utility; *natural capital* is the capacity of nature to provide humans with utility (those parts of nature that fail to do so being disregarded), such as resources, plants, ecosystems, or species; *man-made capital* includes infrastructure such as roads or machines, and *human capital* includes knowledge and skills. Adopting either form of sustainability means insisting that the future be integrated into decision-making. Being committed to *weak sustainability* means insisting on a non-declining stock of total capital; being committed to *strong sustainability* means insisting on a non-declining stock of (some forms of) natural capital. It is by insisting on a *non-declining* stock that we obtain a commitment to intergenerational equality as a lower boundary.

According to weak sustainability, all forms of capital are substitutable for each other and the preservation of anything in particular is not required. Future people cannot complain as long as they are no poorer in total capital. In contrast, the most common version of strong sustainability identifies some forms of natural capital as significant, or "critical" (to make clear that, say, obscure species of beetles do not deserve preservation, a point that presupposes, controversially, that we have a sufficiently good understanding of ecosystems to consider the extinction of such species "non-critical"). So even if future people are richer in terms of overall capital, they can complain if their wealth comes at the expense of such capital.

One reason for supporting strong over weak sustainability turns on the instrumental value of natural resources, insisting that weak sustainability does not optimally secure the future of humanity. What is of concern are biodiversity losses, loss of ecosystems or life-support systems such as the global climate and the ozone layer, and soil erosion. We must ask to what extent protecting these assets requires non-substitutability of natural resources, and how to assess opportunity costs from giving a special status to such resources. Neumayer (2003) insists that "the combination of the distinctive features of natural capital with risk, uncertainty and ignorance suggests the conclusion that there are good reasons for the non-substitutability of specific forms of natural capital" (p 124). These "features" are that those forms of capital (global life-support systems, biodiversity) provide for elementary life functions better than any replacements ever could; that we have no practical way of replacing them; and that it is hard to know which elements of our environment will matter. For instance, the eminent biologist E. O. Wilson refers to biodiversity as "our most valuable but least appreciated resource" (1993, p 281).

So there is a strong rationale for caution about depleting natural capital. But in addition to such instrumental arguments *enlightened anthropocentrism* too supports strong sustainability. Enlightened anthropocentrism, again, finds room for a range of attitudes towards nature, for instance, that nature should be valued intrinsically, as sublime or awesome, or as providing a context where human life obtains meaning. Those ways of valuing nature in turn support the preservation of the natural environment itself.

Singer's argument for equal entitlements to pollution

In *One World* Peter Singer (whose work we already encountered in Chapter 4) asserts that humanity collectively owns the absorptive capacity of the earth, its capacity to absorb greenhouse gases in a way that preserves basic climate conditions, which is one good provided by that part of the earth. Singer advocates a per-capita view as the principle of distribution for this good: each person may consume (or "access") the absorptive capacity to the same degree (i.e., bring about the same volume of emissions). One may implement this approach via a "cap-and-trade" system. We would choose a global limit, each country obtaining an amount of permissible emissions (its "cap") based on population size. Countries that wish to pollute more must purchase additional rights. One way of assigning caps is that each person since, say, the industrial revolution has the same entitlement. We must then determine how much pollution that involves in light of bearable greenhouse gas concentrations. Or one may think of the distribution in terms of current populations. Variations are conceivable: one could index population sizes to a year before which actors could be expected to combat pollution. Or one could index to a future year, to avoid perverse incentives for population policy or accommodate countries with young populations. But in any event, as political scientist Steve Vanderheiden states, "the atmosphere presents a rare example of a pure public good, where no one has a valid claim to larger shares of the good than anyone else" (2008, p 225).

Note some implausible implications of the equal per-capita approach. Countries would obtain allocations regardless of how this affects their economy, how they use them, what importance they have for people's lives, and whether they reduce emissions. At least some of these concerns could be resolved by clever allocation and trading mechanisms. However, there is a more fundamental worry about Singer's approach that draws on the idea of collective ownership of the earth. We can develop this objection in two steps. Note first that Singer's standpoint assumes that there is an entitlement to the atmosphere that all of humanity shares. This is plausible only if humanity owns the *earth as a whole*. After all, one would think the atmosphere (or its absorptive capacity) is collectively owned because everybody needs it for survival, and because it is nobody's accomplishment that it exists to begin with. But the domain for which these claims hold is the earth as such, not the atmosphere or the absorptive capacity in particular. The second step then is this. We noted that collective ownership *of the earth* does not imply that any particular object on or part of it must be divided up. But if not every nugget of gold found on the ocean floor must be shared out, then this inference does not hold for the absorptive capacity either. In light of the initial difficulties and of this fundamental problem I think the idea is untenable that we should think of the distribution of burdens from climate change in terms of everybody having the same right to pollute the atmosphere.

How to regulate access to the absorptive capacity?

Humanity's collective ownership of the earth does bear on the question of how to distribute the burdens from climate change. If we ask that question, among others things we are asking how to regulate access to the absorptive capacity (i.e., how much pollution is permissible). Collective ownership offers one way of explaining why we must find a fair way of distributing access to the absorptive capacity, rather than leaving this matter to self-serving bargaining. However, what collective ownership implies is not as straightforward as suggested by Singer. Instead, we must be open-minded as to what criteria best capture ideas of fairness when it comes to the regulation of access to the absorptive capacity. Generally, one addresses *fair-division problems* by exploring the strength of various initially plausible criteria and by then making a proposal that brings the criteria that pass initial scrutiny into "reflective equilibrium:" one that integrates the criteria and explains precisely how they bear on the distribution. So the process that leads to such reflective equilibrium enumerates and compares the relative strength of different criteria.

The following criteria are the initially more promising ones in this debate about how to divide up the burdens from climate change (including Singer's criterion that we already discussed):

(1) Equal entitlements to the absorptive capacity of the earth
(2) Polluters pay, including past polluters
(3) Polluters pay, but not past polluters
(4) Those pay who are willing to do so, which presumably is a reflection of how much they worry about climate change
(5) Consumers pay for emissions required to produce goods they consume
(6) We respect the status quo: countries are asked to reduce emissions by a fixed percentage of current emissions
(7) Those pay who have the ability to do so

Some criteria can be dismissed quickly. "Willingness-to-pay" (4) disregards causal involvement and capacity to deal with the problem. It should therefore enter any overall proposal at best in a very limited way. My proposal below integrates it in just such a way, in the sense that not all burdens from climate change count as burdens that should be distributed globally. The approach that takes the status quo as starting point (6) merely offers political expediency. The consumer-pays principle (5) is implausible if producers sell voluntarily. Producers control emissions, buyers do not. One might say that if buyers act voluntarily, they control emissions by creating demand. But they only do so mediated through actions of producers. Perhaps it is implausible to say about very poor countries that they "control" emissions since they often have very limited choices in what they can put on world markets. However, as long as those countries need not contribute to a solution to climate change (as they do not on my proposal below), the consumer-pays principle is unacceptable.

So we can readily reduce the longer list to a shorter one:

(2) Polluters pay, including past polluters
(3) Polluters pay, but not past polluters
(7) Those pay who have the ability to do so

These are the serious contenders. To narrow this shorter list down further, let us discuss the importance of historical emissions.

Historical emissions

To begin with, we must assess what should count as historical emissions. What is the relevant time t such that, before t, we should not blame emitters for emissions? Axel Gosseries (2004) mentions various sensible dates, among them 1896 (publication of an article by the chemist Svante Arrhenius on the greenhouse effect, "the first warning of global warming" (Neumayer 2000, p 188)); 1967 (publication of first serious modeling exercise on climate change); 1990, and 1995 (publication of first two IPCC reports). An advocate of historical accountability, Neumayer (2000) thinks it was not before the mid-1980s that the public and decision makers became aware of the greenhouse effect. The 1992 UN Framework Convention on Climate Change too sets a plausible date. The years of the publication of the third and fourth IPCC reports, 2001 and 2007, are also possible since both added much clarity on climate change.

The crucial question is at what time decision makers could be expected to know, specifically, the *dangers* of climate change. By this standard, 1990 is the latest sensible date: the 1990 IPCC report already absorbed a body of insights gathered over years. Any choice of date will trigger the objection that if countries cannot be blamed for emissions prior to Year X, they cannot be blamed for having committed themselves, over generations, to lifestyles that essentially involve massive emissions. Come Year X, they were locked into certain patterns. However, if Year X is fixed as the latest possible year this objection loses its force.

In light of the relevance and visibility of the 1990 IPCC report, and of persistent doubts a choice of date other than the latest sensible one would inevitably create about what decision makers may have been expected to consider, 1990 is also a sensible choice, *provided* the proposal for the distribution of burdens acknowledges reasons other than rectification of wrongful past emissions as reasons for which disadvantaged countries can demand aid. The importance of 1990 can then make us neglect the fact that it is the *latest* sensible date. Put differently: if the only aid available to poor countries on the correct proposal depended on the amount of blameworthy past emissions, then the later we move the date, the less aid poor countries will get. We will then have to worry about choosing the latest sensible date, rather than, say, the earliest. However, we saw in Chapter 1 that there is a duty to help states realize human rights, and thus help them create the *conditions* under which the realization of these rights is possible. (There is in fact a duty of assistance *in building institutions*, a topic we discuss in Chapter 7.) One sensible way of making good on these duties is the sharing of technology and other support to mitigate or adjust to climate change. It is because of these independently existing duties that also affect the distribution of burdens from climate change that the choice of the latest sensible date before which emissions are not blameworthy is not too worrisome.

Let me discuss five problems about holding countries accountable for historical emissions and thus about imposing higher burdens because countries have emitted in the past. Let me begin with three minor problems. First of all, delineating and ascribing damage might be problematic. For instance, soil erosion might have done damage to shorelines if rising sea levels due to climate change had not done so. Second, it is unclear what the unit of analysis should be: should it just be individuals, or also corporations and states? If it should be states, then what about new states (such as those that emerged from the breakup of the Soviet Union and Yugoslavia)? And who should be accountable for damage done by agents who are no longer alive? A third issue is that if we count past polluters they would be counted disproportionately. After all, contemporary industrializers have better technology that draws on past experience.

These problems could probably be solved somehow. But in addition there are also two bigger ones. To begin with, just about everybody has benefitted from the spread of early industrialization. Countries other than those where most emissions occurred have benefited from those emissions via trade, as well as via the spread of technology and scientific understanding. Developing countries now benefit from inventions during earlier industrializations that used inferior technology. Henry Shue (1999) responds to this point that developing countries have paid for the benefits they have received. Singer (2002) insists that in the US most goods and services are for domestic consumption (and thus do not benefit anybody else). However, quality of life has improved everywhere since the industrial revolution, in terms of longevity, child mortality, or literacy. These benefits cannot be detached from industrialization and have been of global reach despite their differential effects.

Most importantly, past emitters, at least in earlier stages of industrialization, did not and (in any relevant sense) *could* not know that greenhouse gases might have catastrophic effects. Nor could they know that fossil fuels would long remain essential: their emissions became problematic only because economies continued to depend on such fuels. Objectively speaking, past emissions may have been wrong. Nonetheless, a set of conditions of *maximally excusatory force* applies to early emitters. The standpoint from which we can say earlier decision makers violated obligations of justice sets aside their scientific limitations. We cannot blame people for failing to regulate access to the absorptive capacity. "[A]ttempts to apply fault-based standards are virtually guaranteed to become embroiled in more or less irresolvable controversy about historical explanations," says Shue, who is one the pioneers of philosophical reflection on environmental issues (1996, p 16). "Yet never to attempt to assess fault is to act as if the world began yesterday." We can indeed assess fault, but although there was wrong-doing in the past, there was no blameworthy fault.

One might say that the tort law sometimes endorses *strict liability*, accountability without fault. One would then be liable to pay for damages one has caused even if one cannot be blamed. Could this notion not allow us to hold people accountable for past emissions although nobody was at fault then? But such strict liability must overcome a strong presumption of unfairness. Minimally, it should not apply without the agents being *aware* of it. Only then can they choose whether to participate in the relevant activities. So strict liability should not apply if people lack the background understanding to act in certain ways. In a nutshell: if we wish to integrate past emissions into an overall proposal for distributing burdens from climate change, we must do so in a way that respects that early emitters cannot be blamed.

Polluter pays, ability to pay, and a proposal

The proposal I am about to make distinguishes between burdens from adaptation and burdens from mitigation. The proposal integrates ideas about who is able to pay ("ability to pay" principle) and ideas in term of current per-capita emissions ("polluter pays" principle). The focus on "polluter pays" and "ability to pay" principles is sensible partly because of the weaknesses of other approaches that we have now explored. But this focus is sensible also because these principles are plausible by themselves. As far as the "polluter pays" principle is concerned: climate change occurs because there are emissions, and they do the damage. The polluters cause the problem and thus should assume responsibility. Who produces them must matter *somehow* to the distribution of burdens (albeit in a way that takes into account whether the polluters were blameworthy). Past polluters have excuses for their actions, polluters after 1990 do not.

One may wonder, however, why the ability to pay bears on the problem at hand. As a matter of justice, collective ownership requires that access to the absorptive capacity be regulated. Collective ownership makes maintaining an atmosphere that sustains human life a globally shared responsibility. Each generation is the keeper of the earth for subsequent generations. For any shared responsibility those who genuinely can contribute more should do so. The plausibility of the "ability to pay" principle is reflected, for instance, in Henry Shue's (1999) point that

> [w]hen some people have less than enough for a decent life, other people have far more than enough, and the total resources available are so great that everyone could have at least enough without preventing some people from still retaining considerably more than others have, it is unfair not to guarantee everyone at least an adequate minimum. (p 541)

Let me consider burdens from adaptation and mitigation separately. Suppose advice is needed concerning a global treaty that distributes burdens from climate change from now on, for an independently fixed overall level of acceptable future emissions (to keep average temperature increases to a bearable minimum). Mitigation concerns future emissions only, and so (I contend) past emissions are (largely) irrelevant to the problem of how to distribute the resulting burdens. Adaptation, however, is (necessarily) adaptation to results of past emissions. So past emissions and associated questions about culpability and wrong-doing become relevant to the question of distributing burdens.

Among burdens from adaptation we can distinguish burdens arising because of emissions that occurred after people became blameworthy (1990), and those from emissions that occurred before. Obviously we can separate these emissions merely for the sake of analysis. Yet we seek principles that guide treaties regulating emissions and possibly also transfers, by offering an idea of what it means to treat people as equals from the standpoint of collective ownership. The path from there to allocations or penalties is thorny, and involves political and economic considerations beyond the scope of our inquiry.

As far as burdens from adaptation are concerned, countries that did not take considerable measures to reduce emissions *after* 1990, the wealthy ones anyway, have a duty to compensate those that have been harmed because of this, with a priority on the poorer ones. Compensation could include financial or technological aid. To the extent that adaptation becomes necessary because of emissions before 1990, no such duty applies. The fact that past polluters did commit a *wrong* enters this proposal (see below, when I discuss mitigation), albeit with less effect than if they owed compensation. Costs of adaptation that arise because of emissions after an agreement has been concluded do not enter my proposal. There are no international duties *merely* because some countries are in less temperate zones, beyond a general duty of aid (or other humanitarian duties) and specific obligations that arise, say, because of trading. Similarly, not all costs of climate change should trigger redistribution. At the same time, the overall level of acceptable future emissions could be fixed in a way that considers the resulting costs of adaptation.

Consider next burdens from mitigation. The goal is to assess which countries need to make how much of a sacrifice, compared to business-as-usual trajectories. This is where the "polluter pays" and "ability to pay" principles enter. Countries that should modify their production are those that, in terms of per-capita wealth, can best afford changes ("ability to pay"), and those that on a per-capita basis emit most ("polluter pays"). These principles must be combined. Axel Michaelowa (2007) plausibly groups countries into categories depending on a combined index, weighing both criteria equally. The amount of reduction for which a country is responsible, by reducing its emissions or by paying *others* to do so, is a function of this index. A country would be the higher on this ranking the higher its per-capita income, and the higher its per-capita emissions. Many countries would incur no obligations because they rank too low.

We should supplement Michaelowa's proposal in such a way that for roughly equal index levels, countries ought to make more sacrifices if they benefit from past (pre-1990) emissions. No blame would be assigned for these emissions. Still, benefitting from them amounts to free-riding on *ill-gotten* gains, and their presence should make a difference somewhere. This is the only way in which emissions from before 1990 appear in my proposal. Historical accountability indeed enters only in a highly qualified way. But this also means the remaining criteria (2), (3) and (7) above all enter my proposal in some way.

We can sum up this proposal as follows:

> Suppose there is a fixed overall level of acceptable future emissions that keeps climate change to a bearable level
>
> *Burdens from adaptation*:
>
> *Adaptation that becomes necessary because of emissions after 1990 but prior to conclusion of major climate treaty:* Countries that did not take considerable measures to reduce emissions after 1990, the wealthy ones anyway, have a duty to compensate those that have been harmed because of this, with a priority on the poorer ones. Since it will be impossible to assess specifically which kinds of adaptation become necessary because of these emissions, at the practical level this duty will generate an obligation to transfer money and technological aid to countries that need to adapt.
>
> *Adaptation that becomes necessary because of emissions that occurred before 1990 or after the conclusion of a climate treaty*: no action required
>
> *Burdens from mitigation*
>
> Must assess which countries need to make how much of a sacrifice, compared to their business-as-usual trajectories so that emissions stay below the overall acceptable level
>
> States that should modify their production are those that, in terms of per-capita wealth, can best afford changes ("ability to pay"), and those that on a per-capita basis emit most ("polluter pays"). The amount of reduction for which a country is responsible, by

reducing its emissions or by paying others to do so, is a function of a ranking of countries in terms of a combined index of these criteria (both being weighted equally). A country would be the higher on this ranking the higher its per-capita income, and the higher its per-capita emissions.

For roughly equal index levels on this list, countries ought to make more sacrifices if they benefit from past emissions.

This proposal brings into reflective equilibrium the morally relevant considerations for regulating access to the absorptive capacity of the atmosphere.

Further reading

Singer (2002) is a wide-ranging philosophical discussion of major issues in world politics. Good discussions of philosophical issues about climate change appear in Gardiner (2011), Vanderheiden (2008) and Page (2006). Attfield (2003) and Rolston (1988) are excellent introductions to environmental ethics. Attfield's chapter 5 is an introduction to the sustainability debate. Callicott (1989) further develops Leopold's "land ethic." Established in 1988, the Intergovernmental Panel on Climate Change (IPCC) is charged with assessing the risks of climate change. The various IPCC reports that have appeared since 1990 are the canonical source for the state of climate science. Aldy and Stavins (2007) contains several proposals for policy responses to climate change. Posner and Weisbach (2010) argue that one should not complicate the debate about appropriate responses to climate change by bringing up considerations of justice. Like this chapter, Caney (2010) makes a hybrid proposal for the distribution of burdens from climate change that integrates a "polluter pays" and an "ability to pay" principle.

6 Immigration

Social-scientific and moral questions about immigration

More often than not, debates about immigration concern disagreement about "what is best for us." The presumption is that immigration policies must be justifiable only to those who already live in a country. "Modern states," writes political theorist Chandran Kukathas, "are like clubs that are reluctant to accept new members unless they can be assured that they have more to gain by admitting people than they have by keeping them out" (2005, pp 209f). What is "best" for a country (its "gain") might be controversial, and turn on conflicting cultural or political considerations. What is beneficial for one segment of the population may not be for others. Yet this standpoint tends to view immigration as a privilege and neglects to ask about possible duties to would-be immigrants. Notice for instance how the economist George Borjas discusses immigration to the US:

> Current immigration policy benefits some Americans (the newly arrived immigrants as well as those who employ and use the services the immigrants provide) at the expense of others (those Americans who happen to have skills that compete directly with those of immigrants). Before deciding how many and which immigrants to admit, the country must determine which groups of Americans should be the winners and which should be the losers. (2001, p xiv)

Borjas counts immigrants among the beneficiaries, but fails to count rejected would-be immigrants among the losers. The laws regulating immigration to the US emphasize family connections, whereas Canada for example formulates a fine-grained view on what kinds of immigrants are needed. The Canadian point system counts educational achievements, prefers younger to older immigrants, weighs occupational background in terms of the current needs of the labor market, and gives weight to years of work experience, as well as to fluency in English and French and to the presence of relatives in the country.

A host of social science questions arises about immigration. We can ask who wants to immigrate to begin with, how immigration affects labor markets, tax revenues and the welfare system, but also how it bears on crime. We can explore how immigrants do or do not assimilate, how their presence bears on demographic change, and what impact the remittances they send home have in their countries of origin. But there are also moral questions. As the French 18th century philosopher Jean-Jacques Rousseau famously remarks in Part II of his *Second Discourse on Inequality*, "The first person who, having fenced off a lot of ground, took it into his head to say *this is mine* and found people simple enough to believe him, was the true founder of civil society." At a larger scale, a similar comment may apply to states. Is it only because of such simplicity (or similarly morally unappealing reasons) that it would be acceptable at all, to those thus excluded, that we draw an imaginary line in the dust and think of it *as a border*?

There are several reasons why immigration constraints require moral scrutiny. First of all, immigration policies limit human freedom. Note for instance that since the late 1970s, Amartya Sen has argued that the appropriate reference space for many evaluative purposes is that of substantive freedoms, or *capabilities*, to choose a life one has reason to value (rather than, say, that of utilities, resources, or other goods capturing achievements within social arrangements). We have encountered this approach briefly in Chapter 1. Martha Nussbaum has offered a list of capabilities she considers central to a life with dignity. "Bodily integrity" appears on her list, and "being able to move freely from place to place" is one instantiation of bodily integrity (2006, p 76). At the same time, immigration policies create "winners" and "losers" in the country of destination, especially on labor markets. If, say, an influx of immigrants makes wages for low-skilled workers decline (as, e.g., Borjas argues for the US), those workers' capabilities presumably decline. Second, in an economically interconnected world where goods and services often move freely, constraints on the movement of people seem like anomalies. Frontiers make sure that goods traded on the world market are produced on labor markets that create considerably better working conditions for some than for others. Third, collective ownership of the earth also creates a need for justification of immigration constraints. Immigration barriers indicate that people can constrain others in the exercise of their ownership rights. And fourth, immigration policies may contribute to our duties toward the global poor, duties many political leaders and citizens, as well as most contemporary philosophers, acknowledge in some form. Immigration, permanent or temporary, serves this function partly because it allows some people access to greener pastures, and partly because of remittances. Wage gaps caused by barriers to movement across borders are large forms of wage differentiation, which means labor mobility can substantially contribute to poverty reduction.

In light of these points we must inquire whether immigration constraints would be acceptable at all. But there are some additional moral questions about immigration. To begin with, there are questions about discretionary immigration. To the extent that a state allows immigration, may it take a stance on "what kind of people" should enter? This is an awkward question especially for liberal states. If such states answer negatively, they will end up with immigrants for whose presence there might be no particular rationale. But otherwise, by giving signals as to what kind of people should enter, liberal states violate the demand for neutrality on such matters. Questions about discretionary immigration may include whether it is permitted to exclude people with AIDS, or whether countries with declining populations may exclude gay immigrants. Moreover, once there are illegal immigrants, we must wonder what to do about them. They may become fully integrated into the economy over the years without adjustments to their legal status. What to do about them is a question of special relevance to the US with its many millions of illegal immigrants.

Immigration: ideal vs. non-ideal theory

One reason why reflection on immigration generates considerable challenges is that proposed changes are often plausible only if other policies also change. For instance, one might argue the wealthier countries had better not admit more immigrants because their inhabitants contribute considerably to climate change. ("The last thing the world needs is more Americans," one may say.) But that argument takes environmentally unfriendly behavior as a given instead of insisting that Americans must pay more heed to the environment anyway. Or suppose somebody advises against more immigration solely because the kind of immigration a country could expect would decrease wages of low-income workers. This argument takes for granted that no additional social policy measures are available to raise wages for these workers (or improve their status otherwise).

We are thinking about immigration under conditions of ideal theory if we can assume that in all other regards the world is as it should be as far as justice is concerned. We would be thinking about immigration under conditions of non-ideal theory if we assume that in some other regards too the world is not as it should be (as far as justice is concerned). For the sake of discussion I assume that, in ideal theory, the world consists of a multitude of states in which everybody has a minimum of provisions to live a decent life (without worrying now what precisely that would mean). In the sections below that are concerned with arguments for closed or open borders we ask what constraints on immigration policy would be acceptable or required *under such conditions*. For proposed measures we must also ask what additional changes (e.g., in social or environmental policies) are needed if such policies were to be implemented (or whether additional measures are required independently). For the non-ideal conditions under which we live such discussions offer only limited guidance. After all, we must assess in relevant situations which other measures that *ideally* should be taken can *in fact* be taken. But that is how it is when we apply philosophical theories to practical politics.

I also assume there is a collective responsibility at the level of the global order to make sure all people can meet basic needs.

There is a duty to make sure people can do so where they live. All countries ought to accept refugees temporarily. Whether in addition immigration policy is a useful device to improve the plight of the poor (and thus a useful device to satisfy human-rights related obligations) is to a large extent a social-science question. Every year remittances are estimated to generate many hundreds of billion of dollars for poor countries. Work permit (guest worker) programs in rich countries could generate much more. However, immigration might also cause brain-drain and thereby increase the need to provide aid to regions thus deprived of precisely those people who would otherwise actively contribute to development. But brain-drain can also trigger positive developments in the country of origin (people might feel motivated to acquire skills for jobs or studies abroad, but only relatively few might be chosen for such careers), or a substantial part of those who leave return eventually or otherwise benefit the country on balance even though they have left. And it is possible that other measures will help the poor better than immigration-related measures (e.g., trade-related policies), or that a combination of various measures does. Again, these are empirical questions whose answer may be highly context-dependent (see Brock 2009 for a discussion of immigration focused on these matters).

The case for closed borders

Let us explore what arguments are available for closed borders, or in any event for the position that states ought to be allowed to regulate access as they please. Again, we are asking this question assuming that we live in a world where everybody has a minimum of provisions to live a decent life, and that immigration measures may be appropriate to create such a world.

One prominent stance on immigration is taken by political theorist Michael Walzer. Walzer's *Spheres of Justice* takes a communitarian stance on immigration. "Communitarians" emphasize the significance of the political and cultural community. For instance, what justice requires depends on the characteristics of the community in question. Walzer believes communities have claims to territory to develop their character. He concedes that not just any number of people can occupy any amount of space, a consideration we reencounter below. For instance, he famously insists that "White Australia could survive only as Little Australia" (1983, p 47), meaning the Australian immigration policy that throughout much of the 20th century kept out no-whites (whatever else might have been wrong with it) could not be legitimately maintained unless Australia relinquished parts of its territory.

But Walzer does not press the implied idea of proportionate use of territory far (contrary to what we do below). He recognizes moral constraints on a community's right to regulate immigration only to the extent that such constraints derive from obligations to mutual aid (mostly directed at refugees) and from what he calls the "meaning of membership" in the respective community. For instance, one might argue a community that derives its identity from being an immigrant nation eager to attract talented immigrants must also bear the "costs" of such policies and admit the immigrants' kin. Similarly, a country that defines its identity in terms of ethnicity should permit immigration by those who share their ethnicity, especially if they are in dire straits where they currently live.

Philosopher David Miller (2005) offers a useful systematic discussion of immigration constraints. First of all, he rejects three common reasons for open borders. The first is an appeal to a plain right to free movement. The second is the claim that a presumed right to exit requires a right to enter other countries. The third is that considerations of international distributive justice require open borders even in a world of multiple states where everybody's basic needs are satisfied. As far as the first is concerned, Miller grants that there is a remedial right to move somewhere else temporarily to avoid persecution or starvation. Short of that, however, freedom of movement *within countries* suffices to meet the basic interest behind freedom of movement. A demand beyond free movement within countries does not reflect a sufficiently basic interest to create a basis for a right.

Second, Miller denies that having a right to exit means there must be an unlimited right to enter anywhere else. For one thing, a right to exit only requires having one other country willing to allow entry. What is more, there are many rights that require that one finds a willing partner for their exercise. This is true of the right to marriage, and as Miller sees it, for the right to immigrate. Miller's position is actually reflected in the UDHR. Article 13 grants the right to leave a country, but not the right to enter a particular country, or even the right to enter *somewhere*. Article 14 merely grants a right to seek and enjoy asylum. Finally, to the extent that a concern about international distributive justice is about equality of opportunity, Miller denies that there is a shared context of valuing goods at the global level to render talk about equality of opportunity applicable. But granting a basic minimum standard, Miller thinks the preferred solution is to help improve conditions where people already live.

Miller also presents two positive reasons for limiting immigration. First, like Walzer, he insists on the importance of a shared public culture that in part constitutes the political identity of people in a given society, something that people have an interest in controlling even as it changes. Moreover, Miller thinks the population in a given country is rightly concerned with its size because both worries about the quality of life and about the preservation of the natural environment relate to population density.

American philosopher Christopher Wellman (2008) argues in support of a state's right to restrict immigration specifically in terms of freedom of association, to such an extent that even refugees can be rejected on this basis. Wellman offers three arguments in support of this position. First of all, a right to self-determination entitles countries to associate (or not) with others as they see fit. If one denies that legitimate states have such a right, one could not explain why they should not be forced into mergers. For instance, it would be unacceptable to force Canada to join the US. Presumably this would be so because Canadians have the right of freedom of association. But then they should also be allowed to regulate immigration as they see fit. The second argument turns on the significance of freedom of association to people's lives. People care deeply about their country. Therefore they also care about policies that shape how their countries will evolve. Wellman considers freedom of association an integral part of self-determination of peoples. As an individual's freedom of association entitles one to remain single, a state's freedom of association entitles it to exclude foreigners. The third argument turns on the weight of responsibility entailed by shared membership in a state. After all, there are special responsibilities of distributive justice to fellow citizens. That generates a good reason to limit the number of people with whom one would share such a relationship.

According to Wellman, the removal of inequalities in life prospects across countries is not important enough to trump freedom of association and self-determination. Wealthier countries need not open their borders to remove such inequalities, let alone at a stage where everybody has a minimum of provisions for a decent life. Wellman acknowledges the arbitrariness of one's place of birth, but denies that this point leads to duties of justice that outweigh concerns of self-determination. Even help for asylum seekers can take the form either of sheltering them, or else of intervening abroad to create a safe place where they came from.

Proportionate use: collective ownership of the earth and immigration

An assessment of the significance of freedom of association is a good way of introducing the standpoint of collective ownership of the earth into the debate about immigration (Risse 2012). As of 2011, the population of the US is at about 313 million. Suppose a mysterious disease first reduces the number of Americans to 3.13 million, then to 313,000, and finally to three. Suppose this disease does not affect people elsewhere. Could these three appeal to freedom of association to keep immigrants out? Most people presumably would answer negatively. The best explanation for this negative answer draws on collective ownership of the earth.

If humanity's collective ownership is plausible at all, we must think of immigration in terms of a fair, proportionate way of sharing the earth. For instance, one should not analyze immigration by way of a parallel to marriage. Marriage is exclusively concerned with two people agreeing to a union. Immigration turns on use of (collectively owned) territory. Freedom of association is not a useful idea to make central to reflection on immigration since it entirely ignores considerations of how much space is occupied. Collective ownership of the earth, to be sure, does not require open borders. A case for that proposal would have to be made independently, and we turn to this below. The goal for now is to develop the ownership approach and to make clear how the case for unilateral border-control must be qualified in light of this approach – again, under conditions where everybody has enough provisions for a decent life.

How should we make sense of the idea that co-owners are *overusing* resources (and so need not admit more people to be able to expect compliance with their immigration policies) or are *underusing* them (so have to)? One might think of developing this idea in terms of population density. However, areas with the same population density differ dramatically: one may consist of arable land with an evenly spread population, another mostly of desert with a population crowded in small fertile areas; one may harbor lots of minerals, another be depleted of them; one may be adjacent to the sea, another landlocked. An approach in terms of population density is not suitable for our purposes. We need a measure that evaluates a region's overall usefulness for human activities. For any state S the desired measure would deliver a measure V_S of the value of the collectively owned resources on S's territory, including the biophysical conditions determining the usefulness of this region for human purposes (such as climate, location on the globe, vegetation, topography, etc).

To assess the extent to which S's territory is used one would divide V_S by the number of people P_S in S. V_S/P_S is *the per-capita use rate* of commonly owned resources on S's territory. Let us think of P_S only in terms of counting people. It would be possible to extend this assessment to certain forms of animal life if one has independent reasons for being inclusive in this way. V_S/P_S includes non-circulating resources (which are not literally used), such as unmined minerals and unextracted oil (suitably discounted). The point is to have a measure of what is at a society's disposal, broadly speaking, actually and potentially, a measure of a stock that takes into account how readily that stock could be transformed into a flow of resources, rather than a measure only of the current flow.

The territory of S is *relatively underused* (or, simply, underused) if V_S/P_S is bigger than the average of these values across states (so the average person uses a resource bundle of higher value than the average person in the average country). It is *relatively overused* (or, simply, overused) if this value is under average. If V_S/P_S is above average, co-owners elsewhere have a pro tanto claim to immigration, in the sense that underusing countries cannot reasonably expect others to comply with immigration policies until such claims are satisfied. It is then a demand of reasonable conduct that the state permit immigration. (I discuss the "pro tanto" character of this claim below.) If a country is not underusing, others can be reasonably expected to accept its immigration policies (if nothing is independently problematic about them). Immigration will be permissible until the values of V_S/P_S are rather close to each other across all states. Individuals would then populate the earth in proportion to the overall usefulness of its regions for human purposes. The intuitive fairness of this way of sharing the collectively owned resources and spaces provides the basic argument in support of this way of approaching immigration.

Global coordination is required for sensible implementation, and sustainability constraints as explored in Chapter 5 will then also have to be integrated. Underusers can relinquish territory, allowing for the founding of other political entities, or admit more people. The world's population may agree that underusers pay others off. However, underusers could not reasonably do so if those others – who after all are co-owners of original resources and spaces – *prefer* immigration.

Since we want to say that one region is taken up to a larger or smaller extent than others, all-things-considered comparability is essential, which is most straightforwardly accomplished by a one-dimensional measure, something like aggregated world market price. We are looking for the value of original resources and spaces in a country, not that of its artifacts. Specifically world-market prices would reflect the usefulness of entities for human purposes in light of limitations on availability. Such prices also reflect technological constraints. Suppose we discover minerals far underground, but lack extractive technology. Such resources would enter in a discounted way. Resources that happen not to be in flow but are part of the stock to which a country controls access should not create *much* pressure regarding immigration. But they should create *some.*

Objectors might argue that little of the world's resources is nationalized, that securitization of resources is increasing, and that barriers to direct foreign investment and ownership of these securities are decreasing. In what sense, then, can the population be said to be underutilizing the three-dimensional space a country occupies, given that many entities within this space trade on the global market and might be controlled by anybody in the world? This problem is structurally parallel to the problem of resources that are difficult to access. Difficulties of access come in degrees, which is why their value must be discounted in an assessment of the value for human purposes of the three-dimensional space in question. The extent to which control from the outside keeps the population of a country from using resources and spaces varies similarly. So discounting again is the correct response.

Some of the required pricing will be novel: biophysical factors shaping the usefulness of locations for human purposes are not normally priced. Humanity has had no trouble attaching price tags to ever more entities. However, reflections on prospects to broaden the US National Income and Product Accounts (measuring activities in the US economy) to include activities and assets not tied to market transactions and thus not captured in those accounts, have revealed difficulties in doing so. Importantly, *no such measure is in use.* We can turn neither to economists for well-established methods of extending pricing in this way, nor to biophysical scientists for strong candidates for such a measure. However, this point by itself does not undermine the normative importance of collective ownership of the earth for immigration. Sometimes the task of philosophy is to argue for the importance of a kind of work whose completion would involve the empirical sciences.

Can we measure proportionate use?

One might question the possibility of measuring over- or underuse meaningfully. Resources and spaces that came into being without human help often are subsequently altered by human activity. The Netherlands became prime land through the polder-dikes. Previously, the area was a wasteland by any indicator assessing the value of original resources. Similarly, eradicating diseases such as malaria changes the value for human purposes of whole regions. The problem is widespread: most farmland, for example, has been improved in some way, even if merely by removing rocks or trees.

How should we think about what to include and exclude in calculating underuse/overuse? The case of the Netherlands also shows that one cannot dismiss the relevance of this question by arguing that only in regions that have a high usefulness for human purposes prior to any human additions can ingenuity increase that usefulness in a way that makes a difference to questions of immigration. The Netherlands, with its high population density, would presumably emerge as a highly overused area relative to the value of resources with human inventiveness factored out, a task we must leave to the biophysical sciences and the ingenuity of econometricians. Can a case be made that, perhaps in time, the value of products of human ingenuity should be included when we measure underuse and overuse?

Suppose a generation has passed: the added value is there but the current generation did nothing to create it. Is it reasonable for this generation to continue to block immigration even if they are enjoying a higher total value of (the now enriched) original resources per capita than everyone else (and thus are underusing)? For this new generation the added value is like the unimproved value in that they were lucky enough to be born into the enjoyment of it. The Dutch could admonish outsiders to add value to other resources. However, those outsiders could respond that such a demand would be unfair because the contemporary Dutch did not have to do so. The Dutch could reply in turn that it is still reasonable for them to block immigration: although they did not create the added value, their predecessors could make their contributions only given their cultural background. What made polder-dikes possible was national unity and stability within which the required skills could flourish. It is because of social, legal, or political conditions that people can improve common resources, or invent things for which resources are necessary *enablers*.

So the reason why the legacy of their predecessors should belong to the current generation of Dutch is the following two-stage argument: First, if commonly owned resources could be improved and other entities invented only because of the culture in which their predecessors participated, *others* have acquired no claim to the value thereby added to the common stock. They have not been relevantly connected to this process. Second, contemporary Dutchmen are relevantly tied to that process. They are the contemporary participants in a culture that made earlier achievements possible and maintains them. Moreover, their predecessors presumably wanted *them* to benefit from these achievements. It is thus up to the current generation of Dutchmen to regulate this legacy, and others have no claim to immigration based on it.

But we can easily create doubts about the strongest version of the view I ascribe to the Dutch: that contemporary Dutchmen have claims to *all* the value their predecessors added and that it is reasonable for this new generation to continue to block immigration even if they are enjoying a higher value of original resources per capita than everyone else. One source of doubt is that this argument makes it appear as if the Dutch had made their accomplishments in isolation although those were made in interaction with others. To the extent that such interaction was voluntary (and thus presumably rewarded appropriately), it does not generate claims by others. To the extent that it was not, it might generate claims to compensation, which, however, is orthogonal to my concerns.

A second source of doubt is more relevant. Regardless of how deserving of the added value the Dutch predecessors were, their acts cannot generate claims that resonate through the ages to the exclusive benefit of relatively few. That the outsiders (had they been allowed in) *could*, and in due course *would*, have added the increased value might not undermine claims of those who did so. But it does weaken the claims of their *offspring*. The point is similar to the objection to first-occupancy theories of acquisition: first-comers can legitimately claim land. Their accomplishments prevent others from doing the same, but that does not undermine desert-based claims they have because of their accomplishments. But such occupation cannot entitle their offspring to exclude others. Like the original value improvers, their heirs bar others from making those same accomplishments. Unlike them, these heirs are tied to the accomplishments only by being offspring of those who made them.

This argument casts doubt on the view that the relevance of national culture for the predecessors' ability to add value to commonly owned resources creates special entitlements for that culture's current participants. But it is a big step from there to the conclusion that with time this added value becomes sufficiently like external resources for all of humanity to have an equal claim to it. So neither would the Dutch have a claim that the features of their culture necessary for the value added by their predecessors to commonly owned resources entitle them to all that value; nor is it plausible that all such value turns into common property because others would have provided it too. We are pointed to some intermediate view on whose details it is hard to be clear. We confront a bewildering array of counterfactuals whose truth and relevance is difficult to assess. Let me only briefly state what seems like an intuitively plausible, if incomplete, view.

Common resources improved by technology or by other means should be counted as common when that technology or those other means *have become readily available*. Polder-dikes should be so counted. The value of common resources should be measured in a manner that incorporates the impact of commonly available technology and other human factors that others could (and in due course would) have provided. But artifacts, ideas, practices and other things for which external resources have been mere enablers should not be counted as common. The value of the Dutch economy beyond the value of improved common resources should not be so counted. Some arbitrariness in drawing the line is inevitable. Drawing a distinction, say, between choice and circumstance (a distinction central to much recent discussion about domestic justice) too encounters this problem. In any event, implementing my proposal requires global coordination. Precisely what counts as common may have to be left to a political process.

Proportionate use: some additional elaboration

The earth must be shared among all human beings. Groups claiming more resources and spaces for their culture than they should reasonably occupy infringe upon others illegitimately. Of course, at this stage in history would-be immigrants do not normally wish to enter countries because those countries leave resources and spaces underused. They wish to enter because of economic opportunities. So my approach does not track the preferences of would-be immigrants. But recall that I have assumed that immigration measures might be among the measures we are required to take to build a world in which everybody has enough resources to lead a decent life, and that there is a collective responsibility to make sure such a world is created. Collective ownership of the earth makes clear that countries do not have unrestricted control over their immigration policies once such a world has been created. Again, the earth must be shared among all human beings, and it must be shared fairly. At the same time, this approach does not acknowledge claims to immigration merely because certain countries are wealthy. Once basic needs are taken care of and people are distributed proportionately across the collectively owned spaces and resources of the earth, valid claims to immigration no longer arise.

Countries have some discretion to choose applicants. (I can now spell out the earlier point that outsiders have a pro-tanto claim to immigration on underusers.) Countries with strong social systems may select immigrants with professional credentials; countries with demographic problems may choose young people; and culturally homogenous countries may prefer applicants who share much of its culture. Countries also have some discretion to channel immigrants to particular regions – to less-populated areas, say. Canada, for instance, seeks to place immigrants in rural areas. It is acceptable to make admission conditional on a prior declaration by would-be immigrants to settle in certain regions. One would have to think carefully about what sanctions could be imposed were immigrants to renege on their commitments, but tax penalties would certainly be acceptable. However, discretion in choosing immigrants is limited. Other things being equal, since the guiding idea of my proposal is proportionate use, applicants from overusing countries have priority.

One might worry that my proposal sets perverse incentives. One way of not underusing resources is to increase one's population. From a global standpoint, a sustainable population size is needed, which is inconsistent with unconstrained population growth. Such growth, however, seems to be in a country's interest if it wants to stop immigration (or bar reasonable demands to permit immigration). However, it seems that the impact of perverse incentives will be minimal. Recall for instance the population decrease facing Germany, Italy or Japan. These countries have trouble adopting policies to increase their population although this is in the current generation's best interest. It is hard to imagine that liberal democracies, at least, could adopt policies that motivate couples to have children as a means of preventing immigration. Individuals would perceive future immigration as a less immediate threat than a decrease in old-age benefits; so if the threat of the latter is not enough to motivate them to procreate, worries about immigration are unlikely to do so.

A related worry is that immigration into rich countries exacerbates environmental burdens. Rich countries should not increase the number of those partaking of unsustainable consumption and production patterns. Yet the transformation of economies into more sustainable operations must occur alongside suitable immigration reforms. Just as states could not reject demands to immigration based on the fact that more immigration requires changes in social policy, environmental duties do not provide states with a legitimate reason to neglect its duties vis-à-vis immigration.

The case for open borders

Countries do have the right to control immigration, but only within the limits set by collective ownership. What seems promising as an account of immigration is the kind of case for limiting immigration made by David Miller above, supplemented with the considerations drawing on collective ownership that we have discussed in between. But let us now discuss some authors who have made further-reaching arguments for open borders.

Political theorist Joseph Carens has presented a challenge to any kind of immigration restriction from the standpoint of liberal justice. Liberalism, Carens notes, condemns the use of morally arbitrary facts about persons to justify inequalities. Examples are race, sex and ethnicity. A community that treated people differently on the basis of such features would be illiberal and unjust. Yet citizenship seems as arbitrary as any of those. None of us chose our place of birth, and we deserve neither advantages nor disadvantages for it. Carens (1987) compares the existence of states to medieval feudalism. Restricting immigration, on this view, is as offensive as other, perhaps more obvious cases of injustice because it differentiates rights based upon one's origins. However, in response to Carens, philosopher Michael Blake (2001a and 2001b) invokes distinction between moral arbitrariness and moral irrelevance. Membership in a state (if one is born into it) is as morally arbitrary as race, sex or ethnicity: nobody has done anything to deserve these features. But whatever might be true of race, sex or ethnicity, membership in a state is not therefore morally irrelevant, any more than family membership is morally irrelevant although it is arbitrary. The moral relevance of shared membership in a state has been discussed in Chapter 3. It is because such shared membership is morally relevant that it generates special obligations that hold among the members and that must be weighed against demands of entry.

In a spirit similar to Carens, Kukathas (2005) presents two reasons for favoring open borders: a principle of freedom, and a principle of humanity. From a standpoint of freedom, restrictive immigration policies are problematic for several reasons: People lose the freedom to leave their country, which among other things implies that oppressive governments have fewer incentives to create bearable living conditions. People also lose the freedom to sell their labor, and are deprived of their freedom of association. The principle of humanity appeals to the fact that moving is often the best way out of poverty. Kukathas does not think economic concerns within the countries of destination override these reasons, nor do considerations of nationality or about the preservation of a certain culture. Kukathas also finds such worries overstated: change brought about by immigration is not necessarily bad. According to him, "many of the reasons open immigration is not possible right now have less to do with the disadvantages it might bring than with an unwarranted concern about its dangers" (p 219). He pushes this consideration quite far. He is aware that one reason why open immigration is not possible is that it is not compatible with the modern welfare state. "While one obvious response to this is to say, 'so much the worse for open immigration,' it is not less possible to ask whether the welfare state is what needs rethinking" (p 219).

But suppose we adopt Kukathas' ideas. What would the world be like if all borders are open? A world with unrestricted freedom of movement would be very different from ours. The philosophical worry is not that creating such a world is politically unrealistic. The worry is instead that we cannot reliably and credibly imagine what a world without borders would be like. This point draws on the general justification of states in Chapter 3. Political philosophy explores utopias. But they should be *realistic utopias*, and one aspect of them being realistic is that they are comprehensible. Open borders are neither required nor advisable beyond what we have arrived at by qualifying David Miller's arguments with considerations drawing on the ownership approach.

Canadian political theorist Arash Abizadeh (2008) argues that unilateral border-control is inconsistent with a democratic theory of popular sovereignty. When institutions coerce, the coerced must have a say about it; there must be *actual* justification to the *demos* (the group of people that is supposed to carry out democratic procedures). It is an essential part of the system of multiple states that there are institutions that coerce people (non-citizens) to whom no such justification is given. These people are coerced, actually or potentially, through the presence of borders. Therefore, the state system – which permits each state to control its borders – ought not to exist, and ought to be replaced with institutions that would give justification to a global demos. For Abizadeh the idea of a *bounded* demos of *democratic* theory is incoherent. If we assume a bounded demos, the justification of the exclusion of some from entering the country in question would only be required vis-à-vis those who already belong to the demos but not to all those affected by it. So a bounded demos cannot democratically legitimize the coercion it exercises.

What kind of legitimization does a demos require? Call a set of people constrained by intense cooperative and coercive structures a *potential demos* of democratic politics. Such a demos is "potential" because I said nothing about the extent to which its members are enfranchised. Coercive and cooperative structures create pressure towards enfranchisement. Enfranchising parts of the potential demos increases the pressure for more complete enfranchisement. Moral arguments demand the transformation of a potential demos into a *demos* of democratic politics. One might object that this process does not deliver a legitimate demos because it has not been democratically constituted: no vote has determined that this circle of people should be united to the exclusion of others. Yet as long as this demos is internally just and its members endorse its institutions, that is unproblematic.

An objection might be that this transformation does not properly consider all affected interests. Mexicans who wish to enter the US never consented to there being an American demos that unilaterally constrains immigration. Yet interests can be considered in domain-specific ways. For instance, to the extent that interests are affected by trade policies, for instance, we should ensure that such policies are fair. Other duties apply for different reasons, and in some cases immigration-related measures may be instrumental to realizing them. But being under such a duty does not mean a demos must enfranchise everybody connected to them through trade.

Discretionary immigration

Discretionary immigration is immigration of people who are not *entitled* to immigrate. States may or may not accept discretionary immigration: by definition, such immigration goes beyond what states are morally required to do. I assume now that discretionary immigration also includes immigration policies adopted by way of discharging an obligation that can be discharged in different ways, such as a duty of assistance. Non-discretionary immigration must aim for making the newcomers full members of society. But what is the state free to offer participants of discretionary programs?

Michael Blake (2002) explores whether the state can offer such immigrants arrangements of partial citizenship, like a guest worker status, or use "suspect categories" such as race and ethnicity to determine who gets to enter. The concerns about partial-citizenship arrangements are that they might well be exploitative if people lack viable alternatives, and that they contribute to an unjust global order by taking advantage of people's economic difficulties that themselves are unjust. But if these concerns do not apply, Blake finds partial-citizenship arrangements unproblematic. However, he concedes that it is hard to assess whether these concerns do apply.

As opposed to Blake, Carens (1992) argues that anybody who resides and works in a country should be allowed to become a citizen after a moderate passage of time and some reasonable formalities. Otherwise such residents would be too vulnerable to all sorts of advantage-taking. However, Carens's position entails that nobody would be allowed to enter a contractual arrangement for partial-citizenship status even where we can plausibly assume that no exploitation occurs. Suppose up-and-coming academics or successful businessmen accept partial citizenship abroad to advance their careers. Surely they are not exploited only because they will not be entitled to citizenship some years later. Of course, circumstances and plans may change after people take up arrangements of partial citizenship. But this is no different in any other contractual arrangements that we would not normally consider void for such reasons. Nonetheless, we may modify Blake's proposal by stipulating that marriage to a permanent resident or parenting a child for whom one is willing to care at a substantial level should suffice to receive citizenship despite earlier arrangements to the contrary. Perhaps we should make room for other exceptions, to avoid undue hardship. But there is in any event no reason to exclude partial-citizenship arrangements categorically.

Many nations prefer immigration by individuals who belong to particular racial or ethnic groups. "White Australia" is an extreme example. In the US, the national origins quotas that were applied between 1921 and 1965 gave differential access based upon nationality, limiting the number of immigrants from any nation to 3% of residents of that nationality in 1910. This system sought to limit the number of immigrants from Africa, the West Indies and other racially "undesirable" locations. Today emphasis upon family reunification privileges those who have already gained access, to that degree perpetuating the exclusionary project of the quota system. But why exactly would the use of race or ethnicity be problematic in immigration policy? After all, the most powerful arguments against discrimination within domestic legal systems draw on shared citizenship. But first of all, a state that prefers one racial group in immigration makes a public statement. Thereby it undermines the ability of citizens with the disfavored identity to see themselves as full participants even if those to whom that message is directly addressed are non-residents. Similarly, indirect racial preferences, like the US national quota system, tell people who are represented in small percentages that that is how it should be.

One other problem in applying such categories is that most countries do not have a homogenous population. Therefore the use of such categories inevitably offends some who are already in the country. For instance, "White Australia" was impermissible also because Australia was never purely white. Aborigines were not properly respected in a state that asked obedience of them while admitting only whites. On the other hand, had Australia been purely white at some point, had Australians desired to keep it that way, and had they limited their territory proportionately, "White Australia" would have been acceptable, but not enduringly so. Australians would have traveled and invited visitors, students, or business partners to visit. Some would have wanted to ask such foreigners to remain in Australia to share their lives with them. Only unacceptable constraints could have prevented this development. A morally acceptable Little White Australia would have been short-lived. Blake rightly argues that suspect categories should be used only under unusual historical or demographic circumstances. If one ethnic or racial group is particularly vulnerable, a state's ethnic or racial preference become defensible as response, very much parallel to affirmative action in university admissions. For example, the Holocaust may serve as a sufficient justification for a Jewish right of return (one that presumably would have to be combined with a suitable arrangement for Palestinians).

To explore discretionary immigration some more, let us briefly consider two specific questions. To begin with, is it permissible to exclude people with AIDS? In the US, being HIV-positive was grounds for denial of admission until 2010. The argument in support of such a measure enlists public health concerns. It seems appropriate to exclude those suffering from AIDS since theirs is a contagious disease. In addition, it seems that no social stigma for those already in the country would be generated in this way. Unlike race or nationality, a disease is not something many people would proudly identify with. However, AIDS is contagious only if one interacts with infected people intimately and thus in ways that can be readily avoided. Unlike diseases that are airborne or transmissible through any kind of physical interaction, AIDS poses no general health risk. Asking people not to spread AIDS is therefore no different from asking them to abide by the law.

A second question is whether it is permissible to exclude gay people in countries with declining populations. This question does not arise forcefully. On the one hand, the percentage of exclusively gay people is relatively small. In addition, it is also the case that many heterosexuals choose not to procreate. If the survival of society depends on reproductive behavior of immigrants, a preference not to admit gay people will be acceptable. (In that case, however, an immigration policy that is strongly focused on population growth would also affect other groups of would-be immigrants with limited or no potential for procreation; there would be no reason whatsoever to single out gay people for special treatment.) But given how unlikely that is, any preference against admitting gay people would more likely express a prejudice than reflect an acceptable political priority.

Illegal immigration

By way of concluding I use collective ownership of the earth to generate a perspective on illegal immigrants in the US (Risse 2008). Note first that although the relevant measure of proportionate use is decidedly not population density, I now use it as a very crude guide. In 2007, Germany and the UK had a population density of about 600 per square mile; for Japan it was 830, for the Netherlands 1,200, and for Bangladesh 2,600. In the US it was 80. Population density varied by state, but only in three states does it surpass 800.

It takes extensive policy changes to accommodate large numbers of immigrants, but if one merely ponders these numbers, the US critically underuses resources. If so, and assuming this will not need to be revised if we obtain better ways of assessing underuse, illegal immigrants (in any event those from overusing countries) cannot be reasonably expected to refrain from seeking entry. One could not resist this conclusion by pointing out that many immigrants would want to settle in the same few locations that in turn are overused. It is a matter of social policy adjustments to solve this problem.

But even if illegal immigration is not wrong from the standpoint of collective ownership, it might be wrong in another way. Perhaps laws of morally acceptable states (including immigration policies) should be respected even where they go astray. However, the usual reasons why laws ought to be obeyed *qua laws* (rather than because they are morally required) only address members of the society. To those one may say that their ongoing presence or participation in economic or political life establishes a tacit acceptance of the law. Fair-play arguments might apply. Perhaps some people, such as naturalized citizens, have explicitly accepted the laws. But none of this gives would-be illegal immigrants reasons not to break laws that bar them *from entering* if they wish to participate in society while abiding by its laws.

Let me offer an argument in support of legalizing illegal immigrants in the country *regardless* of whether US immigration policy is reasonably acceptable as a whole. My argument draws on the civil law notion of "adverse possession." This term refers to the open occupation of property by people who do not own it, assuming the owners know of the situation and do not challenge it. If the situation persists for a certain period, the civil law allows for ownership, or aspects of it, to pass to the occupiers. Like a knowing but non-contesting owner, the US presumably under-occupies its space and has created niches for illegal immigrants. They are a mainstay of parts of the economy. Illegal immigration, in the aggregate, occurs in a manner and on a scale that is known to the public. Such immigrants hold jobs, have licenses, and participate in society in many ways. The US falls short of what it *could* do to enforce immigration laws. A moral form of adverse possession has taken hold. Among co-owners, this situation creates pressure to facilitate adjustment of status for illegal immigrants.

Further reading

Immigration is a relatively recent subject of philosophical inquiry. Barry and Goodin (1992) continues to be a useful resource. The work of Joseph Carens has set the stage for most subsequent philosophical writing on immigration. A view similar to Abizadeh (2008) is also defended by Robert Goodin (2007). The relevance of the ownership approach to immigration is explored in Blake and Risse (2007) and developed systematically in Risse (2012). Dummett (2001) illuminatingly discusses many issues about immigration. Cavallero (2006) offers an approach to immigration that takes the preferences of immigrants more seriously than the account in this chapter.

7 Fairness in Trade

Trade

In Chapter 3 we encountered Kant's *Perpetual Peace*. Published in 1795, this work is often praised for its foresight. After all, Kant suggested the founding of a federation of states charged with the preservation of peace. In the 20th century, the League of Nations (founded after the First World War), and later the United Nations implemented his vision. But Kant was strikingly naïve in other ways, especially in his attitude towards trade. "The spirit of commerce sooner or later takes hold of every people," he wrote, "and it cannot exist side by side with war." Kant seems to have thought a world dominated by trade would inevitably be peaceful. But history unfolded differently. Increasing commercial prospects transformed societies into different classes that were not always at peace. And at the global level, 19th-century imperialism was driven by commercial interests. In many cases trade interests of Western powers were enforced by force ("gun boat diplomacy"). In their 1848 *Communist Manifesto*, Karl Marx and Friedrich Engels already wrote rather differently about trade:

> The bourgeoisie ... has resolved personal worth into exchange value, and in place of the numberless indefeasible chartered freedoms, has set up that single, unconscionable freedom – Free Trade. In one word, for exploitation, veiled by religious and political illusions, it has substituted naked, shameless, direct, brutal exploitation. (McLellan 1977, pp 247f)

International trade amounts to structured and repeated exchanges involving markets and the bodies of law, domestic and international, that regulate them. The potential of trade to contribute to a peaceful and prosperous world is indeed enormous. People in different parts of the world excel at doing different things. Trade creates possibilities for people to obtain goods and services for whose provision they lack the prerequisites. Standard economic theory teaches that trade benefits all countries involved, at least in the long run, and if the country is taken as a whole. If country A is better at producing cheese than wine, it should obtain wine by trading cheese. If the reverse is true for B, B should trade wine for cheese. A has a *comparative advantage* in cheese and B in wine, even if A is better at producing both. While there are other reasons for trade liberalization, this insight, going back to David Ricardo's 1817 *Principles of Political Economy*, underlies international economics. Trade theory supports free trade: barriers like tariffs and quotas obstruct mutually beneficial transactions. Countries should undo them, even unilaterally.

However, trade has also much potential for creating and perpetuating disadvantage around the world. In the past colonial powers took advantage of their military prowess to limit other parts of the world to producing what benefited the colonizers' domestic economy, or to open their markets to products the colonized did not ask for or could have gotten elsewhere on better terms. Much global trade is now regulated by the WTO. In 2010, the WTO had 153 members, representing more than 95% of world trade, and 30 observers, most seeking membership. The WTO came into being in 1995 under the Marrakesh Agreement, replacing and expanding the General Agreements on Tariffs and Trade (GATT) that had existed since 1947. While the GATT only dealt with tariff barriers for trade in goods, the WTO treaty also includes agreements on services, intellectual property and investment measures, as well as agreements on, for instance, sanitary barriers to trade. Agriculture and textiles, though absent from the GATT, are part of the WTO's mandate. The WTO treaty is a "single undertaking:" members must accept the whole package. Through the treaty on Trade-Related Aspects of Intellectual Property (TRIPs), the WTO regulates at least one domain of property.

WTO membership improves ease and security of access to export markets, and involves access to a dispute settlement mechanism for trade issues. If country A is not in the WTO, member countries, including large countries with market power, may impose tariffs on A when times are bad. Moreover, A cannot demand change if policies of member countries frustrate its prospects. So there are considerable advantages to WTO membership. However, for many states joining the WTO as it is, or not joining at all, is a choice between subjection to unwanted and perhaps unreasonable norms, on the one hand, and isolation, on the other. Powerful countries can impose terms on weaker ones that have no realistic alternative to joining the organization largely as it is. "In transnational processes of production, trade and investment," philosopher Richard Miller writes, "people in developed countries take advantage of bargaining weaknesses of individuals desperately seeking work in developing countries, in ways that show inadequate appreciation of their interests and capacities for choice" (2010, p 62).

I discuss two topics: export subsidies and WTO reforms. Subsidies concern us in the next several sections, and our discussion of the WTO takes up the remainder of this chapter. Export subsidies – governmental payments to producers for exporting products – appear prominently in debates about what justice requires when it comes to trade. Also criticized as inefficient and surrounded by much controversy, specifically agricultural export subsidies in the US, EU, and Japan are widely seen as serving the rich at the expense of the poor. Alongside anti-dumping measures, export subsidies are common forms of protectionism. "Dumping" occurs if goods sell at less than "normal" (WTO) or "fair" value (US language). Anti-dumping duties make imported goods more expensive, to help domestic industries. Anti-dumping measures and export subsidies are the primary fairness topics covered by WTO regulations (which constrain both).

Human rights and the duty of assistance

To set the stage, however, we must briefly return to our discussion of human rights. We noted in Chapter 1 that there is a general obligation for all individuals and institutions to do what they can (within limits) to realize human rights. Realizing human rights is a global responsibility. Specifically we noted that states must assist *other* states with the realization of such rights in their (the other states') jurisdiction if those are incapable of doing so themselves. They must interfere if other states are unwilling to maintain an acceptable human rights record. Duties of assistance and interference are held alongside other states, and may be exercised through international organizations, such as the WTO. This generic duty to assist other states implies an obligation to put these states in a position to provide human rights to their citizens. After all, states create the immediate environment for people's lives to unfold. The practical content of that obligation, in turn, is to provide *assistance in building institutions.*

According to the economic historian Douglass North (1990), institutions

> are the humanly devised constraints that shape human interaction. In consequence they structure incentives in human exchange, whether political, social, or economic. Institutional change shapes the way societies evolve through time and hence is the key to understanding historical change. (p 3)

As the economist Dani Rodrik explains, "there is now widespread agreement among economists studying economic growth that institutional quality holds the key to prevailing patterns of prosperity around the world." "Rich countries," he continues, also by way of illuminating what kinds of institutions matter,

> are those where investors feel secure about their property rights, the rule of law prevails, private incentives are in line with social objectives, monetary and fiscal policies are grounded in solid macroeconomic institutions, idiosyncratic risks are appropriately mediated through social insurance, and citizens have civil liberties and political representation. Poor countries are those where these arrangements are absent or ill-formed. Of course, high-quality institutions are perhaps as much a result of economic prosperity as they are its cause. But however important the reverse arrow of causality may be, a growing body of empirical research has shown

that institutions exert a very strong effect on aggregate incomes. Institutions are *causal* in the sense that a poor country that is able to revise the rules of the game in the direction of strengthening the property rights of entrepreneurs and investors is likely to experience a lasting increase in its productive capacity. (2007, p 184)

Good institutions are essential for economic growth, but also provide the background for civil and political rights. Assistance in building institutions is the most sensible investment in the future of troubled countries. Therefore, this duty of assistance is the crucial obligation implied by the conception of human rights we have explored in Chapter 1.

How much of a sacrifice do individuals, states, or other organizations have to make to satisfy a duty of assistance? The political theorist Brian Barry once concluded a discussion of this vexing question by stating, appropriately, that

there is no firm criterion for the amount of sacrifice required to relieve distress. This does not mean that nothing can be said. I think it is fairly clear that there is a greater obligation the more severe the distress, the better off the potential helper would still be after helping, and the higher the ratio of benefit to cost. What is indefinite is where the line is to be drawn. (1982, p 225)

Barry's statement speaks to short-term assistance, but the point applies with even greater force to a duty of assistance in building institutions. Sometimes the duty of assistance will be very demanding, but sometimes no duty applies because outsiders cannot do what requires doing. After all, institutions can emerge and persist only if most individuals support the "rules of the game." This is so especially for institutions that cannot be effectively created by governmental fiat (as, say, market-regulating institutions can), such as a constitution guiding generations through disputes, a legal system enforcing property rights and contracts, as well as a culture of trust, shared understandings of what are reasonable benefits from and sacrifices imposed by cooperation, commitment to the common good, and other hallmarks of civil society. Outside assistance may well be ineffective then: what is needed cannot be "imported," and the stability of institutions might be undermined if those whose participation maintains them rely on outside support. The institutions might collapse once the support is withdrawn. One of the most striking points to note about the morality of international relations is that it is frequently difficult to assess whether a duty of support in institution-building applies, and is demanding, or whether it does not apply because outsiders are in no position to do what is needed.

Agricultural subsidies

Let us turn to subsidies. According to Wolf (2004), a prominent advocate of globalization, the priorities shown in the agricultural policies of the US, EU and Japan are "obscene." "Total assistance to rich country farmers," he tells us,

> was $311 billion in 2001, six times as much as all development assistance, indeed more than the GDP of Sub-Saharan Africa. In 2000, the EU provided $913 for each cow and $8 to each Sub-Saharan African. The Japanese, more generous still, though only to cows, provided $2,700 for each one and just $1.47 to each African. Not to be outdone, the US spent $10.7 million a day on cotton and $3.1 million a day on all aid to Sub-Saharan Africa. (p 215)

Export subsidies benefit domestic producers but harm domestic consumers because there are fewer goods on that market, and so prices rise. Such subsidies are often paired with import restrictions that further increase prices. While redistributing wealth, subsidies also cause "deadweight-losses," distortions arising because restrictions motivate producers to produce more and consumers to consume less. Subsidies also have effects abroad. They harm producers elsewhere by lowering world market prices (if subsidies are large enough), leading to lower wages and limiting employment possibilities. Ipso facto, subsidies benefit consumers elsewhere in the short run. However, they may well also harm these same consumers by worsening their job market prospects if they hamper world market access in the respective country.

Subsidies create a particular situation on world markets that, at the level of countries, benefits some and harms others. Agricultural subsidies benefit net-food-importing countries, which includes most of the least developed countries. How individuals fare depends to a large extent on whether they are producers or consumers. The expiration of the Multi-Fiber-Agreement (which had regulated textiles markets for some decades) benefited China. Similarly, removing subsidies may provide some countries an advantage in agriculture and cause others to alter what they produce. Yet it is hard to predict which countries would make the shift: only retrospectively do we realize that the Multi-Fiber-Agreement had supported its beneficiaries against China. Liberalization may not benefit the countries on behalf of which it is often demanded.

Subsidies create winners and losers, as would their removal. Still, it could be argued that, from a consequentialist standpoint, the case for trade liberalization is straightforward. According to Anderson (2004), estimates of gains from liberalization range from $254 billion annually ($108 billion for non-OECD countries, 1995 dollars), to $832 billion ($539 billion for non-OECD countries, 1997 dollars). Anderson and Martin (2006) say that "[f]reeing all merchandise trade and eliminating agricultural subsidies are estimated to boost global welfare by nearly $300 billion a year by 2015. Additional gains would come from whatever productivity effects that reform would generate" (p 11). They add that 45% of the gains would go to developing countries. As opposed to that, however, Hertel and Keeney (2006) estimate that eliminating agricultural subsidies and liberalizing trade in goods and services would generate gains of $151 billion, $34 billion for developing countries (and thus considerably less than estimated by Anderson and Martin). The degree of variation here is astounding. Each of the economic models used for these predictions makes assumptions about what will happen when subsidies are removed. For some countries it is easy to predict how they will change their production. However, for other countries there might be no way of anticipating what they will do. Yet others will only react to countries that show an immediate response to the removal of subsidies.

A first strategy for defending subsidies: individual claims

A claim to subsidies is stronger and more specific than claims to basic economic protection, which can assume many forms, such as unemployment benefits or funds to enter other lines of work. For claims to subsidies to succeed, individuals must argue that the government is liable for their occupational choice (and for its consequences being unfortunate) as well as that they are entitled to *such* support. Such an argument cannot be that the absence of subsidies harms some people, if only by disadvantaging them relative to others. Most governmental measures do. We need an argument why governments are under this *particular* duty.

We will consider three strategies to provide such an argument on behalf those who seek to benefit from subsidies. First, some might have an actual claim against the government to be put in a position to continue in a line of work that has become unprofitable. Second, the political community as such might have a prerogative to indulge in certain products, and, say, to pay subsidies if this is what it takes to keep farmers in business although payments harm farmers abroad. And third, perhaps subsidies should be paid because the community as a whole has made moral commitments that require protection of members whose individual interests are thwarted by these communal commitments. Domestic producers could make such an argument if their competitiveness suffers because they must comply with higher labor standards than are used abroad, and if these standards are demanded by the community's moral commitments.

Let us begin with the individual-claims-based argument. One might think everybody is on the labor market at her own risk (except that a social system provides basic safeguards) and for her own sake (except that she must help maintain the basic structure through taxes). People acquire skills, and keep the gains, such as salaries (except for taxes). If they fail, the state only owes them protection against hardship. This view is implicit in the political economy of liberal market systems. Yet the so-called *Varieties-of-Capitalism* approach to comparative political economy distinguishes various versions of capitalism (Hall and Soskice 2001, Howell 2003).

Versions of capitalism are characterized by institutional complementarities: one set of institutions operates effectively only (or in any event operates more effectively) if accompanied by other institutions. This especially applies to ownership arrangements and labor markets. Two ideal types are liberal market economies, as in the US, and coordinated market economies, as in Germany. Coordinated economies have rigid labor markets that strongly encourage employees to acquire specialized skills, rewarding them with job security. Other factors that shape the political economy complement such markets. Participants in coordinated economies have a different relationship to the state than those in liberal economies. Note this assessment of labor markets in Germany and Japan:

> Social constraints and opportunities ... typically enforced by social institutions, define the legitimate place and the possible range of market transactions and markets in the economy-cum-society in which they take place. By circumscribing and thereby limiting the role of markets, they typically 'distort' them, for example by shielding desirable social conditions from market fluctuations." (Streeck and Yamamura 2001, p 2)

Workers specialized because legislation made it irrational for them not to. So the state is liable for their inability to find work if their sector collapses. By promoting specialization, the government participates in its citizens' professional decisions. The risk that accompanies specialization, if occurring in response to how labor markets are framed, is justifiable to citizens only if the state offers guarantees if they fail.

One may object that individuals must always make choices in light of legislation. Yet this objection runs together too many legislative acts. Suppose I am Swedish and make life choices based on Swedish liquor laws. As far as legislation is concerned, I am left with many alternatives, namely, those that do not engage liquor laws. (My life, as it is, may not make it easy for me to make choices that do not turn on these laws. I may be a scion of a liquor-selling family: but that is not a matter of legislation, but something about my life.) Suppose I am Japanese and must decide whether to invest in certain skills and find that labor markets make it irrational not to specialize *somehow*. Short of emigrating, or accepting failure, I cannot escape from this choice (which makes this case very different from the Swedish scenario). So laws like those that shape the set-up of labor markets differ from just any law that affects choices.

In liberal market economies individuals can specialize or not, at their own risk. Since the system is prepared to deal with workers who lack specialization and may need additional training on the job, even those who specialize and fail may have an easier time switching sectors than in coordinated economies. But even in liberal market systems states do much to "subsidize" individuals: they provide the infrastructure that enables individuals to go about their lives in the first place, ranging from the provision of education to the construction of roads. Yet support for unprofitable lines of work is beyond the limits of what individuals can legitimately demand.

But even in coordinated economies one may doubt if individuals have claims against the state to let them continue in a line of work. The strength of their claims lies in the trouble of finding other employment once people have specialized. However, perhaps this argument only shows that employees have a claim to a high level of governmental support. Such claims may turn into specific claims to aid to continue in one's line of work only if the costs of change are forbidding for individuals – but in that case they indeed do. Especially for well-trained people who have spent all their life in one niche, these costs may be truly forbidding (a combination of economic costs, such as additional training, and personal costs, such as having to adjust to a new environment, etc.). Still, even in such cases support ought to come with a commitment to simultaneously dissuade others from entering the sector.

A second strategy: collective preferences

Let me offer another strategy to support the view that some should be allowed to continue in a line of work although markets would not allow it. A country may consider redistribution and deadweight-losses acceptable if people disagree with the market about costs or benefits of products. The French may consider such burdens acceptable to continue the production of baguette from French grain, camembert from French cows, or *foie gras* from local ducks. Far from honoring a duty in response to the claims of individuals, they might have a *collective preference* for home-grown products and be willing to pay for them.

Yet the individual-claims-based and the collective-preference-based argument face the same difficulty: as we noted at the beginning of this chapter, there is a duty of assistance that developed countries have towards developing countries. Suppose trade is crucial for growth as well as for other goals of development. Then an overwhelming case emerges for helping developing countries to join markets. However, we must also note that controversial empirical matters are central to this argument, namely, the link between trade, on the one hand, and growth and other development goals, on the other. It is only *to the extent that* trade is tied to these purposes that it bears on the satisfaction of duties to developing countries. It is therefore only *to the extent that* trade is tied to these purposes that liberalization gains in importance vis-à-vis duties a state may have towards its citizens, especially, again, in coordinated market economies.

Disagreements remain about how important trade and liberalization are for development (recall the differences in estimations of benefits from liberalization), and so about how much priority one should put on negotiations to reduce trade barriers, rather than on exploring alternative solutions. These disputes make it hard to reach a verdict about subsidies. In coordinated market economies, individuals have claims to governmental aid if their line of work fails. Yet it depends on the presence of competing claims whether this claim assumes the shape of subsidies. If subsidies are trade-distorting and other forms of support are not, proportionate consideration of different claims requires that citizens be helped in minimally trade-distorting ways. The need to avoid trade-distorting measures and the case for the moral urgency of the termination of subsidies depend on the importance of trade for development.

There is another complication. Suppose the relevance of trade for development is strong enough to warrant the claim that developed countries should abolish trade-distorting subsidies, especially in agriculture. Yet such subsidies also lower prices for net-food-importing countries. If the relevance of trade for development makes it compelling to abolish subsidies, this is because of the *aggregative* importance of trade, not because this will immediately be good for each country. Initially, net-food-importers will be worse off. Gains from the discontinuation of subsidies must be redistributed to countries that suffer. This will cause political problems because gains do not gather in accounts of international agencies, but instead are widely disseminated.

As far as the collective-preference-based argument is concerned, note that the existence of subsidies indicates that, say, the French government thinks this preference should be maintained through its authority, rather than consumer choices. But preferences for home-grown products can be realized without trade-distortions. Farm products can be transformed into (or simply be re-marketed as) gourmet products. Higher prices for "French" products will keep farmers in business if consumers pay for this quality. In any event, however, a stronger argument in favor of state action on behalf of home products stems from values that may *not* appear as frivolous as food preferences. The preservation of food may be part of the preservation of French culture or countryside. Or perhaps the preservation of French food is part of a security strategy of making sure France can survive emergencies.

Such claims warrant governmental protection also in the eyes of many who do not attribute such power to food preferences. Supporters may claim that without government support these goals fall prey to collective action problems. Still, even such stronger claims for governmental action on behalf of social goods must address the claim that trade is relevant to development. Since alleviation of poverty bears more weight than cultural preservation (and as long as concerns about security cannot be made sufficiently urgent, to the extent that they turn on certain countries being able to provide their own food), attempts at preservation ought not to be trade-distorting.

A final strategy in defense of subsidies: moral commitments

Let us explore a final argument in support of the view that some should be supported to continue in a line of work although markets would not allow it. Suppose legislation for social standards is adopted not merely because it expresses what our practices happen to be, but for moral reasons that capture views about how persons ought to be treated. If labor standards abroad differ from those we are collectively committed to, and if domestic producers suffer as a consequence, the harm done should be redistributed among all members of the community. Such redistribution may take the form of export subsidies. In addition, import of goods produced under conditions of which our community disapproves could be restricted. Both measures help domestic industries. A consideration in support of such measures would also be that, in this way, we avoid setting incentives for future treatment of the relevant sort. If lower labor standards are negatively sanctioned in this way, they might change.

This argument falls short of demanding that one prevent others from treating people badly in ways other than by protecting those in the country who act properly and by refusing to set incentives that would instigate such behavior at home and abroad. Consider the fight against corruption. For a long time, many countries treated domestic corruption differently from corruption abroad. Playing along with, and giving rise to, corruption abroad was not punishable (Eigen 2003). Suppose corruption was prohibited in country A because of moral concerns about the conditions under which people should get ahead. A should protect those of its citizens who abide by its norms (for instance, by making sure that those who do not abide by these norms do not gain advantages thereby), and should refrain from setting incentives for corrupt behavior in B by tolerating that its, A's, citizens become complicit with corruption in B. But A need not take additional measures against B. Or consider a case involving animals. Foie gras is duck or goose liver fattened by force-feeding. Some countries have laws against such practices, but not against importing foie gras. Suppose A has prohibited force-feeding because of moral concerns for animals. A should refrain from setting incentives for future production of foie gras by prohibiting imports. But A need not act in other ways to prevent B from producing foie gras.

If legislation of social standards rests on moral reasons, *then* domestic industries deserve protection. Often, however, social standards have been adopted for protectionist reasons, or have arisen from domestic power struggles. Domestic industries then cannot insist on shifting the harm to everybody if competitors abroad benefit from different practices. Only if the intent behind social standards is moral is there an argument to that effect. Consider an excerpt from the 1930 US Tariff Act:

> All goods, wares, articles, and merchandise mined, produced, or manufactured wholly or in part in any foreign country by convict labor or/and forced labor or/and indentured labor under penal sanctions shall not be entitled to entry at any of the ports of the United States, and the importation thereof is hereby prohibited.... [B]ut in no case shall such provisions be applicable to goods, wares, articles, or merchandise so mined, produced, or manufactured which are not mined, produced, or manufactured in such quantities in the United States as to meet the consumptive demands of the United States.[1]

The protectionist intent is easy to track: the legislators have no qualms about importing goods produced by prison labor if demand in the US is higher than supply. Import is prohibited only if the US can satisfy its own demand. So the point is not that there is something morally problematic about using convict labor in this way. But while in this case the protectionist concern is obvious, it will often be hard to tell whether, say, labor legislation has been adopted as a moral view. Generally, identifying collective moral commitments involves both conceptual and practical problems.

However, in many countries it is plausible for cases of severe human rights violations that legislation against such acts was adopted for moral reasons. For instance, Western democracies have adopted legislation against oppressive governance in virtue of a moral view of personhood, captured as early as in the 1789 Declaration of the Rights of Man and of the Citizen, whose Article II lists resistance to oppressive governance as an end of political associations. So if domestic industries suffer set-backs because competitors benefit from severe human rights violations, it seems that they have a claim to the redistribution of the damage thus caused. That is, compensation for their business losses (as well as compensation for losses suffered by the workers) should then become a public expense.

Yet this argument merely delivers pro tanto considerations: indeed, if we are collectively committed to certain moral views, then those of us who suffer harm from our collective commitments can make a strong case that their damages be redistributed. But any response to this demand must not violate our duties of justice. In particular, this kind of argument cannot validate export subsidies if such payments violate a duty of assistance in building institutions. While this third argument does succeed within the constraints set by what justice demands, it succeeds *only* within these constraints.

The WTO as an agent of justice

Export subsidies raise complex issues, and the preceding discussion has tried to capture these complexities that are often ignored when their existence is characterized as a major evil in an era of globalization and their removal praised as a panacea. Let us turn to our second major topic then. Many of those who, in some sense or another, oppose globalization have complained about the WTO's impact on global trade and on the prospects of individuals whose fates depend on trade. So we must ask whether there ought to be an organization like the WTO in the first place, and if so, how the present organization ought to be reformed.

The WTO has a staff of more than 600 and headquarters in Geneva. Its major task is to facilitate trade negotiations. The WTO is often called a "member-driven" organization: the members themselves negotiate and implement agreements. Members commit themselves to non-discriminatory trade practices, using a *most-favored nation rule*: products made in one member country should be treated no less favorably than "like" products (very similar products) made in any other (with few exceptions, such as

preferential treatment for developing countries). A favorable status for one member with regard to some product applies to all.
Members also accept a principle of *national treatment* for foreign
goods, to treat them no less favorably than national ones: domestic taxes or similar measures must not be levied differentially on
domestic and foreign goods. In addition, the WTO applies a principle of reciprocity, which ensures that countries do not unilaterally benefit from non-discrimination but offer equivalent market
access. It is hard to apply this criterion to developing countries
since they often lack the market shares required to respond in
kind if developed countries open markets to them.

Some think the WTO should only concern itself with trade liberalization and be judged in terms of efficiency. But this view is
untenable. First of all, the view of human rights I have defended
implies a generic duty for all entities to do what they can towards
the realization of human rights. This view applies to the WTO. We
can also derive a view about the obligations of the WTO from what
we have said about states. Entities that are empowered by states
and whose activities affect the satisfaction of the obligations to
which states are subject ought to assist states with their duties.
In virtue of having been founded by and receiving power from
states, such entities are subject to demands of justice that apply
to states, namely those with regard to the domain for which they
were founded. So in the domain of trade the WTO ought to help
states realize obligation *they* have, which includes a duty of assistance in building institutions. Therefore we must think of the WTO
as having a *development-oriented mandate*.

The WTO is already quite officially concerned with more than
trade liberalization or efficiency. The preamble of the Marrakesh
Agreement talks about "reciprocal and mutually advantageous
arrangements directed to the substantial reduction of tariffs and
other barriers to trade." But these goals should be pursued "with
a view to raising standards of living, ensuring full employment
and a large and steadily growing volume of real income and effective demand," as well as with the goal of ensuring that "developing
countries, and especially the least developed among them, secure
a share in the growth in international trade commensurate with

the needs of their economic development." Limited as it is, moral language appears in the WTO's mandate. This language also ought to include justice.

From the standpoint of justice, there ought to be a global organization concerned with trade. If no trade organization with global aspirations had been founded yet, we ought to found one now. The realities of domestic politics provide obstacles for governments to take seriously duties of justice pertaining to noncitizens. Let me limit my argument to democracies. A government that is democratically accountable to its citizens for domestic justice has strong incentives to neglect other duties. The problem is not merely that the dynamics of electoral politics – the ability and willingness of political parties to make promises they can realize only by neglecting other duties – might *occasionally* interfere with other values. The real problem is that voters are preoccupied with their own concerns. Politicians cater towards these preoccupations, running the risk of being penalized in elections if they fail to do so. This normally implies a high degree of political inward-directedness. Therefore there should be *transnational* entities where governments both coordinate and account for efforts to realize principles whose scope is not limited to fellow citizens. Because of the *global* nature specifically of trade such coordination and account-giving with regard to matters of trade should occur in a global trade organization. So given that there are multiple states we readily find a justice-based rationale for the existence of the WTO: the existence of such an organization makes it more likely that justice be done as far as trade is concerned.

Reforming the WTO

But perhaps this organization ought to be very different from the current WTO. One crucial issue for the current WTO is the lack of power for poor countries in rule-making. According to Bernard Hoekman (2002), the WTO's member-driven nature strains some national delegations: "Many countries have no more than one or two persons dealing with WTO matters; a large minority has no delegations in Geneva at all" (p 47f). Barton, Goldstein, Joslin and

Steinberg (2006) plainly doubt the WTO's member-driven character, insisting "the reality of a complex organization supported by an educated and sophisticated staff is not entirely consistent with this image" (p 212). Both assessments draw attention to the problem that many decisions are made by informal blocks of powerful nations that meet frequently (and so work in a manner that would overstretch the resources of smaller members) and enjoy the assistance of a sophisticated staff. Officially, the WTO is a one-member-one-vote organization, its decisions being consensus-based. But since many members are effectively excluded from influence, WTO procedures favor the powerful.

Poor countries also face difficulties maneuvering the WTO's dispute settlement system. If one member accuses another of violations, and negotiations fail, the first can request adjudication. The dispute settlement mechanism permits retaliation via trade-related measures. Retaliation can occur across issues, and so can be deployed in ways that hurt. The GATT allowed losing parties simply to block the decisions against them. WTO rulings can only be rejected unanimously. The WTO's dispute settlement mechanism is generally highly regarded. According to Barton et al. (2006), the WTO's process

> is by far the most effective international dispute settlement process. Although it is natural that some of its decisions and processes are criticized, few would say that it is not a basically fair process or that there has been corruption. The system uses high-quality decision makers, has the power to enforce a significant and specific body of international law, and has control over a trade sanction that seems to be of just the right strength both to be politically acceptable and to generally induce compliance. (p 210)

However, the success of the system depends on compliance. Suppose powerful countries fail to comply, and in response smaller countries may retaliate through trade sanctions. But retaliation is of no use for countries without impact on world market prices: they cannot harm or benefit others through trade measures. Monetary compensation would sometimes be preferable for smaller countries. Moreover, since participation requires staff and expertise, countries cannot equally benefit from the system.

Political scientist Amrita Narlikar (2005) characterizes the WTO in terms of an unsustainable discrepancy between "extreme legalization, particularly in the enforcement of its rules through the dispute settlement mechanism, on the one hand, and an inordinate reliance on de facto improvisation in the making of those rules, on the other" (p 42). Under-representation of the poor, unequal capacities to take advantage of the system, and informal exercise of power are widely acknowledged problems. There are various ways of defending the WTO from those charges. To facilitate participation of poor countries, the WTO offers variable transition times. International donors and NGOs aid developing countries with capacity building. In 2001, the Advisory Center on WTO law opened in Geneva. Moreover, proposals to render enforcement of WTO rules independent of economic power have long been around, like the proposal to allow *coalitions* of countries to take responsibility for enforcement. Developing countries themselves have sought better ways of coordinating and articulating stances. But these defenses cannot dispel the worries.

Poor countries plainly must have standing in the WTO. After all, there is a duty of assistance in building institutions that applies to the WTO, and this duty is more successfully realized if the countries that are supposed to benefit are involved in decisions about measures taken to that effect. Developing countries must be properly represented, and the costs of such representation should be borne by the developed countries if developing countries themselves cannot afford it. However, increased empowerment complicates dispute settlements and negotiations. Narlikar (2009) worries that, to the extent that there has been more of it, transparency has come at the expense of efficiency. Not only does increased empowerment (which presumably here involves increased transparency) entail that it takes longer to reach agreement, but inefficiency may decrease commitment to the process. The problem is bigger for rule-making (negotiations) than for dispute settlement, which only involves relatively few actors each time. As far as adjudication is concerned, empowerment means all members can equally take advantage of the WTO machinery. But what are the institutional implications of such empowerment for the rule-making process?

The WTO is governed by a biannual ministerial conference, a general council responsible for administration, and immediately by a director-general appointed by the ministerial conference. Narlikar (2005) argues that the only way of overcoming inefficiency in making decisions (especially were there to be additional empowerment) is to create an executive board. Any such proposal leads to the inevitably controversial question of how that board would be composed. We saw that the WTO has a development-oriented mandate. What this amounts to depends on how trade regulation is best used to that end, which is an empirical question that goes beyond what we can do here. Similarly, precisely how WTO members can be empowered to participate effectively, is a matter of institutional design we cannot further pursue here.

The WTO and a possible linkage between human rights and labor standards

A crucial question is to what extent the intense policy harmonization championed by the WTO constrains the freedom of poor states to take measures that might aid development. For instance, harmonizing commerce infrastructures deprives countries of flexibility in protecting themselves with tariffs during crises. On the one end of the spectrum of views on such harmonization Dani Rodrik proposes to regard the WTO "as an organ that manages the interface between different national practices and institutions," rather than "an instrument for the harmonization of economic policies and practices across countries" (2007, p 215). He finds no convincing evidence associating trade liberalization with subsequent growth ("while global markets are good for poor countries, the rules by which they are being asked to play the game are often not," p 240).

On the other end of that spectrum we find Christian Barry and Sanjay Reddy (2008), who explore ways in which the WTO could help implement a link between trade and labor standards. Alongside the anti-slavery movement and the women's liberation movement, the Red Cross, and other humanitarian or emancipatory movements, the labor movement was one of the issue-specific movements that set the stage for human rights since the late 18th century. After the First World War, the Treaty of Versailles codified the concern for labor rights internationally and founded the International Labor Organization (ILO). The ILO is a permanent organization involving governments, employers, and workers to coordinate progress in the realization of labor rights. Although the ILO is not broadly known to the publics around the world, it is the pioneering and archetypical international organization of the 20th century.

The core labor standards to which the ILO is committed include freedom of association and the right to collective bargaining, elimination of forced and compulsory labor, abolition of child labor, and the elimination of workplace discrimination. The ILO has since passed almost 200 conventions, concerning minimum wages, working conditions, and so on. Each must be ratified separately by each country (the US and China, e.g., have ratified less than a quarter). The ILO was later incorporated into the UN, which endorsed labor rights in the UDHR:

Article 23

1. Everyone has the right to work, to free choice of employment, to just and favorable conditions of work and to protection against unemployment.
2. Everyone, without any discrimination, has the right to equal pay for equal work.
3. Everyone who works has the right to just and favorable remuneration ensuring for himself and his family an existence worthy of human dignity, and supplemented, if necessary, by other means of social protection.
4. Everyone has the right to form and to join trade unions for the protection of his interests.

Article 24

> Everyone has the right to rest and leisure, including reasonable limitation of working hours and periodic holidays with pay.

Alongside other social and economic rights, labor rights are often violated. In many developing countries goods are produced in sweatshops, factories and workshops that operate under abysmal conditions that disregard health and safety of the workers. The much debated proposal to link labor rights and trade is one approach towards improving the realization of labor rights. The "linkage" proposal is to enforce labor standards by linking them with trade contracts. Rights to trade would be conditional upon the promotion of labor standards. An additional idea is to involve the WTO in the oversight of such linkage. Linkage is desirable because it creates incentives for governments of developing countries to improve labor standards. The basic moral argument for linkage is that both trade policy and labor standards get their justification from their importance for improving human welfare. Labor standards protect the welfare of those who produce what is being traded, and linkage makes sure trade benefits all participants so that producers in developing countries are not taken advantage of. Moreover, regulation in many domestic economies makes the ability to produce and trade depending on some labor standards. It is only natural to consider such a proposal for the international context.

Barry and Reddy's "linkage" proposal

It is often the developing countries that reject linkage. They worry that trade conditions would be used to force developing countries to raise labor standards so that the prices for which their products sell would rise. It is for fear of such protectionism that developing countries have exerted influence within the WTO to make sure trade and labor standards will not be linked. However, among other things Barry and Reddy make an organizational proposal designed to respond to standard concerns about linkage. The proposed Agency for Trade and Labor Standards (ATLAS) would be jointly governed by ILO and WTO. ATLAS would be charged with finding ways in which developing countries could obtain greater access to markets in developed countries in exchange for improving labor standards. ATLAS would have the developmental role of proposing measures to promote adherence to labor standards, and the adjudicative role of identifying violations and of prescribing remedies. The ILO has unique monitoring capacities as far as labor standards are concerned, and the WTO has enforcement capacities through its ability to impose trade sanctions. Trade and labor standards are inevitably linked anyway, through questions of product identity. Fair trade coffee, for instance, is coffee produced under particular circumstances. Current trade rules do not allow for the kind of differential market access required by the linkage proposal since it would violate the most-favored nation rule. However, developing countries have often been granted preferential treatment, and there is no reason why this should not be doable in the future.

Developing countries get a comparative advantage on the world market largely through labor. That advantage, however, can be preserved even if labor standards are respected given the considerable differences in labor costs between developing and developed countries. This is so especially if uniform standards apply so that developing countries do not compete with each other by lowering labor standards ("race to the bottom"). ATLAS must be a transparent and rule-based organization that arises from fair negotiations among states and involves adequate international burden-sharing. Developed countries would open their markets, but in exchange developing countries would increase their labor costs by improving labor standards. What they would also get in return is a straightforward possibility to help put developed countries in a better position to realize human rights for their citizens (and thus to discharge their duty to that effect). If workers in developed countries are harmed, social policy must step in.

Developing countries would raise labor standards, but this would not mean they would suffer losses because they get improved market access in return. Care must be taken to make sure ATLAS does not turn out to be a politically imperialistic organization. It must make room for context-specific implementations, and its decisions must result from a consultation-oriented process and from fair negotiations among states. Careful consideration must be given to the consequences of changing labor standards in particular developing countries. For instance, in many countries child labor is common. Increased market access should improve the conditions on the labor market to such an extent that children would no longer have to work. But solutions have to be found for the transition period so that families of children who used to be major breadwinners are not condemned to starvation. Adjudication must be done by an independent panel that is not biased to the concerns of one particular block of countries. In all these ways ATLAS would address the concern that linkage only serves protectionist ends.

In his discussion of fairness in trade, Richard Miller (2010) concludes that "the basic tendency of *reasonable* trade deliberations will be a trade regime whose allocation of openness to goods, exemptions from constraints, and mitigation of burdens of disruptions due to trade must favor the countries where there is most need for growth through trade" (emphasis added, p 74). Miller acknowledges that governments of developed countries have a duty to protect their industries. But developed countries are more receptive to the kind of "creative destruction" that occurs in capitalist economies when one kind of production replaces another. Developing countries often have very limited options to pursue in search of economic improvement. Moreover, in developed countries changes in social policy are possible remedies for harm suffered from competition from abroad.

However, often it is in the interest of certain political circles in developed countries to insist that certain social policy parameters are firmly entrenched so that they can take no measures that would benefit distant strangers while doing harm to compatriots. In many cases this is disingenuous rhetoric. It is in principle possible to raise taxes for the rich in developed countries to pay higher unemployment support or to fund additional professional training for those who must find new work. The moral argument in favor of choosing this avenue is strong if this is what it takes to make sure developing countries can overcome their misery. Since that moral argument is so strong it is a disgrace that alleged domestic constraints in developed countries often serve as pretexts for refusing measures to improve the plight of the poorest.

I submit that Barry and Reddy offer a plausible proposal for a measure that would help make good on Miller's sensible demand (quoted above) that "a trade regime whose allocation of openness to goods, exemptions from constraints, and mitigation of burdens of disruptions due to trade must favor the countries where there is most need for growth through trade." This does not mean nothing else should be done to promote development and to improve the plight of the poorest. In particular, let me again draw attention to the guest worker programs mentioned in Chapter 6. But presumably it will take a variety of measures to make the world a better place, and more specifically, to make globalization work to everybody's benefit.

Further reading

Relatively little work on fairness in trade has been done by philosophers. Brock (2009) offers some interesting discussion. Stiglitz and Charlton (2006) is a wide-ranging account by two non-philosophers who are intimately familiar with the political economy of trade. For more extensive treatment of some the questions explored in this chapter, see Kurjanska and Risse (2008) and Risse (2007). Sen (1999) explores many issues that arise with regard to globalization. Oxfam (2002) is a resounding indictment of wealthy countries for their trade policies.

Epilogue: Pluralist Internationalism

In Chapter 4 we encountered pluralist internationalism as a view about how justice applies at the global level. Pluralist internationalism acknowledges the normative peculiarity of the state, but also recognizes several other grounds of justice, some relational and others not. Respectively different principles are associated with these different grounds, all of which are binding, say, for states and international organizations. In the course of this book we have not systematically pursued pluralist internationalism. However, a plausible way of developing this view is to think of the following as different grounds of justice: common humanity, shared membership in a state, collective ownership of the earth, membership in the global order and subjection to the trading system. We would thereby recognize individuals as human beings, members of states, co-owners of the earth, as subject to the global order, and as subject to a global trading system. Much more needs to be said to complete pluralist internationalism as a theory of global justice (see Risse 2012). What I would like to do here, however, by way of concluding, is to indicate how domestic principles of justice must be expanded to cover concerns of global reach.

Let us continue to assume the principles of justice that apply *domestically* are Rawls's two principles (which is obviously a controversial matter that would need to be argued for separately):

1. Each person has the same indefeasible claim to a fully adequate scheme of equal basic liberties, which scheme is compatible with the same scheme of liberties for all.
2. Social and economic inequalities are to be arranged so that they are both (a) attached to offices and positions open to all under conditions of fair equality of opportunity, and (b) to the greatest benefit of the least advantaged.

Recall that priority is given to the first, and within the second to the first clause. Principles of distributive justice generally are propositions in the first instance about the distribution of some good in some population. They take this generic form: "The distribution of good G in population P is just only if..." (After the "only if" one would then add in particular the two Rawlsian principles). The principle says "only if" because what is to the right of "only if" states one necessary condition of the distribution of G in P being just, not a sufficient condition.

Like other entities, states (that is, their populations) have their own concerns of justice that do not stand out from the standpoint of the universe, but to which they may show partiality in their execution of the duty to do what they can to bring about justice. Many states are destitute. But richer states are extraordinarily powerful, and can shoulder a broad range of duties of justice. Nonetheless, even the most demanding understanding of what can be reasonably expected of them must acknowledge that resources and abilities are limited. In light of these points, I submit the following list of principles of justice that ascribe obligations to states, in order of priority (which reflects my own considered judgment):

1. Within the state, each person has the same indefeasible claim to an adequate scheme of equal basic liberties, which scheme is compatible with the same scheme of liberties for all.
2. (a) The distribution in the global population of the things to which human rights (understood as membership rights) generate entitlements is just only if everyone has enough of them for these rights to be realized.
   (b) The distribution of original resources and spaces of the earth among the global population is just only if everyone has the opportunity to use them to satisfy their basic needs, or otherwise lives under a property arrangement that provides the opportunity to satisfy basic needs.

(These principles are at the same level of priority.)

3. Within the state, each person has the same indefeasible claim to a *fully* adequate scheme of equal basic liberties, which scheme is compatible with the same scheme of liberties for all.

4. Social and economic inequalities are to be arranged so that they are both (a) attached to offices and positions open to all under conditions of fair equality of opportunity, and (b) to the greatest benefit of the least advantaged.

   (4(a) has priority over 4(b)).

The discussions of the components of this list in earlier chapters provide a commentary on their meaning and implications, especially for items 2(a) and (2b). Two grounds do not make an explicit appearance on this list: common humanity and subjection to the trade regime. The implications of common humanity are subsumed under 2(a). And to the extent that trade creates obligations for states pertaining to other states, they too are subsumed under 2(a). To the extent that trade creates domestic obligations, they are subsumed under Principle 4. This does not mean trade does not generate demands of justice; it merely means that the principles on this list are sufficiently general to absorb these demands to the extent that they apply to states.

Rawls's first principle appears in two versions. Principle 1 omits the word "fully." States need not help improve the fates of non-citizens if circumstances do not allow them to realize a *broadly adequate* scheme of equal basic liberties for their citizens, but this scheme does not need to be *fully* adequate before obligations to help improve the fates of others apply. If citizens of a state already are in a position to enjoy a broadly adequate scheme of equal basic liberties, the duties generated by Principle 2 have greater importance than the provision of a *fully* adequate scheme of equal basic liberties. A certain level of deficiency in the realization of Rawls's original first principle should not discourage states from doing their share for obligations in Principle 2. Principle 3 restates Rawls's first principle, including the word "fully," to capture his own prioritizing of his principle over his second principle (my Principle 4).

While the state system per se is justifiable (in the moderate sense explained in Chapter 3), Principle 2 requires *considerable* policy changes vis-à-vis the status quo. We must assess governments in terms of how they foster the realization of all principles that apply to them. Governments are trustees of the earth on behalf of future generations. As a matter of justice, governments are guardians of membership rights in the global order, and partly responsible for the realization of a duty of assistance towards the poor. To the extent that past violence has created difficulties in satisfying this duty, there is a compensatory aspect to this duty. This aspect implies that in many cases where doubts arise if certain measures are required, we should decide that they do. Governments must also assume responsibility for a just trade system, considering the interests of those who live elsewhere. Governments must do their share to foster the flourishing of humanity.

The grounds-of-justice approach dilutes the contrast between domestic and foreign policy. To ensure acceptability of the global order, governments can reasonably be expected to assume responsibility for a globally even-handed (and to some extent harmonized) immigration policy, and to guarantee that humans can live on this planet in accordance with the idea of proportionate use from Chapter 6. Ensuring acceptability also requires the implementation of a climate change policy for instance as sketched in Chapter 5. Governments must not neglect duties to distant strangers even if discharging such duties threatens disproportionately to affect disadvantaged segments of society. Social policy must be reformed then, and especially the domestic tax code must be adjusted accordingly. Inheritance taxes and other taxes targeting the increasingly large share of the very wealthy in rich countries' economies are particularly suitable sources of income that could help with discharging international duties. It is especially in light of the increasingly serious ecological crisis in which we find ourselves that it is fair to conclude that the survival of humanity requires that governments think of matters of domestic and global justice together, rather than in isolation and with distinct priority for domestic matters.

Further reading

Pluralist internationalism is developed in detail in Risse (2012).

Notes

1 Human Rights

1. In the contemporary literature T. M. Scanlon (2003b), Jürgen Habermas (1999), and Joshua Cohen (2004) do the former.
2. A contemporary version of natural law theory has been developed for instance by the legal theorist John Finnis (1980).
3. The American philosopher Alan Gewirth (1978, 1984), for one, has more recently made self-consistency central to his widely-discussed derivation of human rights.
4. The terms I use to characterize the nature of the duties of different entities appear in quotation marks; from Nickel (1993) I adopt the terms "refrain," "protect," and "provide."

3 Why States?

1. Kant references are to the Reiss-edition (Kant 1970) of Kant's political writings.
2. To be sure, Marx and Engels themselves would not have agreed that they were presenting a large-scale utopia. Instead, they regarded their theories as scientific. But their theories could be scientific only to the extent that one would have been willing to accept their theories of history as scientific, theories that claimed that the progression towards communism was historically inevitable given the general patterns of change across societies. But once one abandons that understanding of history (as I think one should), one can only regard a vision of communist society as a political ideal, and thus as a large-scale utopia.
3. Quoted in Herz (1957), p 493, without a reference.

4 Global Distributive Justice

1. Some of my terminology draws on Sangiovanni (2007), yet my usage deviates from his. For instance, globalism, on my account, is by

definition a relationist view. To remember the relationist meaning of this term easily, the reader should connote it with *global order* rather than with *globe.*

2. Any pluralist view of this sort faces the challenge of explaining how the different principles that we obtain in this way fit together. The Epilogue says a bit more on this subject.

7   Fairness in Trade

1. This is Title 19, US Code, chapter 4 – Tariff Act of 1930; Subtitle II – Special Provisions, part I – Miscellaneous, Sec. 1307.

Bibliography

Abizadeh, Arash. 2008. "Democratic Theory and Border Coercion: No Right to Unilaterally Control Your Own Borders." *Political Theory* 36 (1): 37–65.

Aldy, Joseph, and Robert Stavins (eds). 2007. *Architectures for Agreement. Addressing Global Climate Change in the Post-Kyoto World.* Cambridge: Cambridge University Press.

American Anthropological Association Executive Board, 1947, "Statement on Human Rights," *American Anthropologist* 49: 539–43.

Anderson, Kym. 2004. "Subsidies and Trade Barriers." In Bjørn Lomborg (ed.), *Global Crises, Global Solutions.* Cambridge: Cambridge University Press.

Anderson, Kym, and Will Martin. 2006. "Agriculture, Trade Reform, and the Doha Agenda." In Anderson and Martin (eds), *Agricultural Trade Reform and the Doha Development Agenda.* Palgrave Macmillan and the World Bank, 3–37.

Attfield, Robin. 2003. *Environmental Ethics. An Overview for the Twenty-First Century.* Oxford: Polity.

Barry, Brian, and Robert Goodin (eds). 1992. *Free Movement: Ethical Issues in the Transnational Migration of People and of Money.* University Park: Pennsylvania State University Press.

Barry, Brian. 1982. "Humanity and Justice in Global Perspective." In J. R. Pennock and J. W. Chapman (eds), *Ethics, Economics, and the Law. Nomos XXIV.* New York: New York University Press, 219–52.

Barry, Christian, and Sanjay Reddy. 2008. *International Trade and Labor Standards: A Proposal for Linkage.* New York: Columbia University Press.

Barton, John, Judith Goldstein, Timothy Josling, and Richard Steinberg. 2006. *The Evolution of the Trade System. Politics, Law, and Economics of the GATT and the WTO.* Princeton: Princeton University Press.

Beitz, Charles. 2009. *The Idea of Human Rights.* Oxford: Oxford University Press.

Beitz, Charles. 2004. "Human Rights and the Law of Peoples." In Deen Chatterjee (ed.), *The Ethics of Assistance: Morality and the Distant Needy.* Cambridge: Cambridge University Press, 193–214.

Beitz, Charles. 1999. *Political Theory and International Relations* (revised edition). Princeton: Princeton University Press.

Berlin, Isaiah. 1992. "The Pursuit of the Ideal." In *The Crooked Timber of Humanity. Chapters in the History of Ideas.* New York: Vintage.

Berlin, Isaiah. 1981. "Nationalism." In *Against the Current: Essays in the History of Ideas.* Oxford: Oxford University Press.

Blake, Michael. 2002. "Discretionary Immigration." *Philosophical Topics* 30 (2): 273–91.

Blake, Michael. 2001a. "Distributive Justice, State Coercion, and Autonomy." *Philosophy and Public Affairs* 30: 257–96.

Blake, Michael. 2001b. "Immigration." In R. G. Frey and Christopher Wellman (eds), *A Companion to Applied Ethics.* London: Blackwell.

Blake, Michael, and Mathias Risse. 2007. "Migration, Territoriality, and Culture." In Jesper Ryberg, Thomas Petersen, and Clark Wolf (eds), *New Waves in Applied Ethics.* Ashgate Publishers, 153–82.

Borjas, George. 2001. *Heaven's Door. Immigration Policy and the American Economy.* Princeton: Princeton University Press.

Brock, Gillian. 2009. *Global Justice: A Cosmopolitan Account.* Oxford: Oxford Univesity Press.

Brock, Gillian. 1998. "Introduction." In Brock (ed.), *Necessary Goods: Our Responsibilities to Meet Others' Needs.* New York: Rowman and Littlefield, 1–18.

Callicott, J. Baird. 1989. *In Defense of the Land Ethic: Essays in Environmental Philosophy.* Albany: SUNY Press.

Caney, Simon. 2010. "Climate Change and the Duties of the Advantaged." *Critical Review of International Social and Political Philosophy* 13 (1): pp 203–28.

Caney, Simon. 2005. *Justice Beyond Borders: A Global Political Theory.* Oxford: Oxford University Press.

Carens, Joseph. 1992. "Migration and Morality: A Liberal-Egalitarian Perspective." In Barry and Goodin (1992), 25–47.

Carens, Joseph. 1987. "Aliens and Citizens: The Case for Open Borders," *Review of Politics* 49: 251–73.

Cavallero, Eric. 2006. "An Immigration-Pressure Model of Global Distributive Justice." *Politics, Philosophy, and Economics* 5 (1): 97–127.

Charny, Israel (ed.). 1999. *Encyclopedia of Genocide.* Santa Barbara: ABC-CLIO.

Coetzee, J. M. 2000. *Disgrace.* New York City: Penguin.

Cohen, Joshua. 2010. "Philosophy, Social Science, Global Poverty." In Allison Jaggar (ed.), *Thomas Pogge and His Critics.* Malden: Polity, 18–45.

Cohen, Joshua. 2006. "Is there a Human Right to Democracy?" In Christine Sypnowich (ed.), *The Egalitarian Conscience: Essays in Honor of G. A. Cohen.* Oxford: Oxford University Press, 226–49.

Cohen, Joshua. 2004. "Minimalism about Human Rights: the Most We Can Hope For?" *Journal of Political Philosophy* 12: 190–213.

Cohen, Joshua, and Charles Sabel. 2006. "Extra Rempublicam, Nulla Justitia?" *Philosophy and Public Affairs* 34 (2): 147–75.

Diamond, Jared. 2005. *Collapse. How Societies Choose to Fail or Succeed.* New York: Penguin.

Doyal, Len, and Ian Gough. 1991. *A Theory of Human Need.* London: Palgrave Macmillan.

Dummett, Michael. 2001. *On Immigration and Refugees.* New York: Routledge.

Eigen, Peter. 2003. The Web of Corruption. Frankfurt/New York: Campus Verlag.

Feinberg, Joel. 1973. *Social Philosophy.* Englewood Cliffs: Prentice Hall.

Finnis, John. 1980. *Natural Law and Natural Rights.* Oxford: Clarendon.

Fleischacker, Samuel. 2004. *A Short History of Distributive Justice.* Cambridge: Harvard University Press.

Forsythe, David. 2006. *Human Rights in International Relations.* Cambridge: Cambridge University Press.

Freeman, Samuel. 2007. *Justice and the Social Contract. Essays on Rawlsian Political Philosophy.* Oxford: Oxford University Press.

Gardiner, Stephen. 2011. *A Perfect Moral Storm. The Ethical Tragedy of Climate Change.* Oxford: Oxford University Press.

Gellner, Ernest. 1983. *Nations and Nationalism.* Oxford: Blackwell.

Geuss, Raymond. 2005. *Outside Ethics.* Princeton: Princeton University Press.

Geuss, Raymond. 2001. *History and Illusion in Politics.* Cambridge: Cambridge University Press.

Gewirth, Alan. 1984. "The Epistemology of Human Rights." In E.F. Paul, J. Paul, F.D. Miller (eds), *Human Rights.* Oxford: Blackwell.

Gewirth, Alan. 1978. *Reason and Morality.* Chicago: University of Chicago Press.

George, Henry. 1871. *Our Land and Land Policy, National and State.* San Francisco: White & Bauer.

Glendon, Marie Ann. 2001. *A World Made New: Eleanor Roosevelt and the Universal Declaration of Human Rights.* New York: Random House.

Goodin, Robert. 2007. "Enfranchising all Affected Interests, and its Alternatives." *Philosophy and Public Affairs* 35 (1): 40–69.

Goodin, Robert. 1988. "What is So Special about Our Fellow Countrymen?" *Ethics*: 663–86.

Gosseries, Axel. 2004. "Historical Emissions and Free Riding," In Lukas Meyer (ed.), *Justice in Time: Responding to Historical Injustice*. Baden-Baden: Nomos, 355–80.

Griffin, James. 2008. *On Human Rights*. Oxford: Oxford University Press.

Habermas, Jürgen. 1999. "Zur Legitimation durch Menschenrechte." In H. Brunkhorst and P. Niesen (eds), *Das Recht der Republik*. Frankfurt: Suhrkamp.

Hall, Peter, and David Soskice (eds). 2001. *Varieties of Capitalism: The Institutional Foundations of Comparative Advantage*. Oxford: Oxford University Press.

Harman, Gilbert. 2000. *Explaining Value*. Oxford: Oxford University Press.

Hathaway, Oona. 2002. "Do Human Rights Treaties Make a Difference?" *Yale Law Journal* 111: 1935–2042.

Hayek, F. A. 1973. *Law, Legislation, and Liberty: A New Statement of the Liberal Principles of Justice and Political Economy*, Vol. 1. Chicago: University of Chicago Press.

Henkin, Louis. 1990. *The Age of Rights*. New York: Columbia University Press.

Hertel, Thomas, and Roman Keeney. 2006. "What is at Stake: The Relative Importance of Import Barriers, Export Subsidies, and Domestic Support." In Thomas Hertel and Alan Winters (eds), *Poverty and the WTO: Impacts of the Doha Development Agenda*. Washington, D.C.: World Bank, 37–63.

Herz, John. 1957. "Rise and Demise of the Territorial State." *World Politics* 9: 473–93.

Hirschman, Albert. 1991. *The Rhetoric of Reaction. Perversity, Futility, Jeopardy*. Cambridge: Harvard University Press.

Hobbes, Thomas. 1991. *Leviathan*. Ed. by Richard Tuck. Cambridge: Cambridge University Press.

Hoekman, Bernard. 2002. "The WTO: Functions and Basic Principles." In Hoekman, Bernard, Aadiya Mattoo, and Philip English (eds). *Development, Trade, and the WTO: A Handbook*. Washington, D.C.: World Bank, 41–50.

Howell, Chris. 2003. "Review Article: Varieties of Capitalism. And Then There Was One?" *Comparative Politics* 36 (1): 103–25.

Jamieson, Dale. 2002. "Sustainability and Beyond." In Jamieson, Dale, *Morality's Progress: Essays on Humans, Other Animals, and the Rest of Nature*. Oxford: Clarendon Press, 321–34.

Kant, Immanuel. 1970. *Kant. Political Writings.* Edited by Hans Reiss. Cambridge: Cambridge University Press.

Keller, Simon. 2005. "Patriotism as Bad Faith," *Ethics* 115: 563–92.

King, Martin Luther Jr. 1963. *Why We Can't Wait.* New York: Harper and Row.

Kolakowski, Leszek. 2005. *Main Currents of Marxism: The Founders, The Golden Age, The Breakdown.* New York: Norton.

Kukathas, Chandran. 2005. "The Case for Open Immigration." In Andrew Cohen (ed.), *Contemporary Debates in Applied Ethics.* Oxford: Blackwell.

Kurjanska, Malgorzata, and Mathias Risse. 2008. "Fairness in Trade II: Export Subsidies and the Fair Trade Movement." *Politics, Philosophy, and Economics* 7 (1): 29–56.

Lauren, Paul Gordon. 2003. *The Evolution of International Human Rights.* Philadelphia: University of Pennsylvania Press.

Leopold, Aldo. 1949. *A Sand Country Almanac.* Oxford: Oxford University Press.

McLellan, David. 1977. *Karl Marx: Selected Writings.* Oxford University Press.

Merry, Sally. 2006. *Human Rights and Gender Violence: Translating International Law into Local Justice.* Chicago: University of Chicago Press.

Michaelowa, Axel. 2007. "Graduation and Deepening." In Aldy and Stavins (2007), 81–105.

Mill, John Stuart. 1991. *Considerations on Representative Government.* Buffalo: New York.

Miller, David. 2007. *National Responsibility and Global Justice.* Oxford: Oxford University Press.

Miller, David. 2005. "Immigration: The Case for Limits." In Andrew Cohen (ed.), *Contemporary Debates in Applied Ethics.* Malden: Blackwell.

Miller, David. 1995. *On Nationality.* Oxford: Clarendon.

Miller, Richard. 2010. *Globalizing Justice: The Ethics of Poverty and Power.* Oxford: Oxford University Press.

Morsink, Johannes. 1999. The *Universal Declaration of Human Rights; Origin, Drafting, and Intent.* Philadelphia: University of Pennsylvania Press.

Moellendorf, Darrel. 2002. *Cosmopolitan Justice.* Boulder: Westview.

Nagel, Thomas. 2005. "The Problem of Global Justice." *Philosophy and Public Affairs* 33 (2): 113–47.

Narlikar, Amrita. 2009. "Law and Legitimacy: the World Trade Organization." In Armstrong (2009), 294–303.

Narlikar, Amrita. 2005. *The World Trade Organization: A Very Short Introduction*. Oxford: Oxford University Press.

Neumayer, Eric. 2003. *Weak vs. Strong Sustainability*. 2nd edition. Cheltenham: Elgar.

Neumayer, Eric. 2000. "In Defense of Historical Accountability for Greenhouse Gas Emissions." *Ecological Economics* 33: 185–92.

Nickel, James. 1993. "How Human Rights Generates Duties to Protect and to Provide." *Human Rights Quarterly* 15 (1): 77–86.

Nietzsche, Friedrich. 1998. *On the Genealogy of Morality* (Maudemarie Clark and Alan Swensen, transl.). Indianapolis: Hackett Publishing.

North, Douglass. 1990. *Institutions, Institutional Change, and Economic Performance*. Cambridge: Cambridge University Press.

Nozick, Robert. 1974. *Anarchy, State, and Utopia*. New York: Basic Books.

Nussbaum, Martha. 2006. *Frontiers of Justice: Disability, Nationality, Species Membership*. Cambridge: Harvard University Press.

Nussbaum, Martha. 2000. *Women and Human Development: The Capabilities Approach*. Cambridge: Cambridge University Press.

Nussbaum, Martha, 1996. "Double Moral Standards?" *Boston Review*, October/November 1996; http://bostonreview.net/BR21.5/nussbaum.html, last accessed June 2, 2012.

O ' Neill, Onora. 1986. *Faces of Hunger*. London: Allen & Unwin.

Oxfam. 2002. *Rigged Rules and Double Responsibilities*. Oxford: Oxfam International.

Page, Edward. 2006. *Climate Change, Justice, and Future Generations*. Cheltenham: Edward Elgar.

Passmore, John. 1974. *Man's Responsibility for Nature. Ecological Problems and Western Traditions*. London: Duckworth.

Perry, Michael. 2000. *The Idea of Human Rights: Four Inquiries*. Oxford: Oxford University Press.

Pogge, Thomas. 2008. 2nd edition. *World Poverty and Human Rights*. Oxford: Polity.

Pogge, Thomas. 2002. *World Poverty and Human Rights*. Cambridge: Polity.

Pogge, Thomas. 1994. "Cosmopolitanism and Sovereignty." In Chris Brown (ed.), *Political Restructuring in Europe: Ethical Perspectives*. London: Routledge, 89–122.

Pogge, Thomas. 1989. *Realizing Rawls*. Ithaca: Cornell University Press.

Posner, Eric, and David Weisbach. 2010. *Climate Change Justice*. Princeton: Princeton Universiy Press.

Rawls, John. 2001. *Justice as Fairness: A Restatement*. Ed. by Erin Kelly. Cambridge: Harvard University Press.

Rawls, John. 1999a. *A Theory of Justice*. Revised Edition. Cambridge: Harvard University Press.

Rawls, John. 1999b. *The Law of Peoples*. Cambridge: Harvard University Press.

Risse, Mathias. 2012. *On Global Justice*. Princeton: Princeton University Press.

Risse, Mathias. 2009. "The Right to Relocation: Disappearing Island Nations and Common Ownership of the Earth." *Ethics and International Affairs* 23 (3): 281–300.

Risse, Mathias. 2008. "On the Morality of Immigration." *Ethics and International Affairs* 22 (1): 25–33.

Risse, Mathias. 2007. "Fairness in Trade I: Obligations from Trading and the Pauper Labor Argument." *Politics, Philosophy, and Economics* 6 (3): 355–77.

Risse, Mathias. 2005. "How Does the Global Order Harm the Poor?" *Philosophy and Public Affairs* 33 (4): 349–76.

Risse, Thomas, Stephen Ropp, and Kathryn Sikkink (eds). 1999. *The Power of Human Rights: International Norms and Domestic Change*. Cambridge: Cambridge University Press.

Rivoli, Pietra. 2005. *The Travels of a T-shirt in the Global Economy*. Hoboken: Wiley.

Rodrik, Dani. 2007. *One Economics, Many Recipes: Globalization, Institutions, and Economic Growth*. Princeton: Princeton University Press.

Rolston, Holmes. 1988. *Environmental Ethics: Duties to and Values in the Natural World*. Philadelphia: Temple University Press.

Rorty, Richard. 1993. "Sentimentality, Rationality, and Sentimentality." In S. Shute and S. Hurley (eds), *On Human Rights*. New York: Basic Books.

Rothbard, Murray. 1996. *For a New Liberty. The Libertarian Manifesto*. San Francisco: Fox and Wilkes.

Ruggie, John. 2008. *Promotion and Protection of Human Rights: Human Rights Questions, Including Alternative Approaches for Improving the Effective Enjoyment of Human Rights and Fundamental Freedoms*. 63rd session of the General Assembly, Third Committee, United Nations, October 28, 2008.

Ruggie, John. 2007. "Business and Human Rights: The Evolving International Agenda." *The American Journal of International Law* 101 (4): 819–40.

Rummel, R. J. 1994. *Death by Government*. New Brunswick: Transaction Publishers.

Said, Edward. 1978. *Orientalism*. New York: Pantheon.

Sangiovanni, Andrea. 2007. "Global Justice, Reciprocity, and the State." *Philosophy and Public Affairs* 35 (1): 3–39.

Scanlon, T. M. 2003a. "Rights, Goals, and Fairness." In Scanlon (2003c), 26–42.

Scanlon, T. M. 2003b. "Human Rights as a Neutral Concern." In Scanlon (2003c), 113–24.

Scanlon, T. M. 2003c. *The Difficulty of Tolerance. Essays in Political Philosophy*. Cambridge: Cambridge University Press.

Scanlon, T.M. 2003d. "The Diversity of Objections to Inequality." In Scanlon (2003c), 202–19.

Scheffler, Samuel. 2001. *Boundaries and Allegiances. Problems of Justice in Liberal Thought*. Oxford: Oxford University Press.

Sen, Amartya. 2004. "Elements of a Theory of Human Rights." *Philosophy and Public Affairs* 32 (4): 315–57.

Sen, Amartya. 1999. *Development as Freedom*. New York: Anchor.

Sen, Amartya. 1985. *Commodities and Capabilities*. Amsterdam: North Holland.

Shaw, William. 1999. *Contemporary Ethics: Taking Account of Utilitarianism*. Malden: Blackwell.

Sher, George. "Ancient Wrongs and Modern Rights." *Philosophy and Public Affairs* 10 (1980): 3–17.

Shue, Henry. 1999. "Global Environment and International Inequality." *International Affairs* 75 (3): 531–45.

Shue, Henry. 1996. "Environmental Change and the Varieties of Justice." In Fen Osler Hamilton and Judith Reppy (eds), *Earthly Goods. Environmental Change and Social Justice*. Ithaca: Cornell University Press, 9–29.

Simmons, A. John. 2001a. "Human Rights and World Citizenship: Human Rights in Locke and Kant." Chapter 9 in Simmons (2001b).

Simmons, A. John. 2001b. *Justification and Legitimacy: Essays on Rights and Obligations*. Cambridge University Press.

Simmons, Beth. 2009. *Mobilizing for Human Rights: International Law in Domestic Politics*. New York: Cambridge University Press.

Singer, Peter. 2002. *One World: The Ethics of Globalization*. New Haven: Yale University Press.

Singer, Peter. 1972. "Famine, Affluence, and Morality," *Philosophy & Public Affairs* 1 (3): 229–43.

Spruyt, Hendrik. 1994. *The Sovereign State and Its Competitors*. Princeton: Princeton University Press.

Steiner, Hillel. 1994. *An Essay on Rights*. Oxford: Blackwell.

Stiglitz, Joseph, and Andrew Charlton. 2006. *Fair Trade for All. How Trade Can Promote Development*. Oxford: Oxford University Press.

Streeck, Wolfgang, and Kozo Yamamura (eds). 2001. *The Origins of Nonliberal Capitalism: Germany and Japan in Comparison*. Ithaca: Cornell University Press.

Tamir, Yael. 1996. "Hands Off Clitoridectomy," *Boston Review*, Summer 1996 http://bostonreview.net/BR21.3/Tamir.html, last accessed June 2, 2012.

Tan, Kok-Chor. 2004. *Justice Without Borders. Cosmopolitanism, Nationalism, and Patriotism*. Cambridge: Cambridge University Press.

Timmons, Mark. 2002. *Moral Theory: An Introduction*. Lanham: Rowman & Littlefield.

Tilly, Charles. 1990. *Coercion, Capital, and European States, AD 990–1990*. Cambridge: Blackwell.

Turnbull, Colin. 1972. *The Mountain People*. New York: Simon and Schuster.

Vanderheiden, Steve. 2008. *Atmospheric Justice. A Political Theory of Climate Change*. Oxford: Oxford University Press.

Waldron, Jeremy. 1993. *Liberal Rights. Collected Papers, 1981–1991*. Cambridge: Cambridge University Press.

Walzer, Michael. 1983. *Spheres of Justice*. New York: Basic Books.

Walzer, Michael. 1977. *Just and Unjust Wars: a Moral Argument with Hisotrical Illustrations*. New York: Basic Books.

Walzer, Michael. 1970. *Obligations*. Cambridge: Harvard University Press.

Weil, Simone. 1986. "Human Personality." In Sian Miles (ed.), *Simon Weil: An Anthology*. New York: Groves Press, pp 49–79.

Wellman, Christopher. 2008. "Immigration and Freedom of Association." *Ethics* 119: 109–41.

Wellman, Christopher. 2003. "Nationalism and Secession." In R. G. Frey and C. Wellman (eds), *A Companion to Applied Ethics*. Oxford: Blackwell, 267–78.

Wenar, Leif. 2006. "Why Rawls is Not a Cosmopolitan Egalitarian." In R. Martin and D. Reidy (eds), *Rawls' Law of Peoples: A Realistic Utopia?* Oxford: Blackwell.

White, Lynn. 1967. "The Historical Roots of Our Ecological Crisis." *Science* 10, March 1967, 1203–7.

Wiggins, David. 1987. "Claims of Need." In Wiggins, *Needs, Values, Truth*. Oxford: Oxford University Press, 1–57.

Williams, Bernard. 2005. "Human Rights and Relativism." Chapter 6 *In the Beginning was the Deed. Realism and Moralism in Political Argument.* Ed. by Geoffrey Hawthorn. Princeton: Princeton University Press.

Williams, Bernard. 1995. "Must a Concern for the Environment be Centered on Human Beings?" In *Making Sense of Humanity and other Philosophical Essays.* Cambridge: Cambridge University Press, 233–41.

Williams, Bernard. 1993. *Morality: An Introduction to Ethics.* Cambridge: Cambridge University Press.

Wilson, Edward. 1993. *The Diversity of Life.* New York: Norton.

Wolf, Martin. 2004. *Why Globalization Works.* New Haven: Yale University Press.

Wolff, Jonathan. 1996. "Anarchism and Skepticism." In John Sanders and Jan Narveson (eds), *For and Against the State. New Philosophical Readings.* London: Rowman and Littlefield, 99–119.

Ypi, Lea, Robert Goodin, and Christian Barry. 2009. "Associative Duties, Global Justice, and the Colonies." *Philosophy and Public Affairs* 37 (2): 103–35.

Index

ability to pay principle, 135–43
Abizadeh, Arash, 161, 167
absorptive capacity, of the atmos-
      phere, 133–43
adverse possession, 167
Agreement on Trade-Related
      Aspects of Intellectual
      Property Rights (TRIPs), 169
agricultural subsidies, 170, 173–4
Alliance of Small Island States
      (AOSIS), 130
American Anthropological
      Association, 10, 40, 44
anarchism, 63–4, 74
Anthropocene, 4, 119–20
antidumping measures, 170
Aristide, Jean-Bertrand, 116
Aristotle, 6
Arrhenius, Svante, 136
assistance, duty of, 137, 170–3
      compensatory aspect of, 118, 196
      for human rights protection,
         29–31
      immigration policy and, 147–50
      for institution building, 171–2
      Rawls on, 95
      shared past as context for,
         117, 196
      trade and, 170–3, 183
Australia, 149, 164–5

bad faith, 86
Barry, Brian, 167, 172

Barry, Christian, 115–17,
      187–92
basic needs, *see* needs
basic structure of society, 72,
      94–5, 175
Baywatch (TV series), 59
Beitz, Charles, 15–16, 39, 96,
      105–6, 118
Berlin, Isaiah, 80, 111
Bible, 33, 43, 127
biodiversity, 133
Blake, Michael, 118, 160,
      163–5, 167
borders, 3, 145
      case for closed, 148–51
      case for open, 159–62
      inability to imagine a world
         without, 161
Borjas, George, 144
brain drain, 148
Bretton Woods, 2
Brock, Gillian, 24, 118, 148, 192
Brundtland Report (1987), 132
Burke, Edmund, 84
businesses, human rights
      responsibilities of, 30

Calvin, John, 127
Caney, Simon, 98–9, 109–11,
      118, 143
cap-and-trade system, 133
capabilities, 21, 27, 145
capital, 132

capitalism, and institutional
  complementarities, 175–6
Carens, Joseph, 160, 163, 167
Categorical Imperative, 22–3
Cavallero, Eric, 167
Charny, Israel, 76
China, 81, 174, 188
circumstances of justice, 96–7
climate change, 120–43
  background on, 120
  burdens from adaptation to
    emissions, 139–43
  burdens from mitigation of
    emissions, 139–43
  and collective ownership of the
    earth, 126–9, 134
  and disappearing islands,
    129–30
  distribution of burdens from,
    135–43
  and free riding, 142
  and moral corruption, 124
  as perfect moral storm, 121–4
  as problem of justice, 124–6, 140
coercion-based statism, 102–4, 107
Coetzee, J. M., 88
Cohen, Joshua, 14, 19, 39, 61, 103,
  114, 118
collective ownership of the earth,
  33–5, 126–9, 193
  and climate change, 126–9,
    134–5
  conceptions of, 127–8
  God and, 33; and enlightened
    anthropocentrism, 131–3; and
    environmental values, 131–3
  and human chauvinism, 127
  and human rights, 32–5
  and immigration, 33, 146, 151–4,
    166–7
  Kant on, 68–9

libertarianism and, 74–5, 128–9
  reductio ad absurdum of, 128–9
colonialism, 2, 58, 63, 115–17,
  126, 169
common humanity, 18, 24, 51–4,
  94, 108, 109, 193, 195
Common Ownership, 128
  Equal Division vs., 128–9
communitarianism, 148–9
comparative advantage, 169
Congo, 48, 116
conservative attitudes, 80
consumer pays principle, 136
cooperation, *see* reciprocity
cooperation-based statism, *see*
  reciprocity-based statism
coordinated market economies,
  176–7
corruption, 180
cosmopolitanism, 68, 97–8
Cost-Benefit Analysis, 122–4

Declaration of the Rights of Man
  and of the Citizen (1789), 181
demos of democratic theory,
  161–2
development, 114, 132, 148, 192
  trade policies and, 178–9, 183–7
Diamond, Jared, 121, 125
difference principle, 70–1
dignity, 20
disappearing islands, 129–30
discounting the future, 122–4
distinctively human life, 18–21,
  24–8
  and relativism, 51–4; global
    order and, 31–2
distributive justice, 3, 88, 194
  different grounds of, 92–4
  modern conception of, 88–9;
    domestic vs. global, 89

principles for global order,
194–6
Rawlsian principles of, domestic, 70–3, 104, 108–9, 193
Rawls on domestic vs. global,
95–6
Doyal, Len, 26
Dummett, Michael, 167
dumping, 170

earth, the, 119
dangers to, 119–21
see also collective ownership of
the earth
emissions, accountability for,
136–43
emissions, historical, 136–9
enlightened anthropocentrism,
131–3
enlightened self-interest, 36, 125
environmental values, 131–3
Equal Division, 128–9
equality
Feinberg on, 23
intergenerational, 132
Locke on, 20
moral equality and
cosmopolitanism, 97–8
and Principle of Sympathy, 110
Rawls on, 69–74
Scanlon on, 101
European Parliament, 104
European Union, 107, 170, 173

Fabre, Cecile, 7
fair division, 135
fallacy of restricted
universalism, 99
false consciousness, 57
Faulkner, William, 117
Feinberg, Joel, 23

female genital cutting, 45, 58–60
Fleischacker, Samuel, 89
France, 63, 84, 115–16, 178–9
free trade, 168–9
freedom, 5, 20–1, 34, 65–71, 72–3,
145, 150–1, 160–1
Freeman, Samuel, 94–5
French Revolution, 84
front-loaded goods, 122
future generations
climate change and, 122
discounting costs and benefits
of, 122–3
sustainability and, 132–3
wealthier than current
generation, 123–4, 132

Gardiner, Stephen, 121–4, 143
Gellner, Ernest, 112
General Agreement on Tariffs and
Trade (GATT), 2, 169
geo-engineering, 124
George, Henry, 33
Germany, 54, 84, 159, 166, 176
Geuss, Raymond, 13, 80–3
Glendon, Mary Ann, 9
global governance, 1
global order, 1, 3, 6, 29, 31–8, 47, 93,
103, 107, 193
difference to states, 103–6
as having collective
responsibility vis-à-vis
satisfaction of basic needs,
129, 147–8
principles of justice for, 193–6
as wrongfully harming the poor,
113–15
Global Resource Dividend, 113
global state, *see* world state
global warming, *see* climate
change

globalism, 93, 97
  Beitz as advocate of, 105
  vs. statism, 102–9
globalization, 1, 6, 173, 182, 192
Goodin, Robert, 85, 115–17, 167
Gosseries, Axel, 136
Gough, Ian, 26
graded internationalism, 107–8
greenhouse gases, 122
Griffin, James, 18, 20, 24, 39, 51
Grotius, Hugo, 33
ground of justice, 92–4, 193–6
  circumstances vs., 96–7
  nonrelationism about, 92–102
  pluralistic view of, 106–9
  principles of justice in relation
    to, 93, 96–7, 106–7, 193
  Rawls and the debate about, 104
  relationism about, 92–102
  scope and, 93–4, 107
guest worker programs, *see* work
  permit programs

Habermas, Jürgen, 99
Haiti, 115–16
Hampton, Jean, 7
Harman, Gilbert, 61
Hathaway, Oona, 39
Hayek, F. A., 84
Hegel, G.W.F., 84
Henkin, Louis, 10
Hirschman, Albert, 80
Hobbes, Thomas, 1, 6, 33, 63–6,
  76–7, 87
Homo sapiens, 119
human capital, 132
human needs, *see* needs
human rights
  acceptance around the world,
    48–51
  agency and, 20, 25

  assignment of duties, 29–31
  basis-driven conceptions of, 15
  business and, 30
  citizenship rights vs., 28, 32
  collective ownership of the
    earth and, 33–5
  concept of, 14
  conceptions of 14–15
  and duty of assistance, 170–3
  features of, 13–14
  global order membership rights
    as, 31–8
  immigration and, 149–50
  ineliminably religious, 18–19
  individuals and, 29
  international organizations
    and, 30
  intervention and, 31, 58
  list-driven conceptions of, 17
  and natural rights, 29
  orthodox conceptions of, 15–28,
    31, 32
  practical conceptions of, 15–16
  principle-driven conceptions
    of, 16
  to relocation, 130
  sources of, 32–3, 36
  states and, 11, 30, 34
  trade and, 170–3, 183
  vernacularization of, 61
  violations of, 54–5
human trafficking, 5, 37
Hume, David, 96

ideal theory, 147–8
immediacy, *see* legal immediacy;
  political immediacy
immigration
  to Australia, 149, 164–5
  border controls and, 144–6
  to Canada, 144–5, 158

and collective ownership, 151–4, 164–5
constraints requiring moral scrutiny, 145
discretionary, 158–9, 162–6
and duties to the poor, 146, 160
environmental impact of, 147, 159
and freedom of association, 150–1
of gay people to countries with declining populations, 165–6
of HIV-positive applicants, 165
and ideal/non-ideal theory, 147–8
illegal, to United States, 166–7
liberal justice and restrictions on, 160
over- or underuse of resources and spaces and, 151–4
perverse incentives for denying, 159
social-science questions about, 145, 148
and suspect categories, 163–5
to United States, 164, 166–7
India, 9, 115
inequality
Rawls and, 71–2, 101
Scanlon and, 101–2
institutions
defined, 171
duties to aid in building, 172
interconnectedness, 1, 5, 29, 47–51, 64, 146
as source of human rights, 37
see also global order
Intergovernmental Panel on Climate Change (IPCC), 120, 136–7, 143
International Covenant on Civil and Political Rights, 11

International Covenant on Economic, Social and Cultural Rights, 11
International Criminal Court, 31, 38, 50
International Labour Organization -(ILO), 188, 189–92
International Monetary Fund (IMF), 2–3, 48, 104
international organizations, 2, 9, 11, 30–2, 50, 61, 83, 104, 109, 130, 171, 193
internationalism, see graded internationalism; monist internationalism; nongraded internationalism; pluralist internationalism
IPCC, see Intergovernmental Panel on Climate Change

Jamieson, Dale, 131–2
Japan, 130, 170, 173, 176
justice, see distributive justice
justification, 63

Kant, Immanuel, 20–3, 39, 66–9, 73, 76–7, 87, 168
Keller, Simon, 86
Kennedy, John F., 35
King, Martin Luther, Jr., 36, 43
Kipling, Rudyard, 58
Kiribati, 129–30
Kolakowski, Leszek, 82
Kukathas, Chandran, 144, 160–1
Kymlicka, Will, 7

labor standards, 180–2, 187–92
land ethic, 131
League of Nations, 36, 168
left-libertarianism, 75

legal immediacy, 105–8
Lennon, John, 85
Leopold, Aldo, 131, 143
Leopold II, 116
liberal market economies, 176–7
libertarianism, 74–5
    see also left-libertarianism;
        right-libertarianism
liberty, *see* freedom
linkage between human rights
        and labor standards, 187–92
Locke, John, 20, 33, 69, 87
Lumumba, Patrice, 117

Malik, Charles, 9–10
man-made capital, 132
Mao's Great Leap Forward, 81
Marrakesh Agreement, 169, 183
Marx, Karl, 81–3, 168
Marxism, 81–3
maximin approach, 70, 108
Maya culture, 4
McCarthy, Cormac, 97
membership rights, in global
        order
    holding of, 31–2
    and human rights, 31–8
    pluralist internationalism and,
        109, 193
    sources of, 32–3
Michaelowa, Axel, 142
Mill, John Stuart, 113
Miller, David, 8, 21, 24–5, 112–13,
        118, on immigration, 149–50,
        160, 161
Miller, Richard, 91, 110, 118,
        170, 191
Mobutu Sese Seko, 117
Moellendorff, Darrel, 118
monist (nongraded)
        internationalism, 107–8

moral equality, 97
moral progress, 46, 57
most-favored nation rule, 182
Multi-Fiber Agreement, 174

Nagel, Thomas, 95, 103–4
national treatment, 183
nationalism, 111–13
natural capital, 132
natural law, 19, 22
natural resources, *see*
        proportionate use of
        resources and spaces of earth
natural rights, 19, 27, 29, 31, 100
needs, 21, 24–7, 34, 90–2, 110–11
    collective responsibility at the
        level of the global order
        vis-à-vis, 147–8
Netherlands, 155–8
Neumayer, Eric, 132–3, 136
Nietzsche, Friedrich, 76
Niue Declaration on Climate
        Change (2008), 130
nongovernmental organizations
        (NGOs), 50, 55, 59, 186
nongraded (monist)
        internationalism, 107–8
nonideal theory, 147–8
nonrelationism, 92–102
    Caney's, 98–9, 110–11
    and pluralist internationalism,
        107–8
normative peculiarity of the state,
        94, 102, 105, 107, 108–12, 193
North, Douglass, 171
Nozick, Robert, 87
Nussbaum, Martha, 21, 24,
        60, 145

O'Neill, Onora, 24
orientalism, 58

original ownership, *see* collective ownership of the earth
original resources and spaces of the earth, *see* collective ownership of the earth
original position, 69–70, 106
Our Common Future (Brundtland Report), 132
ownership, *see* collective ownership of the earth

partial citizenship, 163–4
Passmore, John, 33
past injustice, 115–18
    compensatory aspect of duties of distributive justice and, 118, 196
path-dependency, 117
patriotism, 85–7
per-capita approach to climate change accountability, 133–4
Perry, Michael, 18
pluralist internationalism, 6, 106–9, 193–6
    relational and nonrelational grounds of, 107–8
Pogge, Thomas, 13, 96–7, 113–14, 118
political and civil rights, 10, 71, 99–100, 171
political constructivism, 95
political immediacy, 105–8
polluter pays principle, 135–43
popular sovereignty, 161
population density, 152, 166
pragmatism, 17
Principle of Sacrifice, 91, 110
Principle of Sympathy, 110
principles of justice
    Rawlsian, for domestic context, 70–3, 104, 108–9, 193; for global order, 194–6

procedural sources of membership rights, 37–8
proportionate use of resources and spaces of earth
    illegal immigration to the US and, 166–7
    immigration and, 130, 151–4
    measurement of, 155–8
    Walzer on, 149
protectionism, *see* subsidies
pure time preference, 123

Rawls, John, 69–74, 87, 118
    and basic structure, 72, 95
    Beitz on, 106
    driving intuition about moral arbitrariness of natural assets and social status, 71
    and duties of assistance, 95
    and human rights, 74; and social primary goods, 72, 108; and the two principles of justice, domestic, 70–3, 104, 108–9, 193
    and principles for ordering international relations, 73
    on realistic utopias, 73, 84
    and relationism, 94–6
    and statism, 95
realism in international relations, 60–1, 66
realistic utopia, 73, 79–83, 161
reciprocity, 105, 108
reciprocity-based statism, 102–7
rectificatory justice, 88
Reddy, Sanjay, 187–92
reflective equilibrium, 135
refugees, 148

relationism, 92–102
  defense of, 100–2
  and pluralist internationalism,
    107–8
  Rawls and, 94–6
relativism, 40–3
  cultural superiority and, 54–8
  cultural vs. moral or normative,
    40–1
  distinctively human life and,
    51–4; vs. Einstein's relativity
    theory, 43–4
  difficulties with, 43–6
  inconsistency of, 46–7
  Universal Declaration of
    Human Rights and, 60
remittances, 148
resources, *see* proportionate use of
    resources and spaces of earth
"responsibility to protect"
    principle, 38
Ricardo, David, 169
right to exit, 149–50
right-libertarianism, 75
rights
  account of, 25
  assignment of duties, 29–31
  moral, 12–13
  natural, 19, 27
  see also human rights; political
    and civil rights
Risse, Mathias, 87, 105–6, 108, 118,
    129, 151, 166, 167, 192, 193, 196
Risse, Thomas, 39, 61
Rodrik, Dani, 171, 187
Rorty, Richard, 17
Rothbard, Murray, 75, 129
Rousseau, Jean-Jacques, 69, 87, 145
Ruggie, John, 30
Rummel, Rudolph, 76

Sabel, Charles, 103
sacred, 18–19
Said, Edward, 58
Sangiovanni, Andrea, 105
Sartre, Jean-Paul, 86
Scanlon, T. M., 25, 55–6, 101–2
Scheffler, Samuel, 102
self-consistency, and basis of
    human rights, 21–2
self-determination of peoples,
    150–1
self-ownership, 75
Sen, Amartya, 17, 21, 24,
    145, 192
Shakespeare, William, 3
shared membership in a state
  coercion as characteristic of,
    104–8
  and immigration, 151, 160
  justified bias vis-à-vis, 111
  nationalism not a contributor
    to, 112
  principles of justice as
    characteristic of, 108, 193
  reciprocity as characteristic of,
    105–8
Sher, George, 116–17
Shue, Henry, 138–9
Simmons, Beth, 39
Simmons, John, 8, 15, 63, 76–7
Singer, Peter, 90–2, 109–12, 133–5,
    138, 143
skepticism, moral, 41
skepticism from above, 64, 78
skepticism from below, 63, 74–7
slavery, 37
social contract, 64–77
social justice, 88
Spruyt, Hendrik, 62
Stalinism, 82

states
  borders of, 3, 145
  coercive character of, 105
  contingency of, 62–3
  cooperative character of, 105
  criticisms of, 63–4, 74–7
  global order compared to, 103–6
  and human rights, 30, 34, 170–3
  immediacy of interaction
    between individuals and, 105
  immigration policies of, 5,
    145–6, 151–4, 158, 162–5
  justifications of, 63–79; and
    nationalism, 111
  medieval feudalism compared
    to existence of, 160
  normative peculiarity of, 93,
    102, 105, 107, 108–12, 193
  principles of justice applicable
    to, 70, 104, 108–9, 193–4
  responsibilities of, in global
    order, 31, 34
  shared membership in, 104–8
  skepticism about, 74–7
  and trade, 170–82
  see also statism; system of states
statism, 93, 97
  coercion-based vs. cooperation-
    based, 102–4
  vs. globalism, 102–9
  Rawls and, 95
Steiner, Hillel, 127–8
strict liability, 139
stringent claims, 3, 88, 93, 100, 103
strong sustainability, 132–3
subsidies, 170–82
  agricultural, 173–4
  claims to, 175–7
  collective preferences and, 177–9
  cultural preservation and, 179

  and development, 178
  economics of, 173
  security and, 179
substantive sources of member-
    ship rights, 31–8
sustainability, 131–3
Swift, Adam, 8
system of states, 64
  contingency of, 62–3
  inability to imagine alternatives
    to, 79–85
  justification of, 78–85
  principles of justice for, 194–6
  skepticism about, 74
  see also global order

Tamir, Yael, 58–60
Tan, Kok-Chor, 118
Tilly, Charles, 63
tolerance, 42
trade, 168–70
  and development, 178–9
  fairness in, 5–6, 170, 190–1
  and human rights, 182–3
  liberalization of, 169, 183
  subsidies in, 170–82
  WTO and, 182–9
TRIPs, *see* Agreement on Trade-
    Related Aspects of Intellectual
    Property Rights

United Nations, 2, 9, 21, 168
  Charter of, 1, 9
United Nations Development
    Programme, 21
United Nations Framework
    Convention on Climate
    Change (1992), 35, 137
United States, 4, 164, 166–7, 170,
    173, 176, 181, 188

United States Tariff Act (1930), 181

Universal Declaration of Human Rights, 2, 9–11, 17, 28, 36, 38, 39, 40, 49, 60, 150, 188

universal jurisdiction, 38

universalism, 41
  vs. moral skepticism and tolerance, 41; and interconnectedness, 47–54; distinctively human life and, 51–4

unreasonableness, and basis of human rights, 23–4

utilitarianism, 61, 126

utopian thinking, 79–85

Vanderheiden, Steve, 134, 143

veil of ignorance, 69–70

Waldron, Jeremy, 29

Walzer, Michael, 61, 76
  on immigration, 148–50

weak sustainability, 132–3

Weil, Simone, 18

Wellman, Christopher, 85, 112
  on immigration, 150–1

Wenar, Leif, 96

White, Lynn, 120

White Australia policy, 149, 164–5

Whitman, Walt, 127

Wiggins, David, 26

Williams, Bernard, 61, 131

Wilson, E. O., 133

Wolf, Martin, 173

Wolff, Jonathan, 8, 77

work permit programs, 148, 163, 192

World Bank, 2, 48, 104

world state, 2, 64–6, 68, 73, 83

World Trade Organization (WTO), 2–3, 5, 30, 48, 104, 107, 169–70
  and justice, 182–4
  and linkage between human rights and labor standards, 187–92
  reform of, 184–7

Ypi, Lea, 115–17

34728455R00128

Made in the USA
Middletown, DE
02 September 2016